STAR WARS
DOCTOR APHRA

THE ENGINE JOB

Writer
ALYSSA WONG

Pencilers
RAY-ANTHONY HEIGHT (#6, #10), **ROBERT GILL** (#6) & **MINKYU JUNG** (#7-9)

Inker
VICTOR OLAZABA

Color Artist
RACHELLE ROSENBERG

Letterer
VC's JOE CARAMAGNA

Cover Art
LEINIL FRANCIS YU & **SUNNY GHO** (#6); and
JOSHUA "SWAY" SWABY (#7-10) with **RACHELLE ROSENBERG** (#9) & **GURU-eFX** (#10)

Recap Design
CARLOS LAO

Assistant Editor
TOM GRONEMAN

Editor
MARK PANICCIA

Collection Editor **JENNIFER GRÜNWALD**
Assistant Editor **DANIEL KIRCHHOFFER**
Assistant Managing Editor **MAIA LOY**
Assistant Editor **LISA MONTALBANO**
VP Production & Special Projects **JEFF YOUNGQUIST**
Book Designer **ADAM DEL RE**
SVP Print, Sales & Marketing **DAVID GABRIEL**
Editor in Chief **C.B. CEBULSKI**

For Lucasfilm:
Senior Editor **ROBERT SIMPSON**
Creative Director **MICHAEL SIGLAIN**
Art Director **TROY ALDERS**
Lucasfilm Story Group **MATT MARTIN**
PABLO HIDALGO
EMILY SHKOUKANI
Lucasfilm Art Department **PHIL SZOSTAK**

STAR WARS: DOCTOR APHRA VOL. 2 — THE ENGINE JOB. Contains material originally published in magazine form as STAR WARS: DOCTOR APHRA (2020) #6-10. First printing 2021. ISBN 978-1-302-92305-1. Published by MARVEL WORLDWIDE, INC., a subsidiary of MARVEL ENTERTAINMENT, LLC. OFFICE OF PUBLICATION: 1290 Avenue of the Americas, New York, NY 10104. STAR WARS and related text and illustrations are trademarks and/or copyrights, in the United States and other countries, of Lucasfilm Ltd. and/or its affiliates. © & TM Lucasfilm Ltd. No similarity between any of the names, characters, persons, and/or institutions in this magazine with those of any living or dead person or institution is intended, and any such similarity which may exist is purely coincidental. Marvel and its logos are TM Marvel Characters, Inc. Printed in Canada. KEVIN FEIGE, Chief Creative Officer; DAN BUCKLEY, President, Marvel Entertainment; JOE QUESADA, EVP & Creative Director; DAVID BOGART, Associate Publisher & SVP of Talent Affairs; TOM BREVOORT, VP, Executive Editor; NICK LOWE, Executive Editor, VP of Content, Digital Publishing; DAVID GABRIEL, VP of Print & Digital Publishing; JEFF YOUNGQUIST, VP of Production & Special Projects; ALEX MORALES, Director of Publishing Operations; DAN EDINGTON, Managing Editor; RICKEY PURDIN, Director of Talent Relations; JENNIFER GRÜNWALD, Senior Editor, Special Projects; SUSAN CRESPI, Production Manager; STAN LEE, Chairman Emeritus. For information regarding advertising in Marvel Comics or on Marvel.com, please contact Vit DeBellis, Custom Solutions & Integrated Advertising Manager, at vdebellis@marvel.com. For Marvel subscription inquiries, please call 888-511-5480. Manufactured between 6/4/2021 and 7/6/2021 by SOLISCO PRINTERS, SCOTT, QC, CANADA.

10 9 8 7 6 5 4 3 2 1

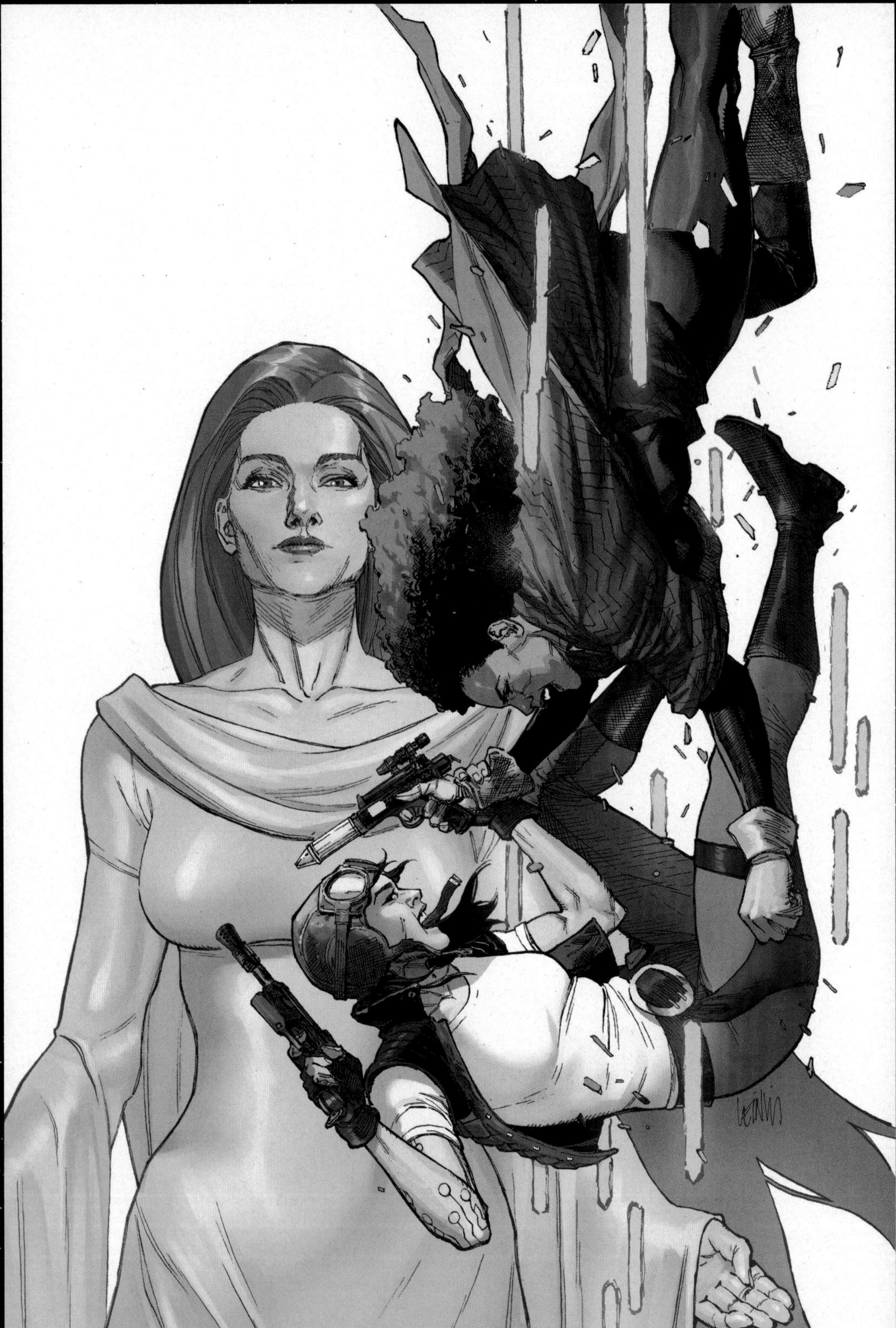

6 — HEADHUNTED

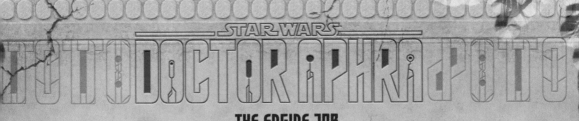

STAR WARS

DOCTOR APHRA

THE ENGINE JOB

After narrowly escaping Darth Vader and doing a huge solid for the Rebellion, Doctor Aphra's cut all ties to her past and is trying to go back to what she does best: hunting down the most valuable treasures in the galaxy.

But the rogue archaeologist is also exceedingly good at making enemies. Aphra's latest misadventure to find the mythical Rings of Vaale put her at odds with Ronen Tagge, the insanely powerful scion of the Tagge dynasty.

And the Tagges do not forgive. Nor do they forget. . . .

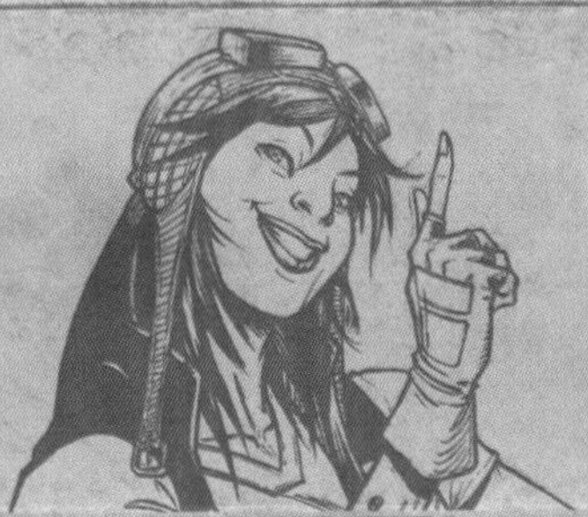

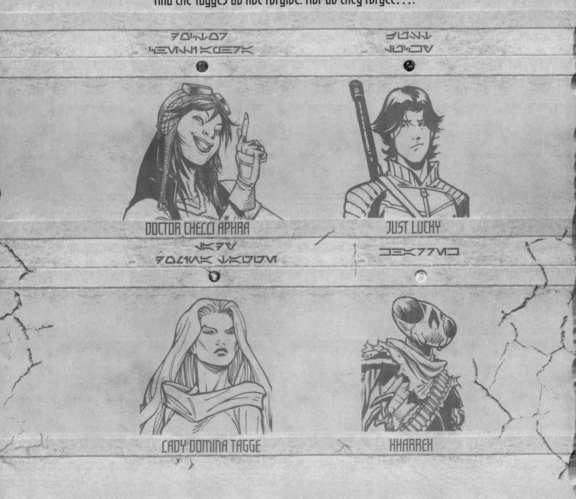

DOCTOR CHELLI APHRA

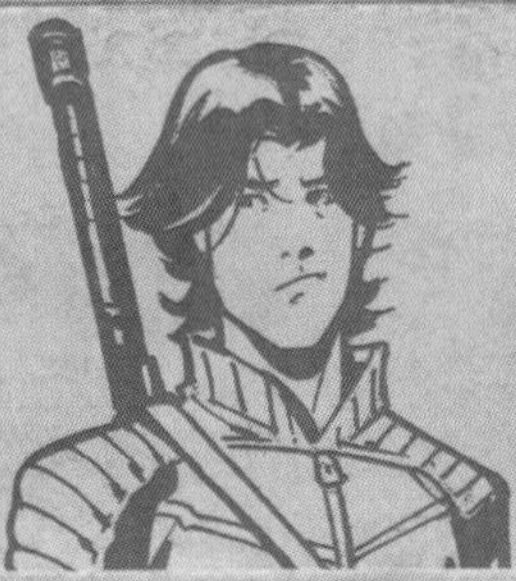

JUST LUCKY

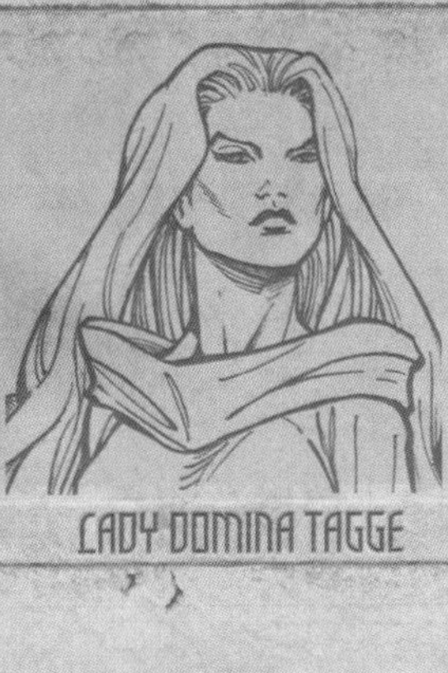

LADY DOMINA TAGGE

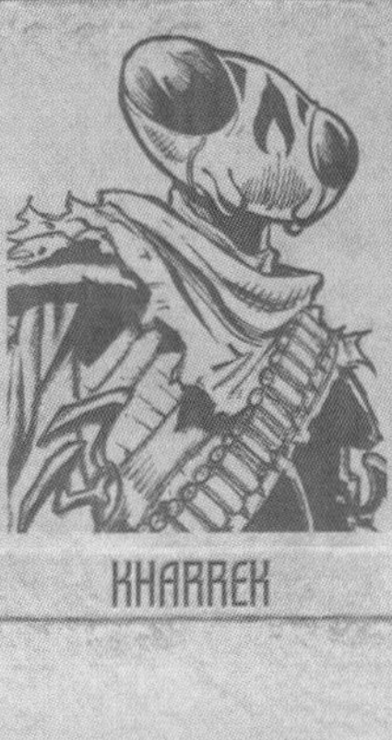

KHARREK

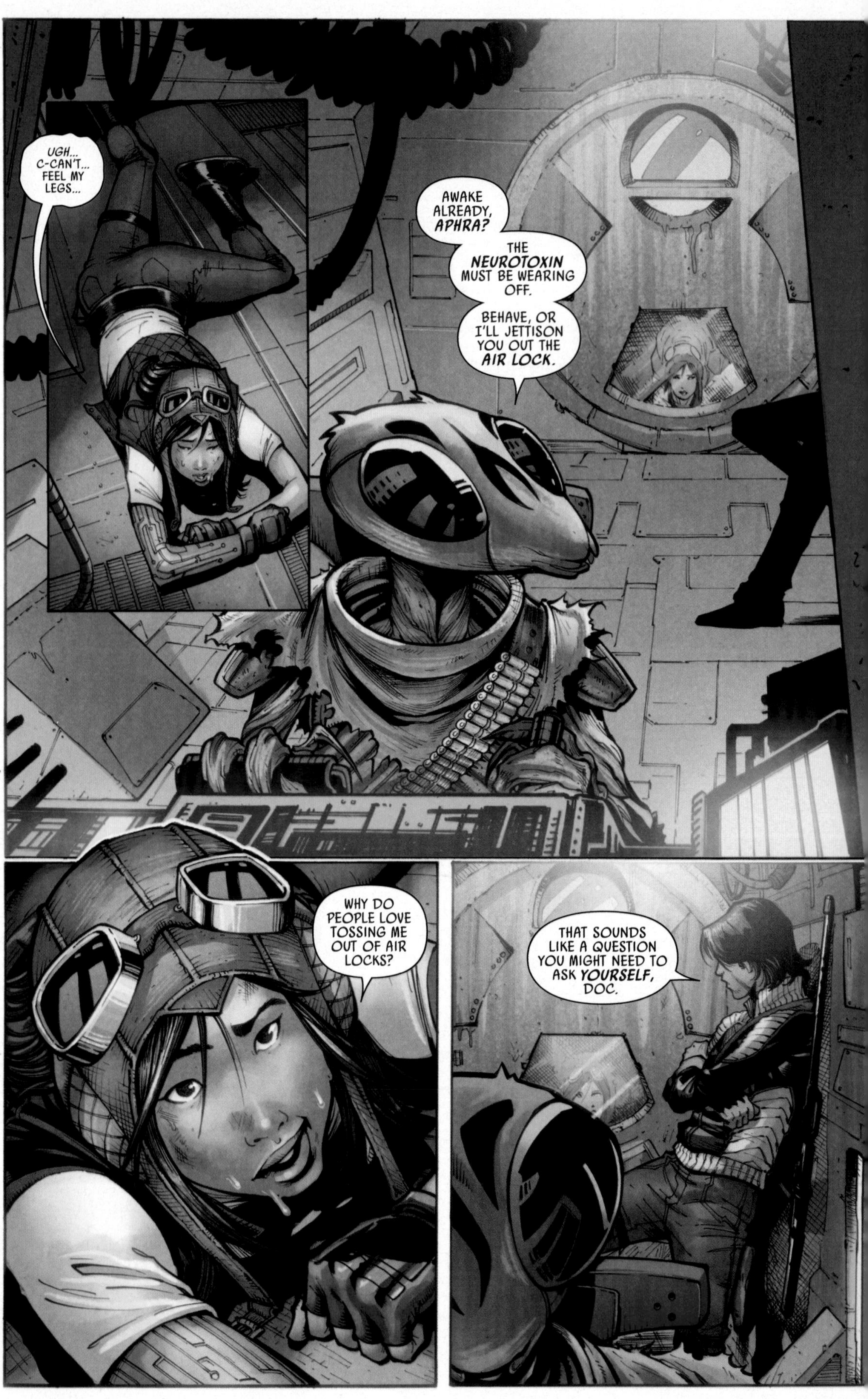
UGH... C-CAN'T... FEEL MY LEGS...
AWAKE ALREADY, APHRA?
THE NEUROTOXIN MUST BE WEARING OFF.
BEHAVE, OR I'LL JETTISON YOU OUT THE AIR LOCK.
WHY DO PEOPLE LOVE TOSSING ME OUT OF AIR LOCKS?
THAT SOUNDS LIKE A QUESTION YOU MIGHT NEED TO ASK YOURSELF, DOC.

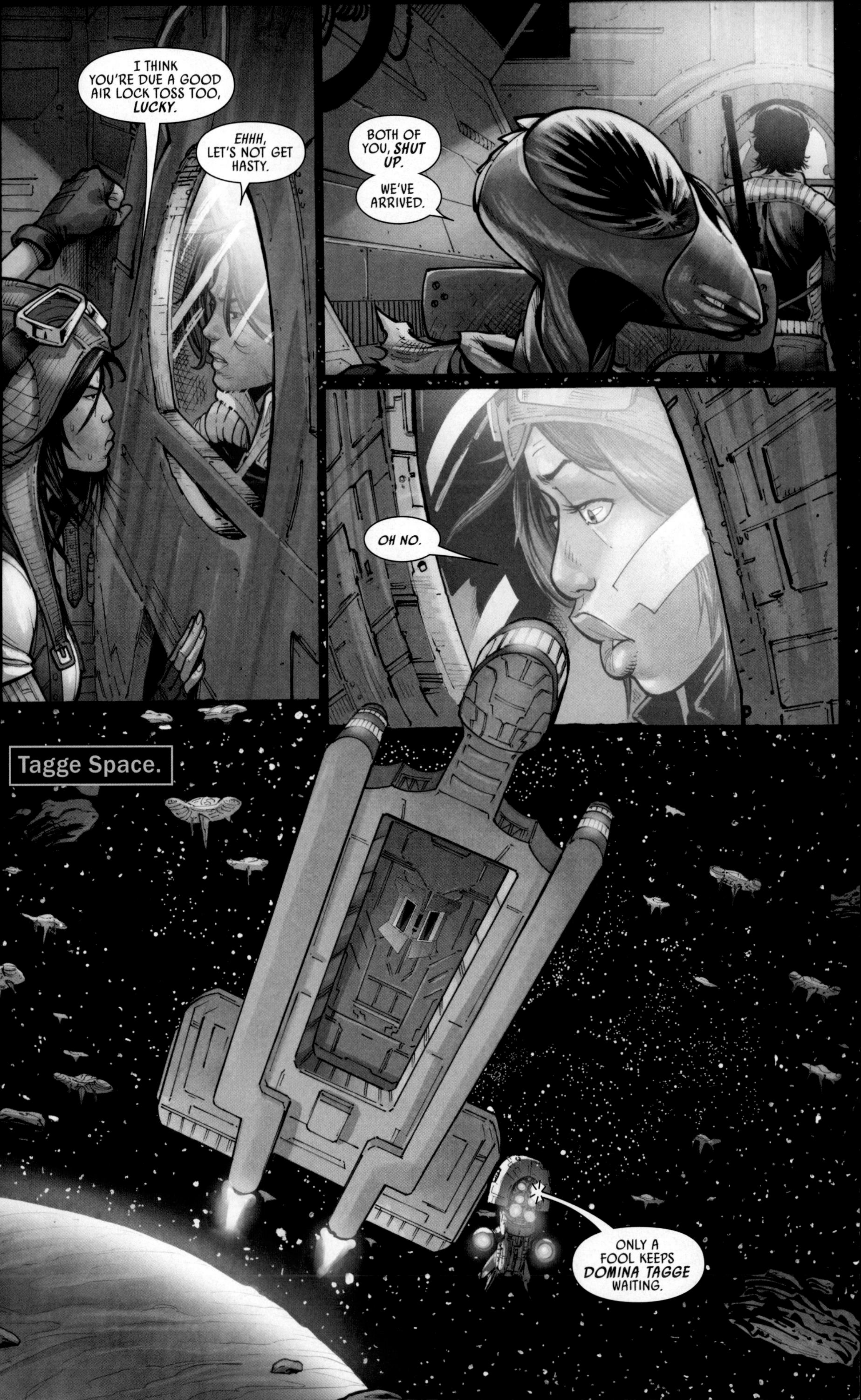
I THINK YOU'RE DUE A GOOD AIR LOCK TOSS TOO, LUCKY.
EHHH, LET'S NOT GET HASTY.
BOTH OF YOU, SHUT UP.
WE'VE ARRIVED.
OH NO.
Tagge Space.
ONLY A FOOL KEEPS DOMINA TAGGE WAITING.

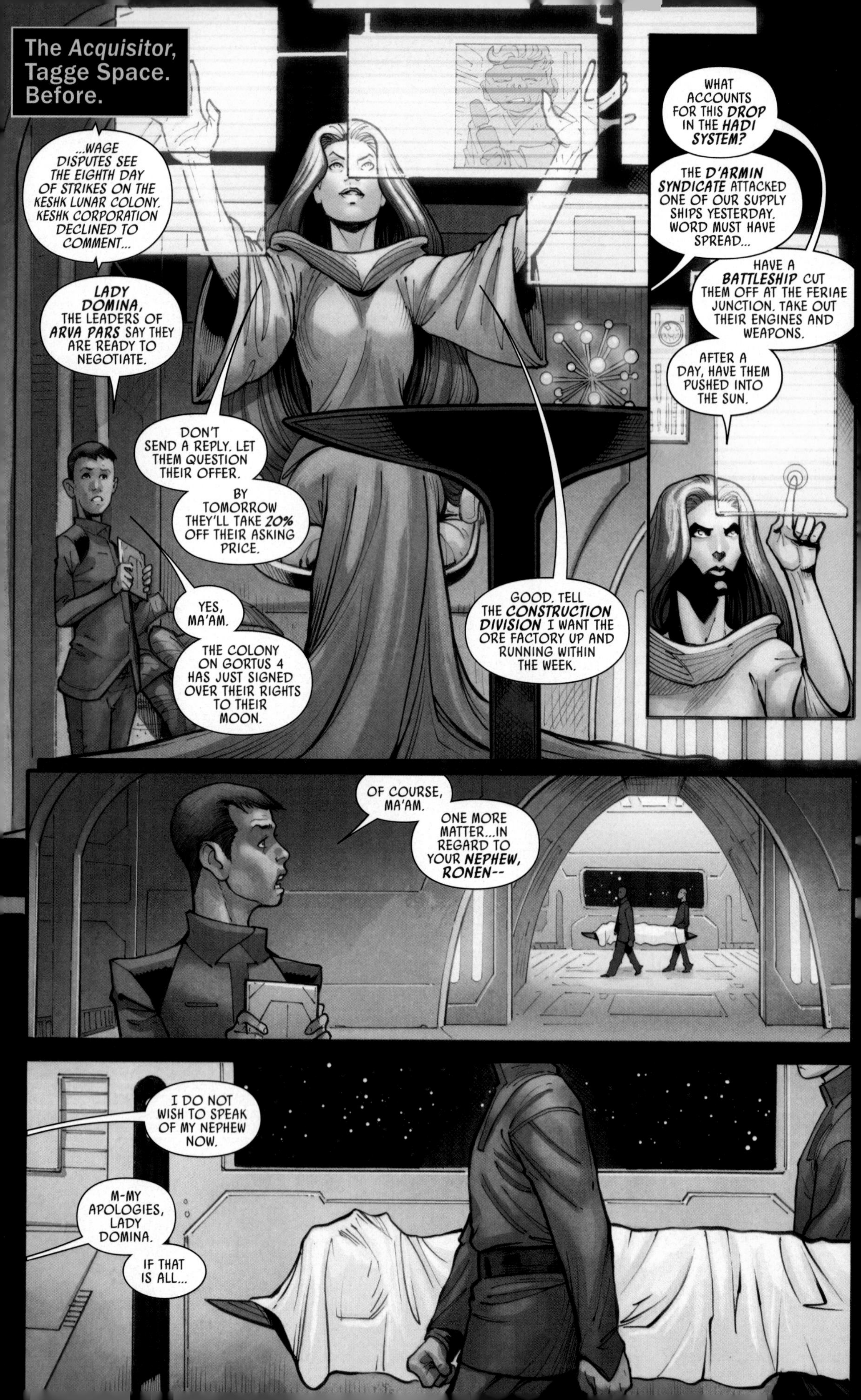
The *Acquisitor*, Tagge Space. Before.
...WAGE DISPUTES SEE THE EIGHTH DAY OF STRIKES ON THE KESHK LUNAR COLONY. KESHK CORPORATION DECLINED TO COMMENT...
LADY DOMINA, THE LEADERS OF ARVA PARS SAY THEY ARE READY TO NEGOTIATE.
DON'T SEND A REPLY. LET THEM QUESTION THEIR OFFER.
BY TOMORROW THEY'LL TAKE 20% OFF THEIR ASKING PRICE.
YES, MA'AM.
THE COLONY ON GORTUS 4 HAS JUST SIGNED OVER THEIR RIGHTS TO THEIR MOON.
GOOD. TELL THE CONSTRUCTION DIVISION I WANT THE ORE FACTORY UP AND RUNNING WITHIN THE WEEK.
WHAT ACCOUNTS FOR THIS DROP IN THE HADI SYSTEM?
THE D'ARMIN SYNDICATE ATTACKED ONE OF OUR SUPPLY SHIPS YESTERDAY. WORD MUST HAVE SPREAD...
HAVE A BATTLESHIP CUT THEM OFF AT THE FERIAE JUNCTION. TAKE OUT THEIR ENGINES AND WEAPONS.
AFTER A DAY, HAVE THEM PUSHED INTO THE SUN.
OF COURSE, MA'AM.
ONE MORE MATTER...IN REGARD TO YOUR NEPHEW, RONEN--
I DO NOT WISH TO SPEAK OF MY NEPHEW NOW.
M-MY APOLOGIES, LADY DOMINA.
IF THAT IS ALL...

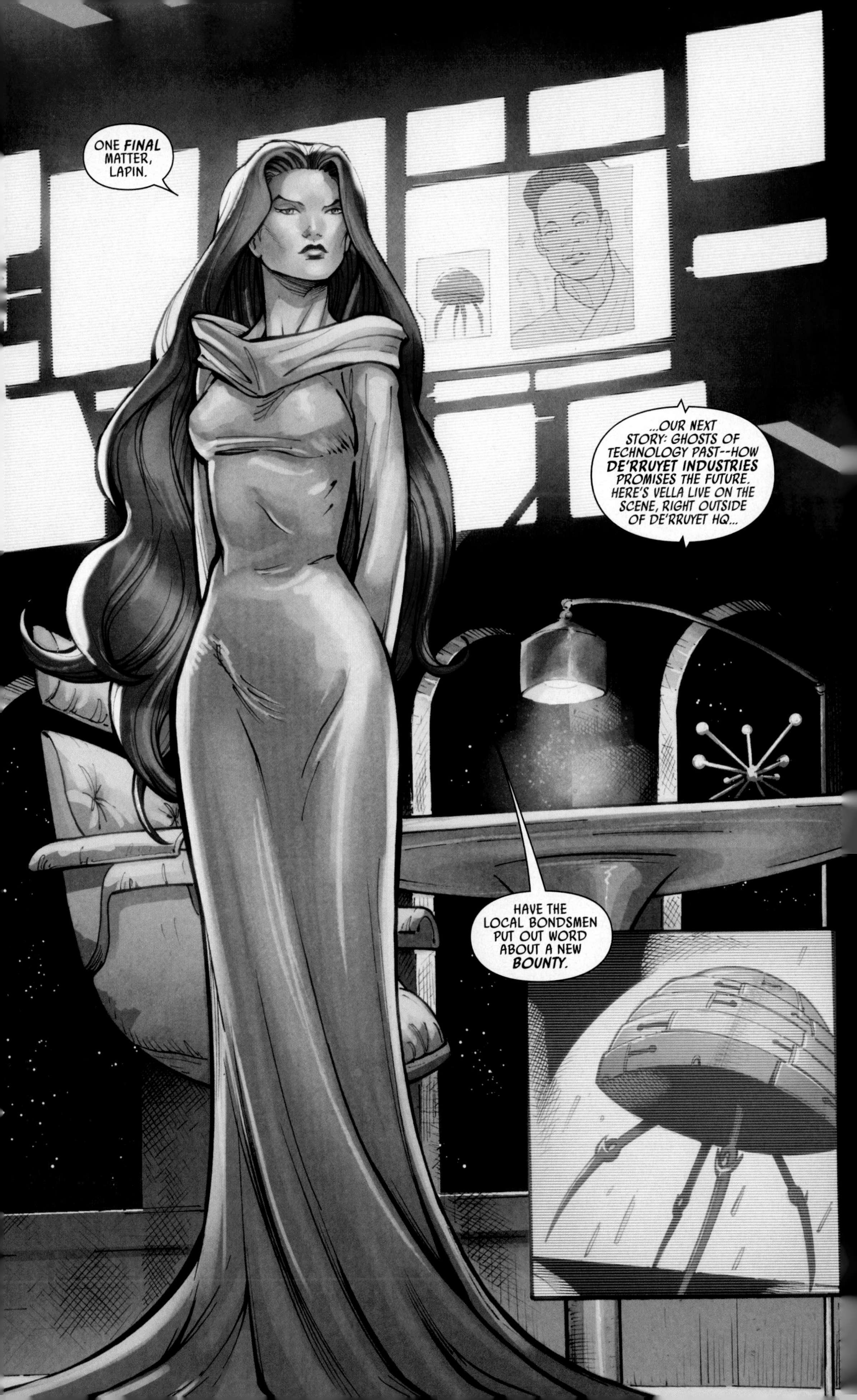
ONE *FINAL* MATTER, LAPIN.
...OUR NEXT STORY: GHOSTS OF TECHNOLOGY PAST--HOW **DE'RRUYET INDUSTRIES** PROMISES THE FUTURE. HERE'S VELLA LIVE ON THE SCENE, RIGHT OUTSIDE OF DE'RRUYET HQ...
HAVE THE LOCAL BONDSMEN PUT OUT WORD ABOUT A NEW *BOUNTY*.

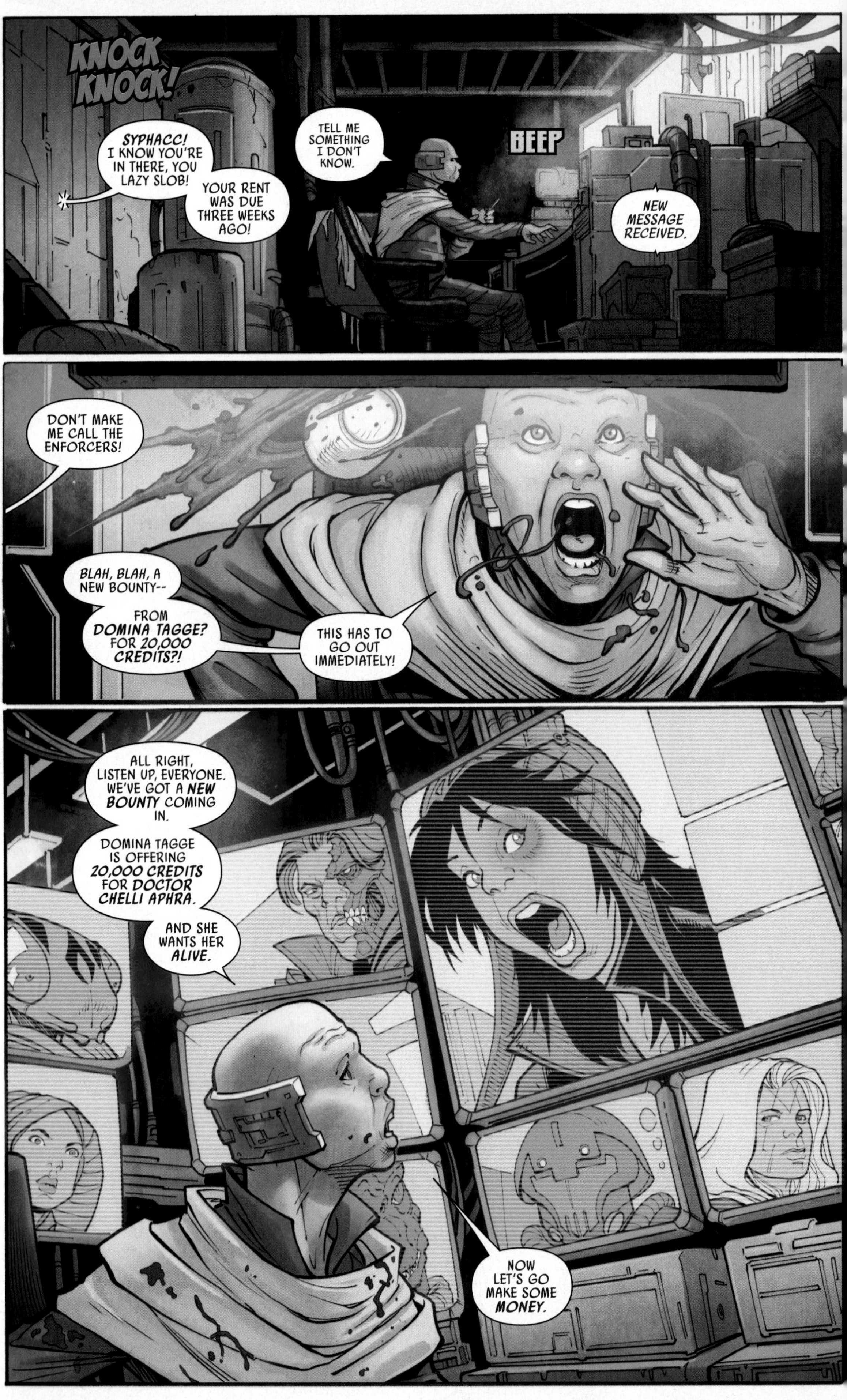
KNOCK KNOCK!
SYPHACC! I KNOW YOU'RE IN THERE, YOU LAZY SLOB!
YOUR RENT WAS DUE THREE WEEKS AGO!
TELL ME SOMETHING I DON'T KNOW.
BEEP
NEW MESSAGE RECEIVED.
DON'T MAKE ME CALL THE ENFORCERS!
BLAH, BLAH, A NEW BOUNTY--
FROM DOMINA TAGGE? FOR 20,000 CREDITS?!
THIS HAS TO GO OUT IMMEDIATELY!
ALL RIGHT, LISTEN UP, EVERYONE. WE'VE GOT A NEW BOUNTY COMING IN.
DOMINA TAGGE IS OFFERING 20,000 CREDITS FOR DOCTOR CHELLI APHRA.
AND SHE WANTS HER ALIVE.
NOW LET'S GO MAKE SOME MONEY.

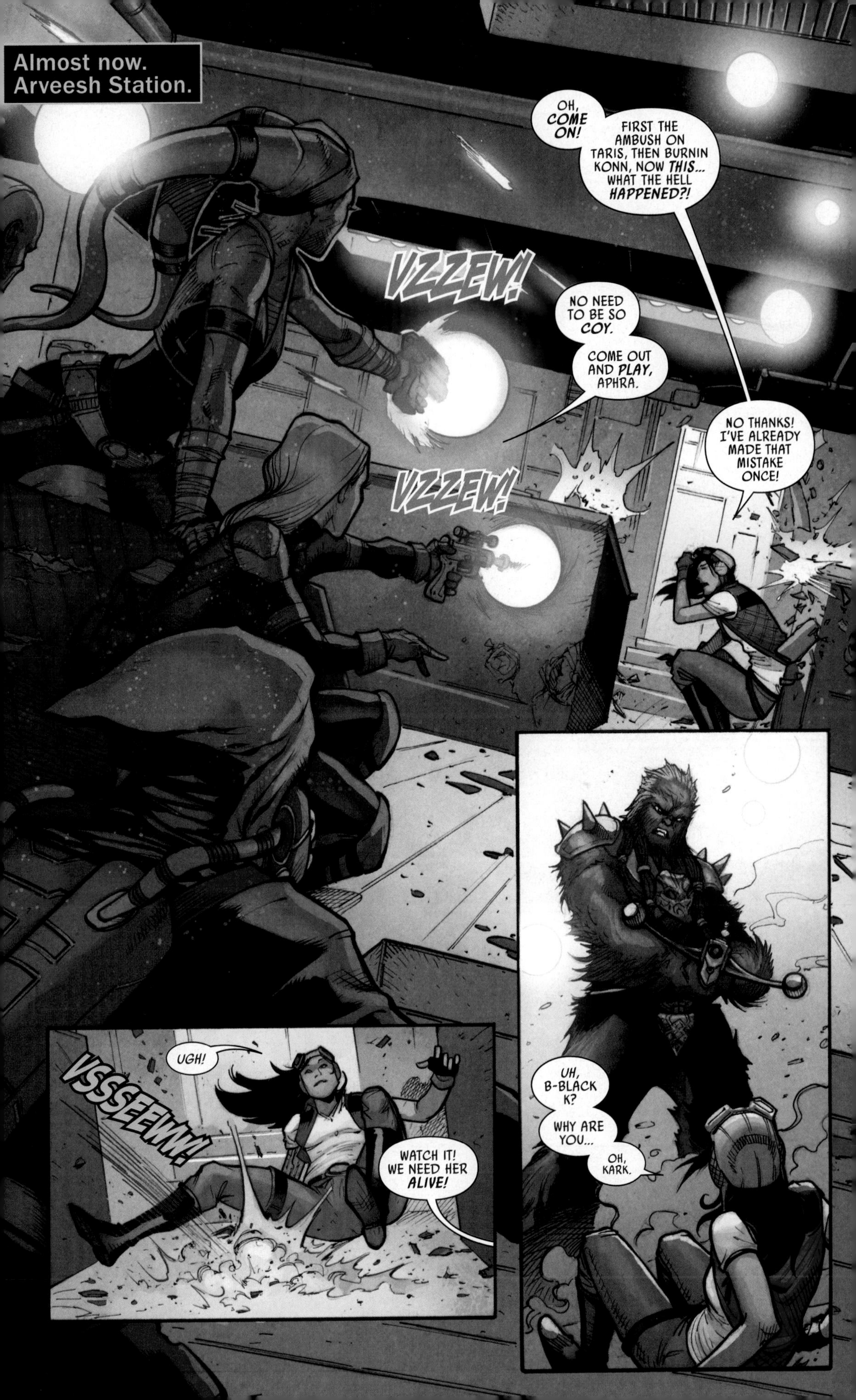
Almost now.
Arveesh Station.
OH, COME ON!
FIRST THE AMBUSH ON TARIS, THEN BURNIN KONN, NOW THIS... WHAT THE HELL HAPPENED?!
VZZEW!
NO NEED TO BE SO COY.
COME OUT AND PLAY, APHRA.
VZZEW!
NO THANKS! I'VE ALREADY MADE THAT MISTAKE ONCE!
VSSSEEWW!
UGH!
WATCH IT! WE NEED HER ALIVE!
UH, B-BLACK K?
WHY ARE YOU...
OH, KARK.

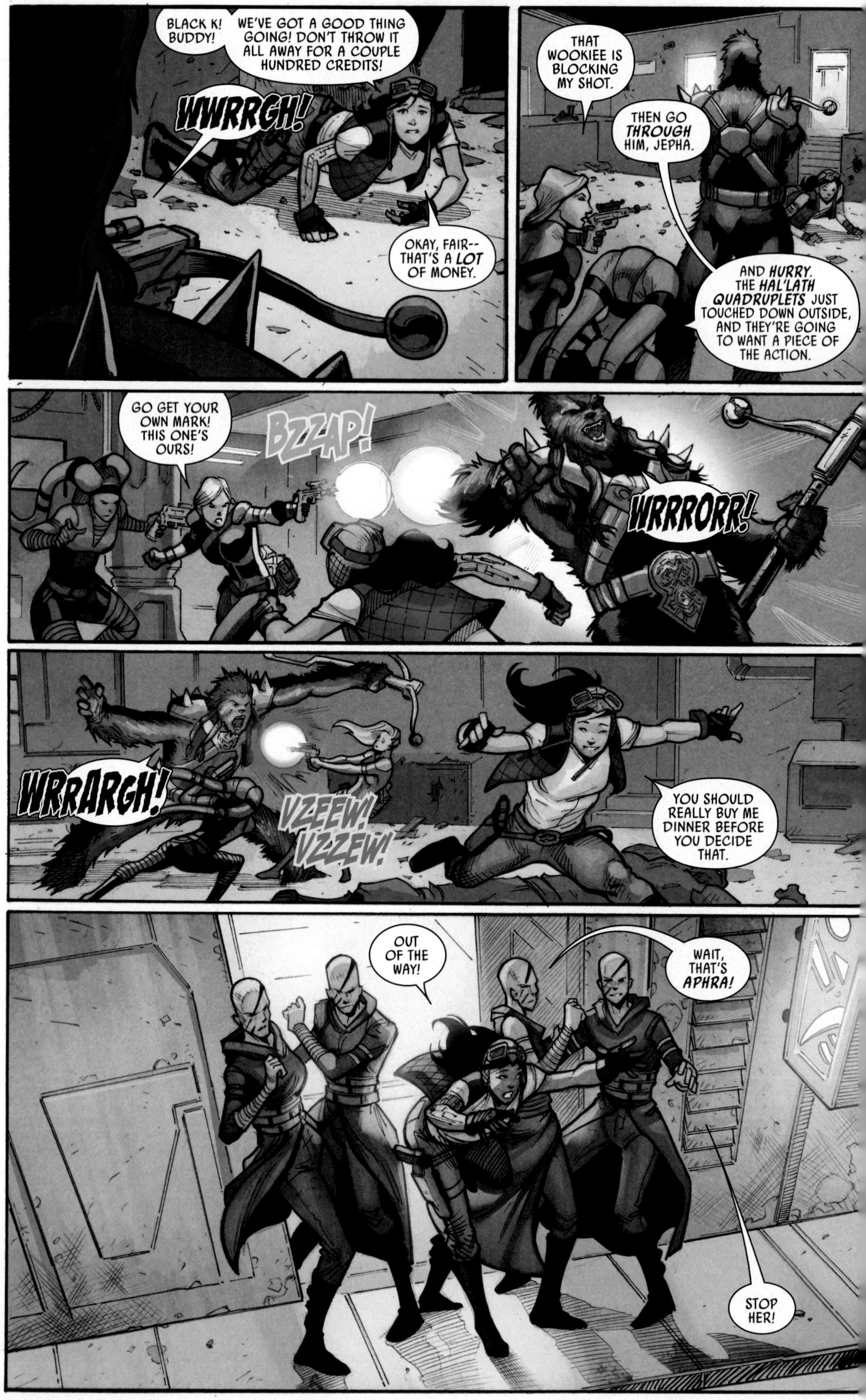

BLACK K! BUDDY!
WE'VE GOT A GOOD THING GOING! DON'T THROW IT ALL AWAY FOR A COUPLE HUNDRED CREDITS!
WWRRGH!
OKAY, FAIR-- THAT'S A LOT OF MONEY.
THAT WOOKIEE IS BLOCKING MY SHOT.
THEN GO THROUGH HIM, JEPHA.
AND HURRY. THE HAL'LATH QUADRUPLETS JUST TOUCHED DOWN OUTSIDE, AND THEY'RE GOING TO WANT A PIECE OF THE ACTION.
GO GET YOUR OWN MARK! THIS ONE'S OURS!
BZZAP!
WRRRORR!
WRRARGH!
VZZEW! VZZEW!
YOU SHOULD REALLY BUY ME DINNER BEFORE YOU DECIDE THAT.
OUT OF THE WAY!
WAIT, THAT'S APHRA!
STOP HER!

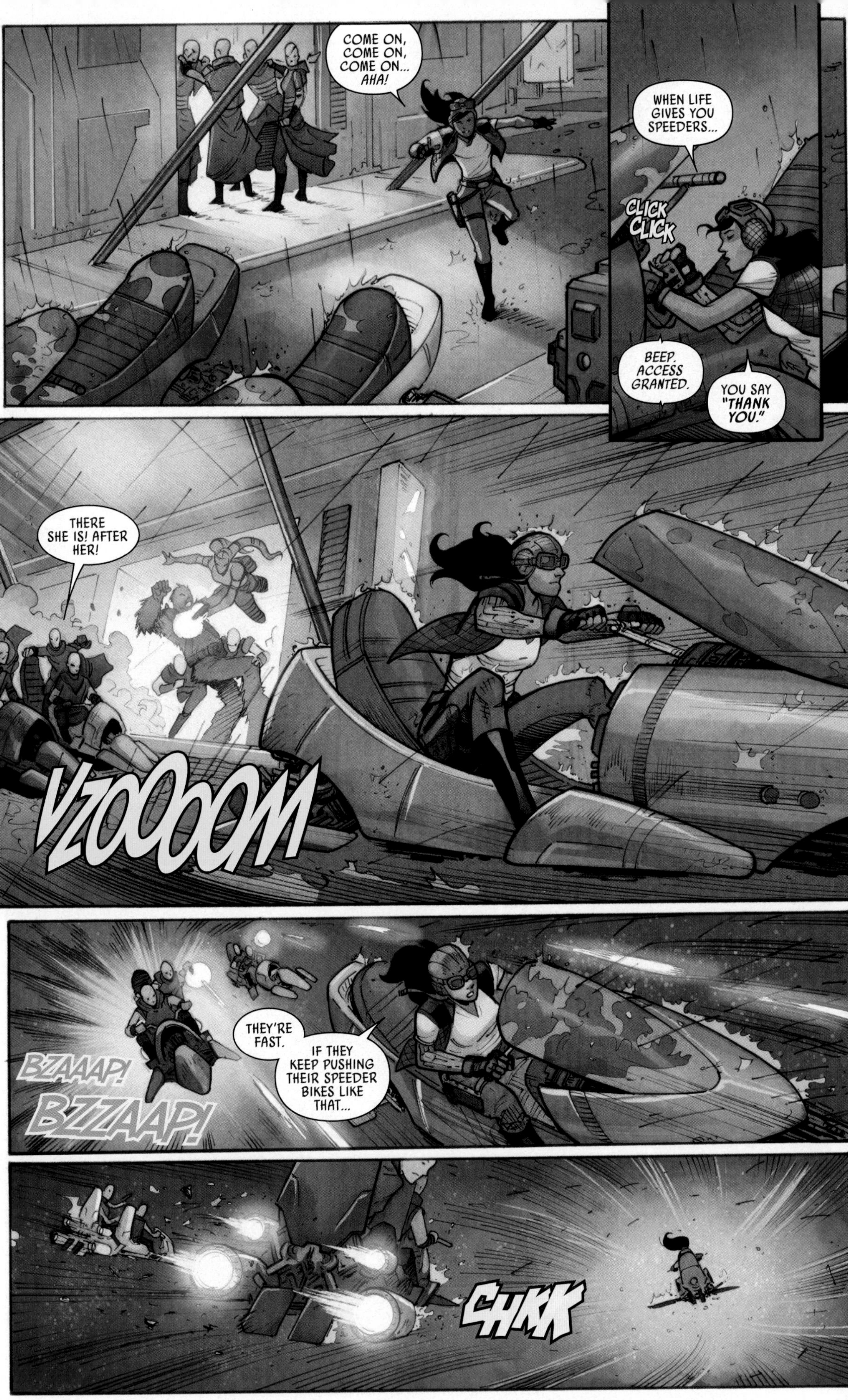
COME ON, COME ON, COME ON... AHA!
WHEN LIFE GIVES YOU SPEEDERS...
CLICK CLICK
BEEP. ACCESS GRANTED.
YOU SAY "THANK YOU."
THERE SHE IS! AFTER HER!
VZOOOOM
BZAAAP! BZZAAP!
THEY'RE FAST.
IF THEY KEEP PUSHING THEIR SPEEDER BIKES LIKE THAT...
CHKK

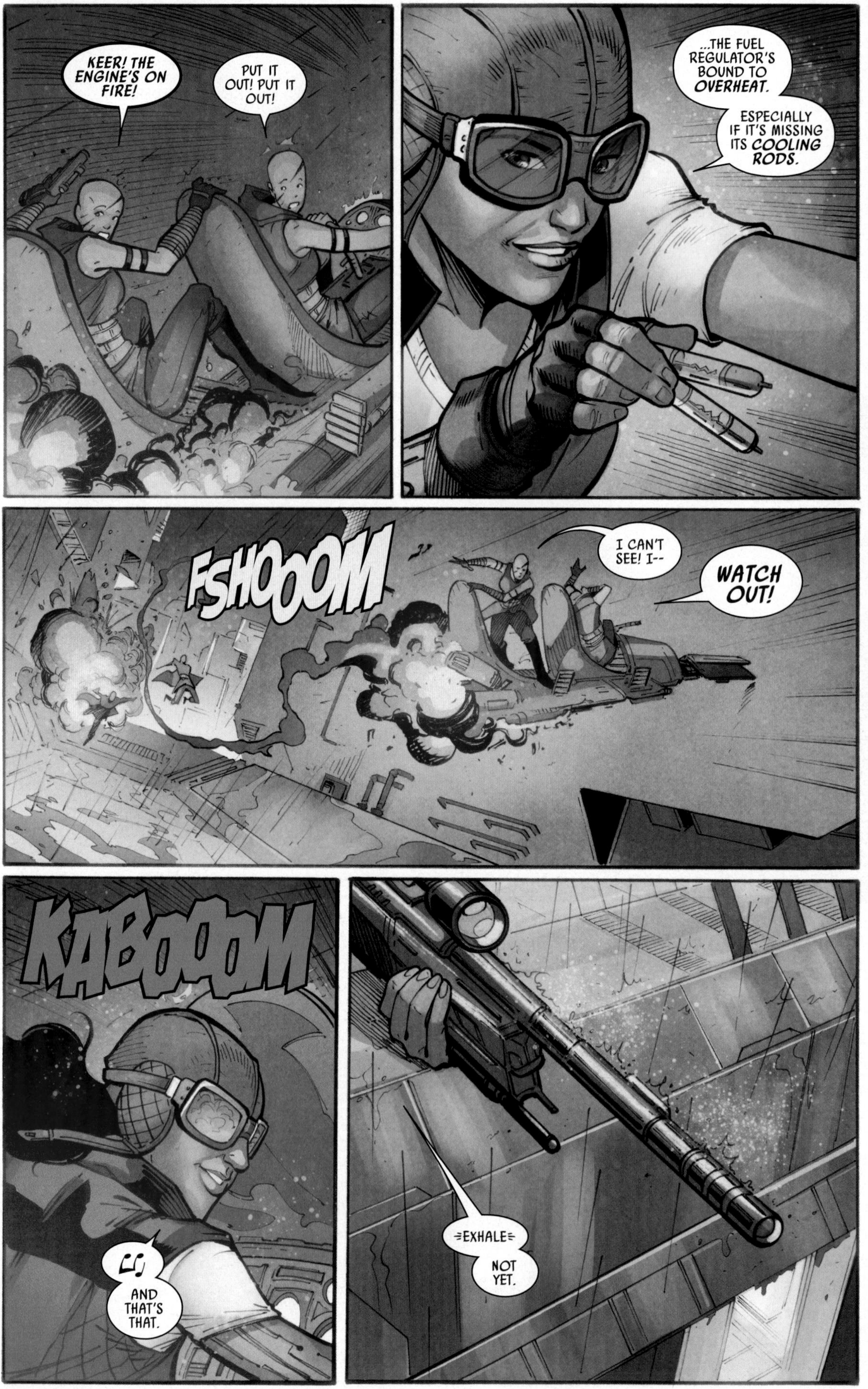
KEER! THE ENGINE'S ON FIRE!
PUT IT OUT! PUT IT OUT!
...THE FUEL REGULATOR'S BOUND TO OVERHEAT.
ESPECIALLY IF IT'S MISSING ITS COOLING RODS.
FSHOOOM
I CAN'T SEE! I--
WATCH OUT!
KABOOOM
AND THAT'S THAT.
EXHALE
NOT YET.

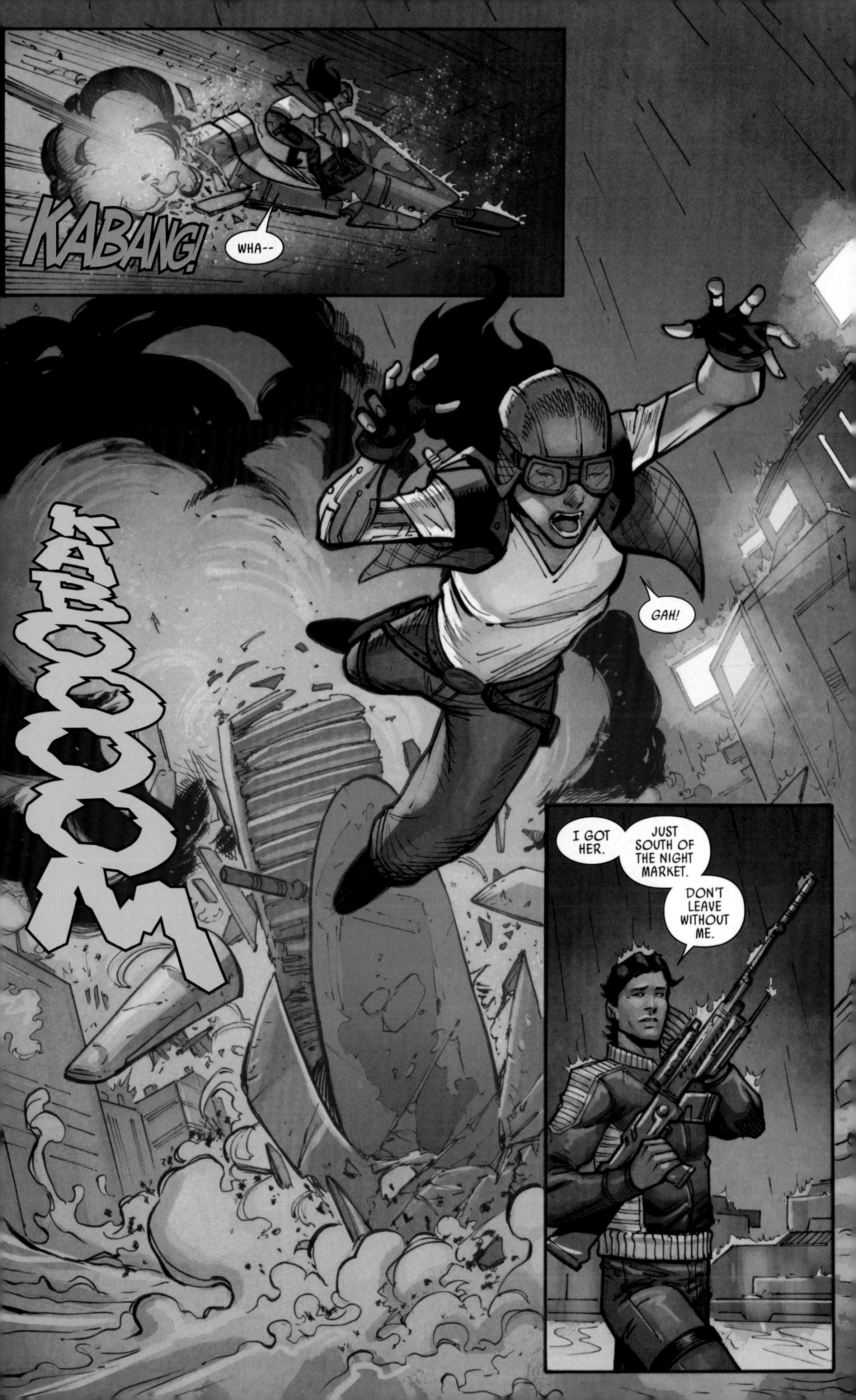
KABANG!
WHA--
GAH!
KABOOOOM
I GOT HER.
JUST SOUTH OF THE NIGHT MARKET.
DON'T LEAVE WITHOUT ME.

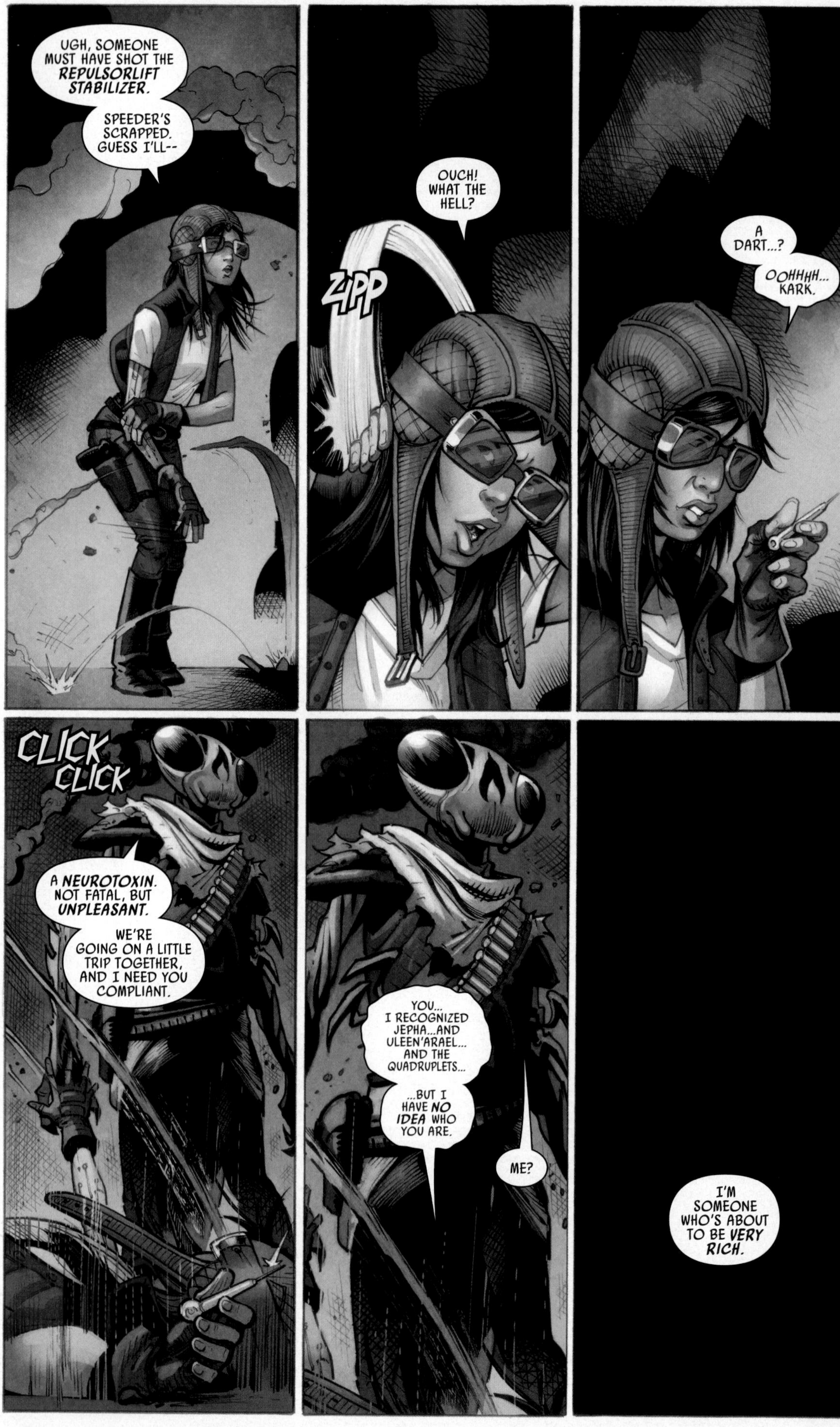
UGH, SOMEONE MUST HAVE SHOT THE REPULSORLIFT STABILIZER.
SPEEDER'S SCRAPPED. GUESS I'LL--
ZIPP
OUCH! WHAT THE HELL?
A DART...?
OOHHHH... KARK.
CLICK CLICK
A NEUROTOXIN. NOT FATAL, BUT UNPLEASANT.
WE'RE GOING ON A LITTLE TRIP TOGETHER, AND I NEED YOU COMPLIANT.
YOU... I RECOGNIZED JEPHA...AND ULEEN'ARAEL... AND THE QUADRUPLETS...
...BUT I HAVE NO IDEA WHO YOU ARE.
ME?
I'M SOMEONE WHO'S ABOUT TO BE VERY RICH.

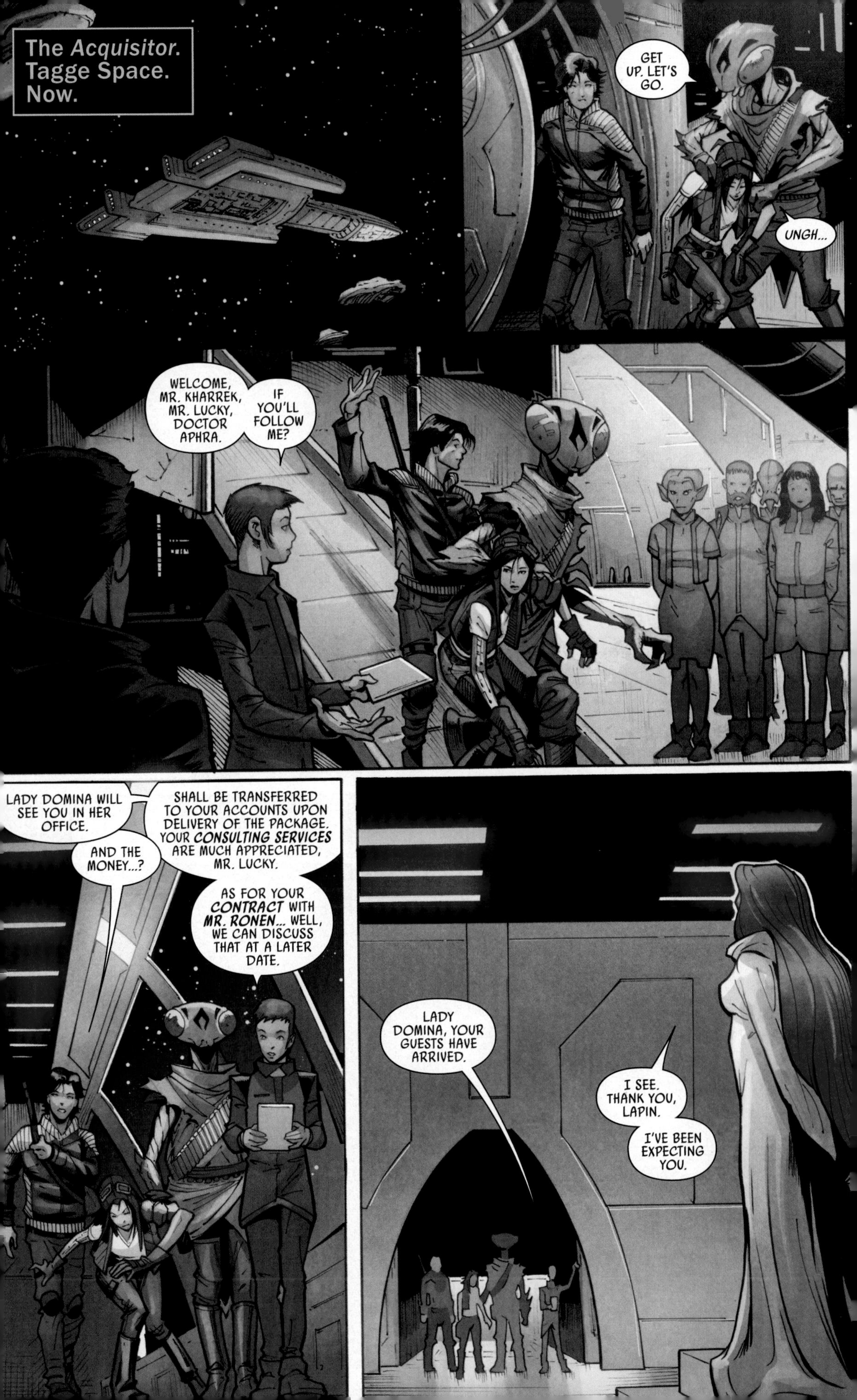
The *Acquisitor*. Tagge Space. Now.
GET UP. LET'S GO.
UNGH...
WELCOME, MR. KHARREK, MR. LUCKY, DOCTOR APHRA.
IF YOU'LL FOLLOW ME?
LADY DOMINA WILL SEE YOU IN HER OFFICE.
AND THE MONEY...?
SHALL BE TRANSFERRED TO YOUR ACCOUNTS UPON DELIVERY OF THE PACKAGE. YOUR ***CONSULTING SERVICES*** ARE MUCH APPRECIATED, MR. LUCKY.
AS FOR YOUR ***CONTRACT*** WITH ***MR. RONEN***... WELL, WE CAN DISCUSS THAT AT A LATER DATE.
LADY DOMINA, YOUR GUESTS HAVE ARRIVED.
I SEE. THANK YOU, LAPIN.
I'VE BEEN EXPECTING YOU.

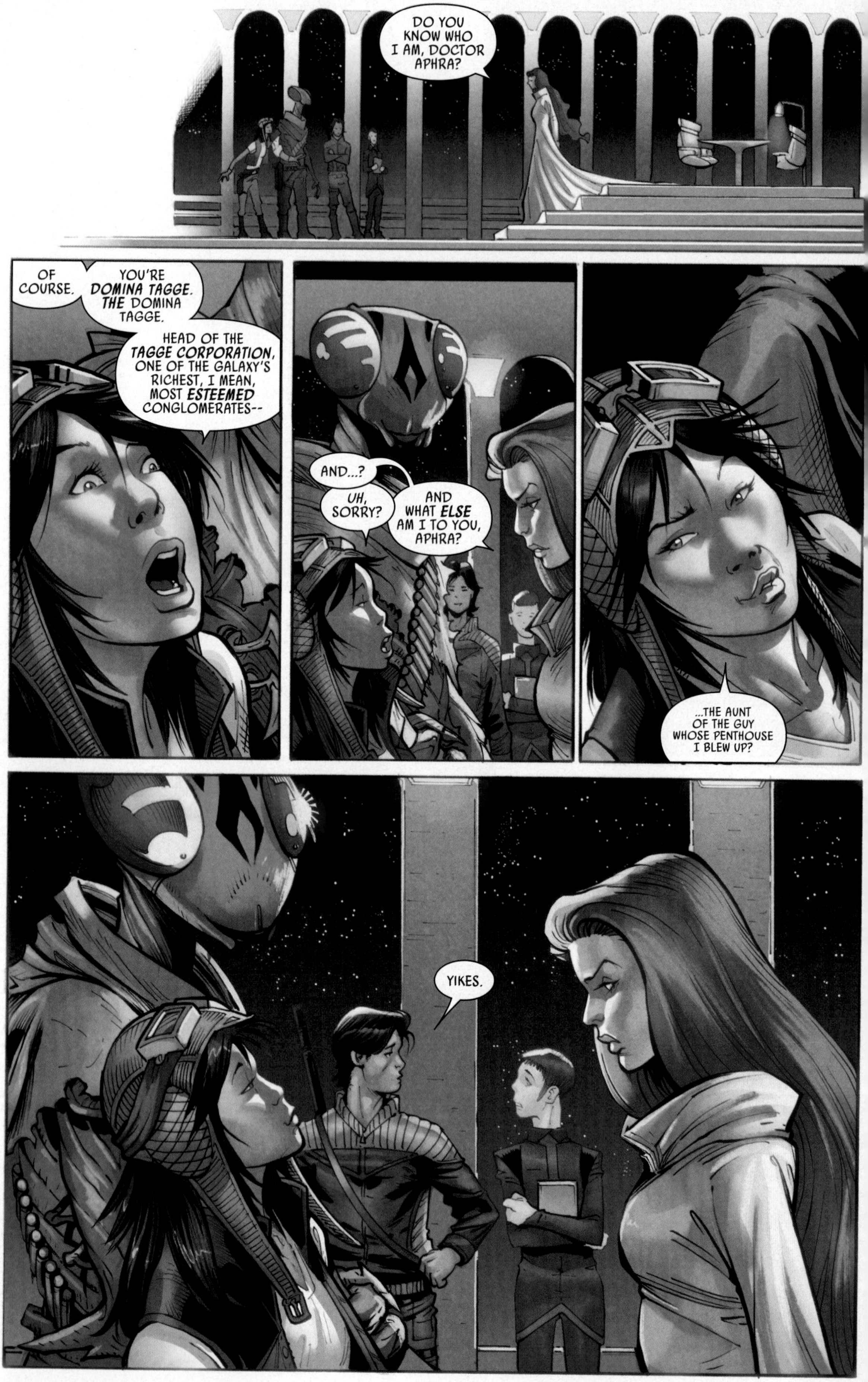
DO YOU KNOW WHO I AM, DOCTOR APHRA?
OF COURSE.
YOU'RE DOMINA TAGGE. THE DOMINA TAGGE.
HEAD OF THE TAGGE CORPORATION, ONE OF THE GALAXY'S RICHEST, I MEAN, MOST ESTEEMED CONGLOMERATES--
AND...?
UH, SORRY?
AND WHAT ELSE AM I TO YOU, APHRA?
...THE AUNT OF THE GUY WHOSE PENTHOUSE I BLEW UP?
YIKES.

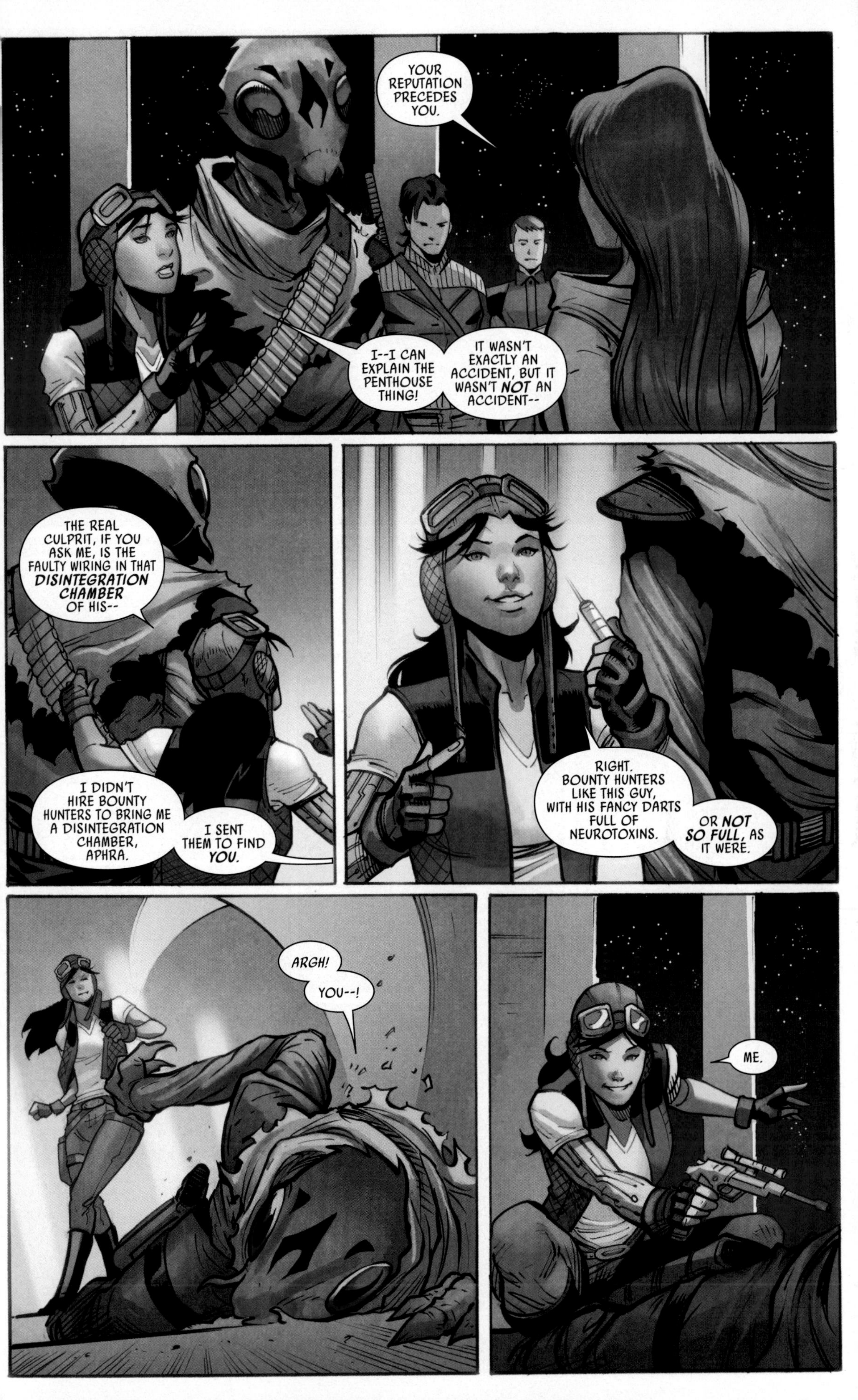
YOUR REPUTATION PRECEDES YOU.
I--I CAN EXPLAIN THE PENTHOUSE THING!
IT WASN'T EXACTLY AN ACCIDENT, BUT IT WASN'T NOT AN ACCIDENT--
THE REAL CULPRIT, IF YOU ASK ME, IS THE FAULTY WIRING IN THAT DISINTEGRATION CHAMBER OF HIS--
I DIDN'T HIRE BOUNTY HUNTERS TO BRING ME A DISINTEGRATION CHAMBER, APHRA.
I SENT THEM TO FIND YOU.
RIGHT. BOUNTY HUNTERS LIKE THIS GUY, WITH HIS FANCY DARTS FULL OF NEUROTOXINS.
OR NOT SO FULL, AS IT WERE.
ARGH!
YOU--!
ME.

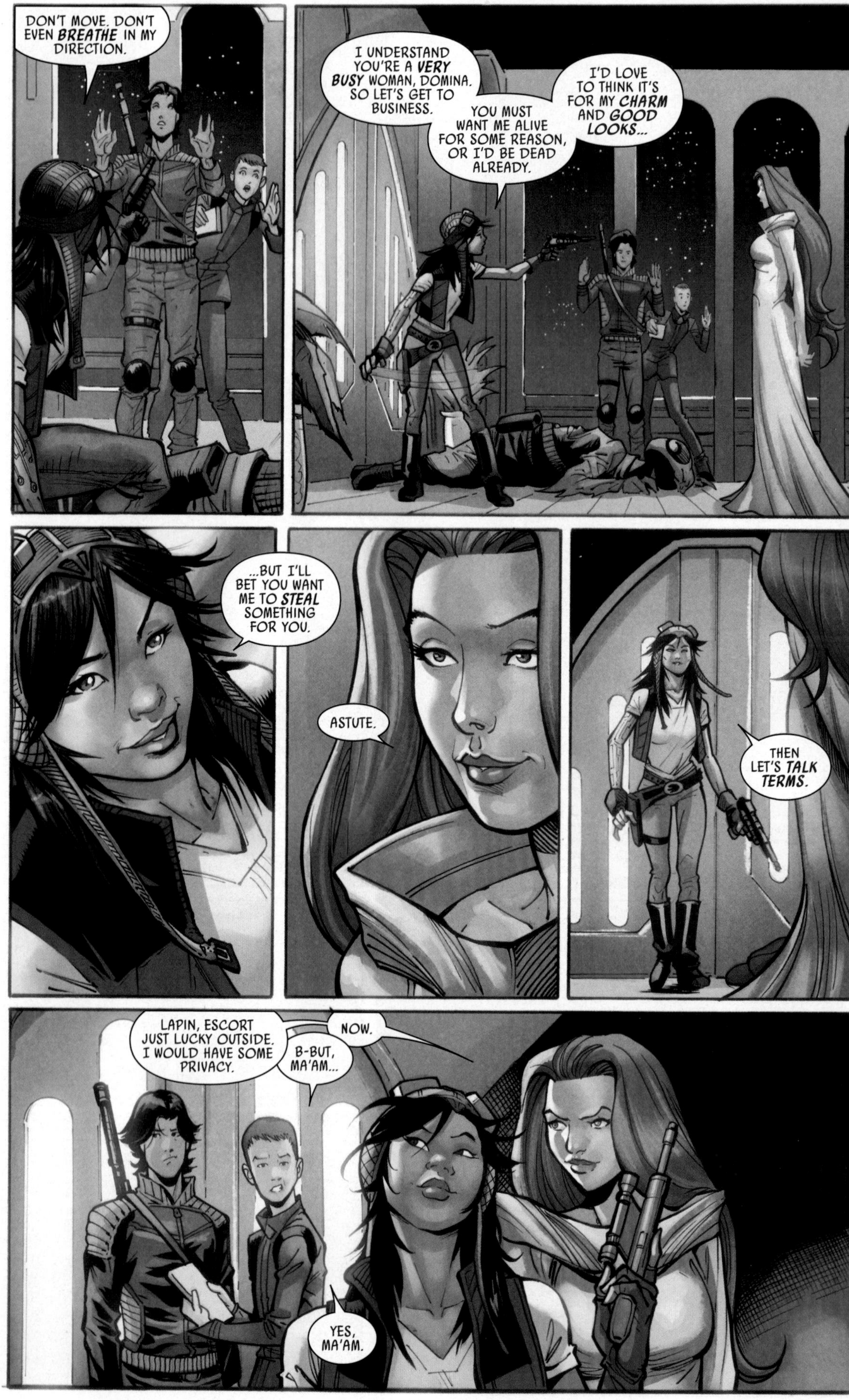

DON'T MOVE. DON'T EVEN BREATHE IN MY DIRECTION.
I UNDERSTAND YOU'RE A VERY BUSY WOMAN, DOMINA. SO LET'S GET TO BUSINESS.
YOU MUST WANT ME ALIVE FOR SOME REASON, OR I'D BE DEAD ALREADY.
I'D LOVE TO THINK IT'S FOR MY CHARM AND GOOD LOOKS...
...BUT I'LL BET YOU WANT ME TO STEAL SOMETHING FOR YOU.
ASTUTE.
THEN LET'S TALK TERMS.
LAPIN, ESCORT JUST LUCKY OUTSIDE. I WOULD HAVE SOME PRIVACY.
B-BUT, MA'AM...
NOW.
YES, MA'AM.

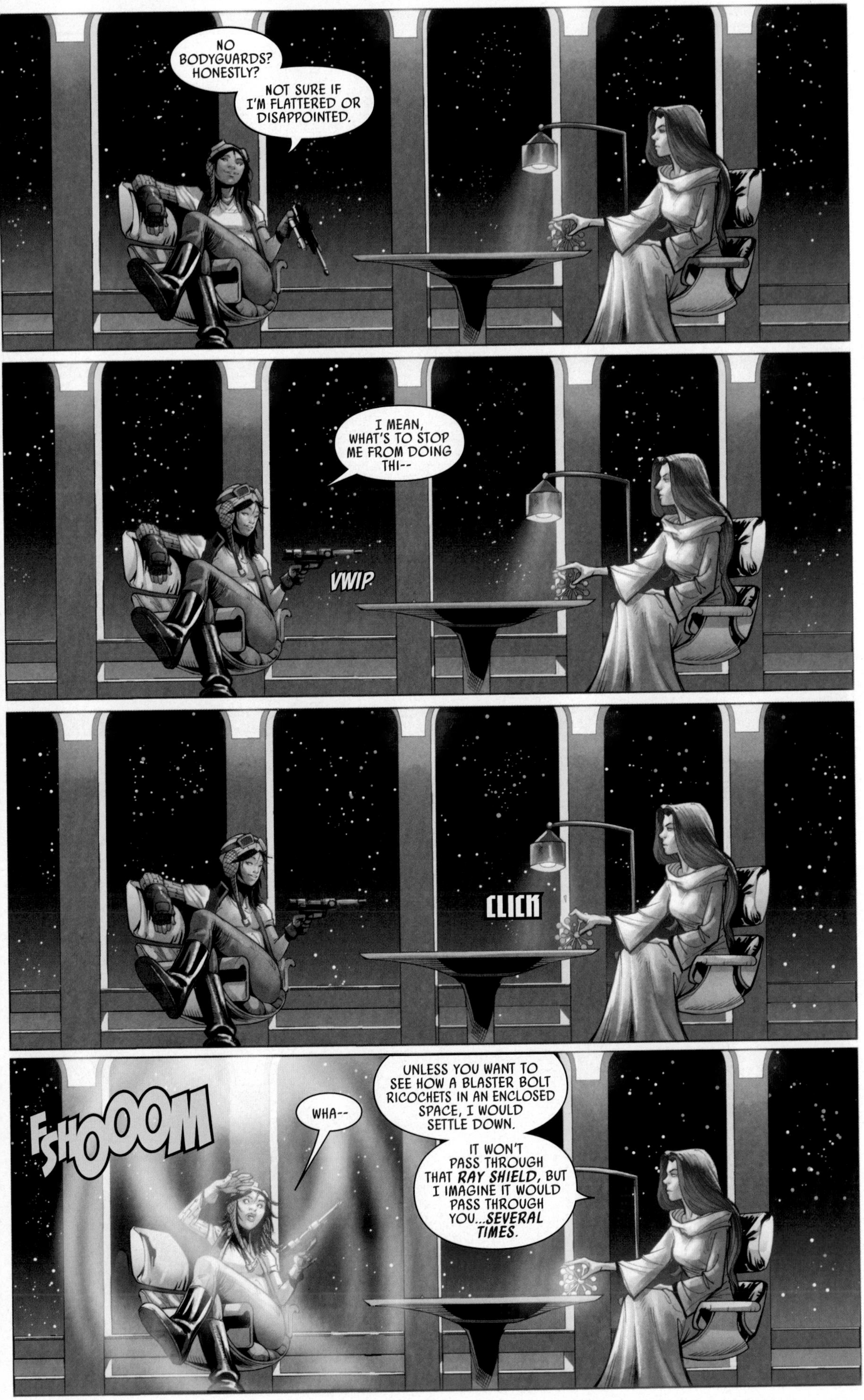
NO BODYGUARDS? HONESTLY?
NOT SURE IF I'M FLATTERED OR DISAPPOINTED.
I MEAN, WHAT'S TO STOP ME FROM DOING THI--
VWIP
CLICK
FSHOOOM
WHA--
UNLESS YOU WANT TO SEE HOW A BLASTER BOLT RICOCHETS IN AN ENCLOSED SPACE, I WOULD SETTLE DOWN.
IT WON'T PASS THROUGH THAT RAY SHIELD, BUT I IMAGINE IT WOULD PASS THROUGH YOU...SEVERAL TIMES.

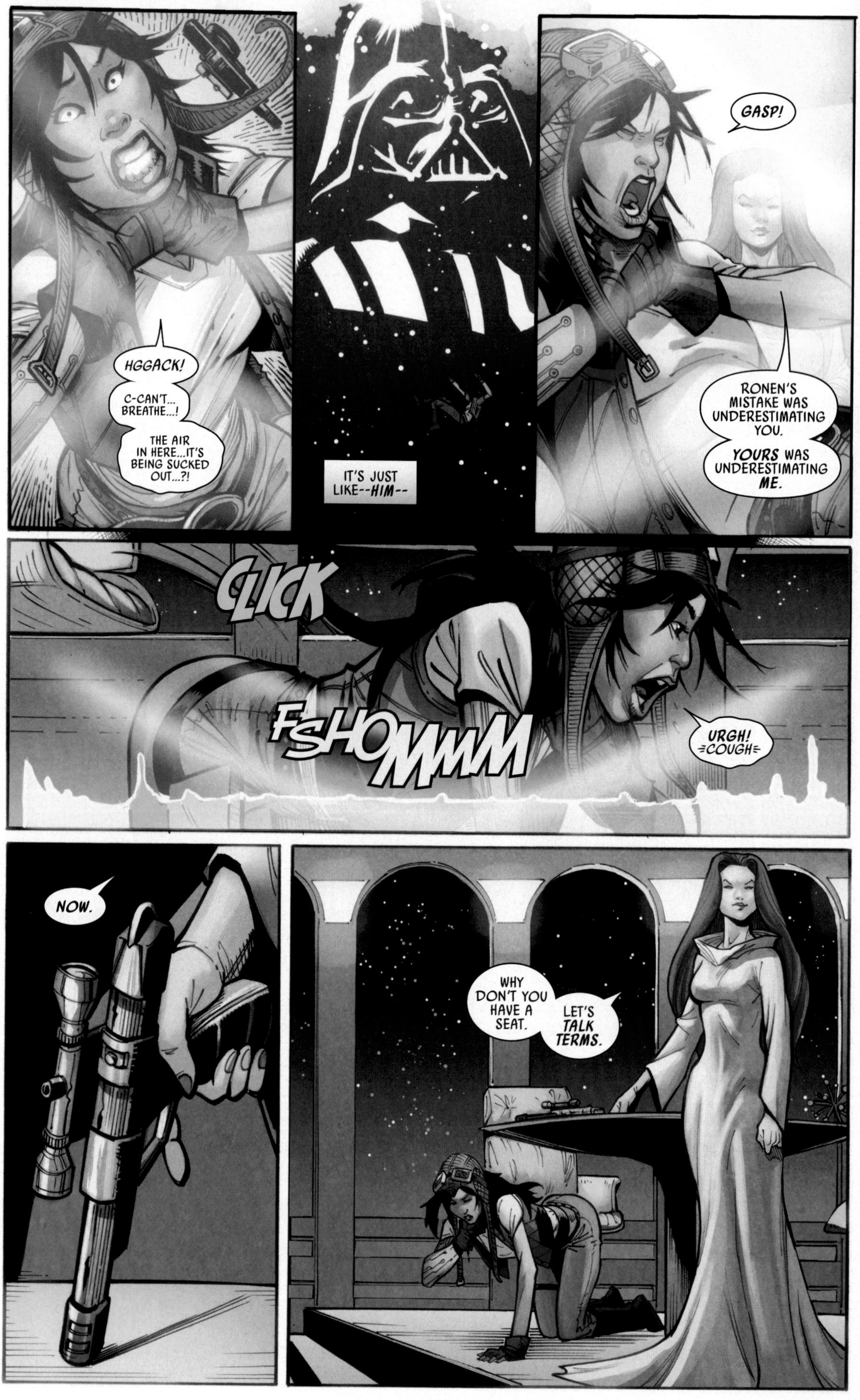
HGGACK!
C-CAN'T... BREATHE...!
THE AIR IN HERE...IT'S BEING SUCKED OUT...?!
IT'S JUST LIKE--HIM--
GASP!
RONEN'S MISTAKE WAS UNDERESTIMATING YOU.
YOURS WAS UNDERESTIMATING ME.
CLICK
FSHOMMM
URGH! COUGH
NOW.
WHY DON'T YOU HAVE A SEAT.
LET'S TALK TERMS.

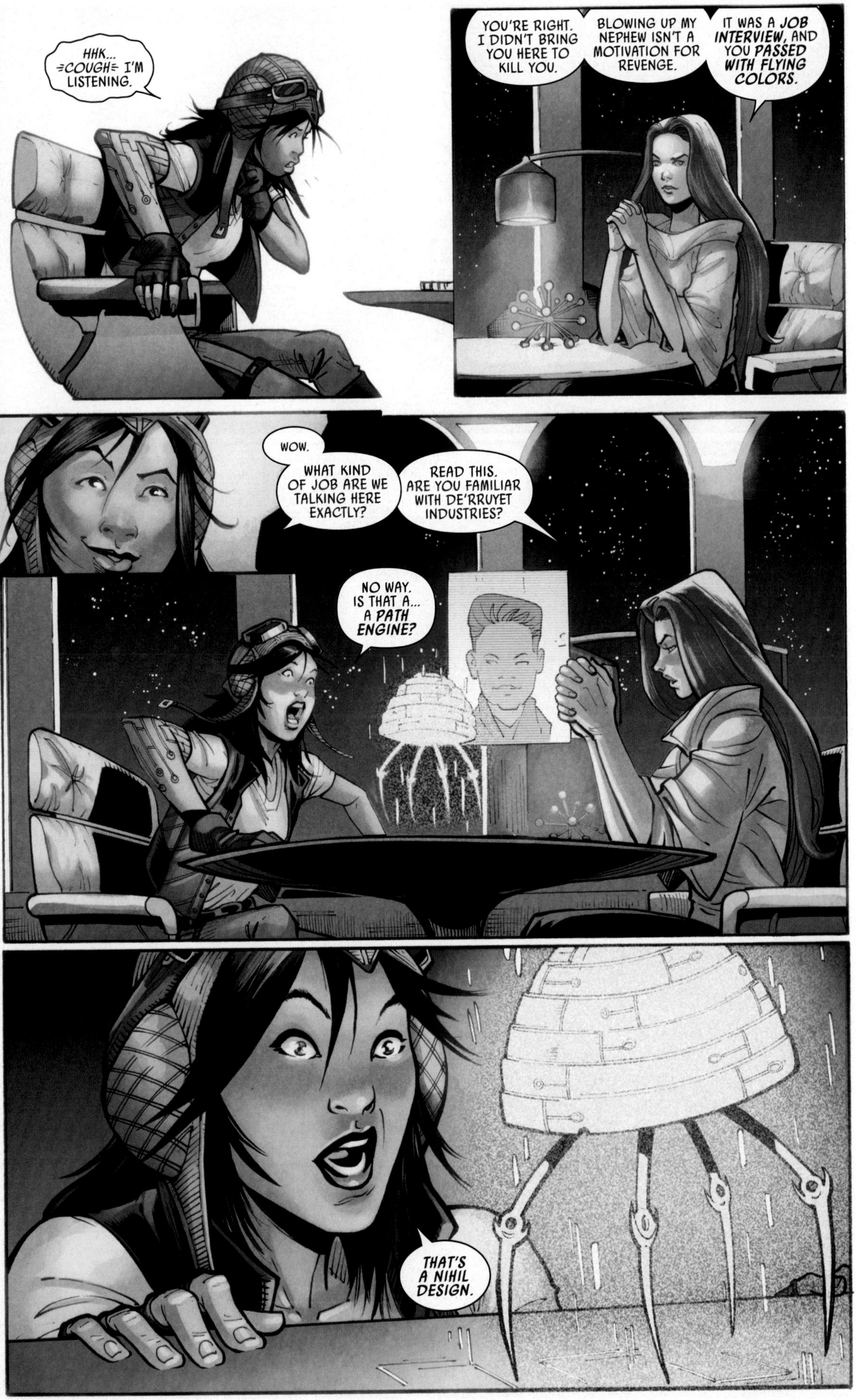
HHK... =COUGH= I'M LISTENING.
YOU'RE RIGHT. I DIDN'T BRING YOU HERE TO KILL YOU.
BLOWING UP MY NEPHEW ISN'T A MOTIVATION FOR REVENGE.
IT WAS A JOB INTERVIEW, AND YOU PASSED WITH FLYING COLORS.
WOW.
WHAT KIND OF JOB ARE WE TALKING HERE EXACTLY?
READ THIS. ARE YOU FAMILIAR WITH DE'RRUYET INDUSTRIES?
NO WAY. IS THAT A... A PATH ENGINE?
THAT'S A NIHIL DESIGN.

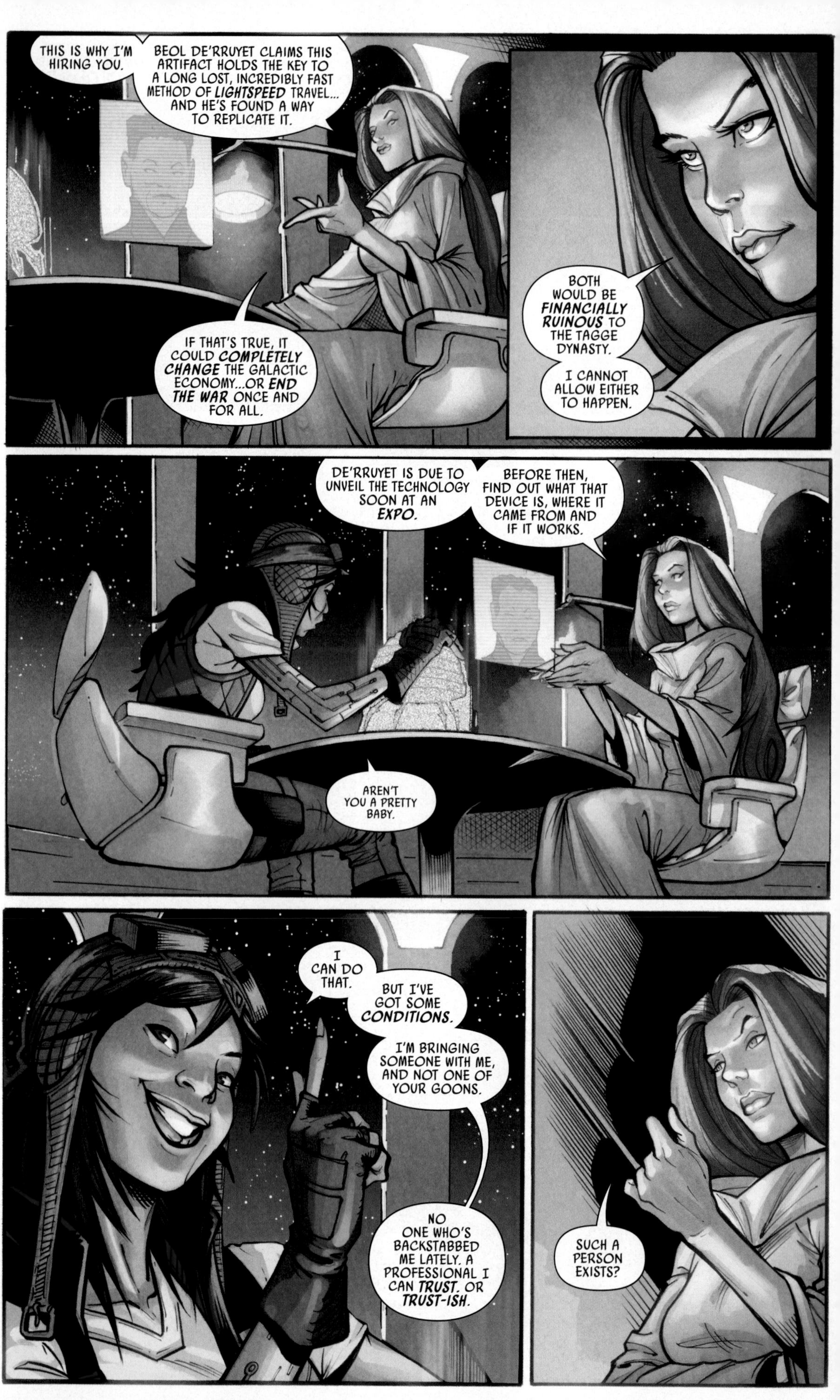

THIS IS WHY I'M HIRING YOU.
BEOL DE'RRUYET CLAIMS THIS ARTIFACT HOLDS THE KEY TO A LONG LOST, INCREDIBLY FAST METHOD OF LIGHTSPEED TRAVEL... AND HE'S FOUND A WAY TO REPLICATE IT.
IF THAT'S TRUE, IT COULD COMPLETELY CHANGE THE GALACTIC ECONOMY...OR END THE WAR ONCE AND FOR ALL.
BOTH WOULD BE FINANCIALLY RUINOUS TO THE TAGGE DYNASTY.
I CANNOT ALLOW EITHER TO HAPPEN.
DE'RRUYET IS DUE TO UNVEIL THE TECHNOLOGY SOON AT AN EXPO.
BEFORE THEN, FIND OUT WHAT THAT DEVICE IS, WHERE IT CAME FROM AND IF IT WORKS.
AREN'T YOU A PRETTY BABY.
I CAN DO THAT.
BUT I'VE GOT SOME CONDITIONS.
I'M BRINGING SOMEONE WITH ME, AND NOT ONE OF YOUR GOONS.
NO ONE WHO'S BACKSTABBED ME LATELY. A PROFESSIONAL I CAN TRUST. OR TRUST-ISH.
SUCH A PERSON EXISTS?

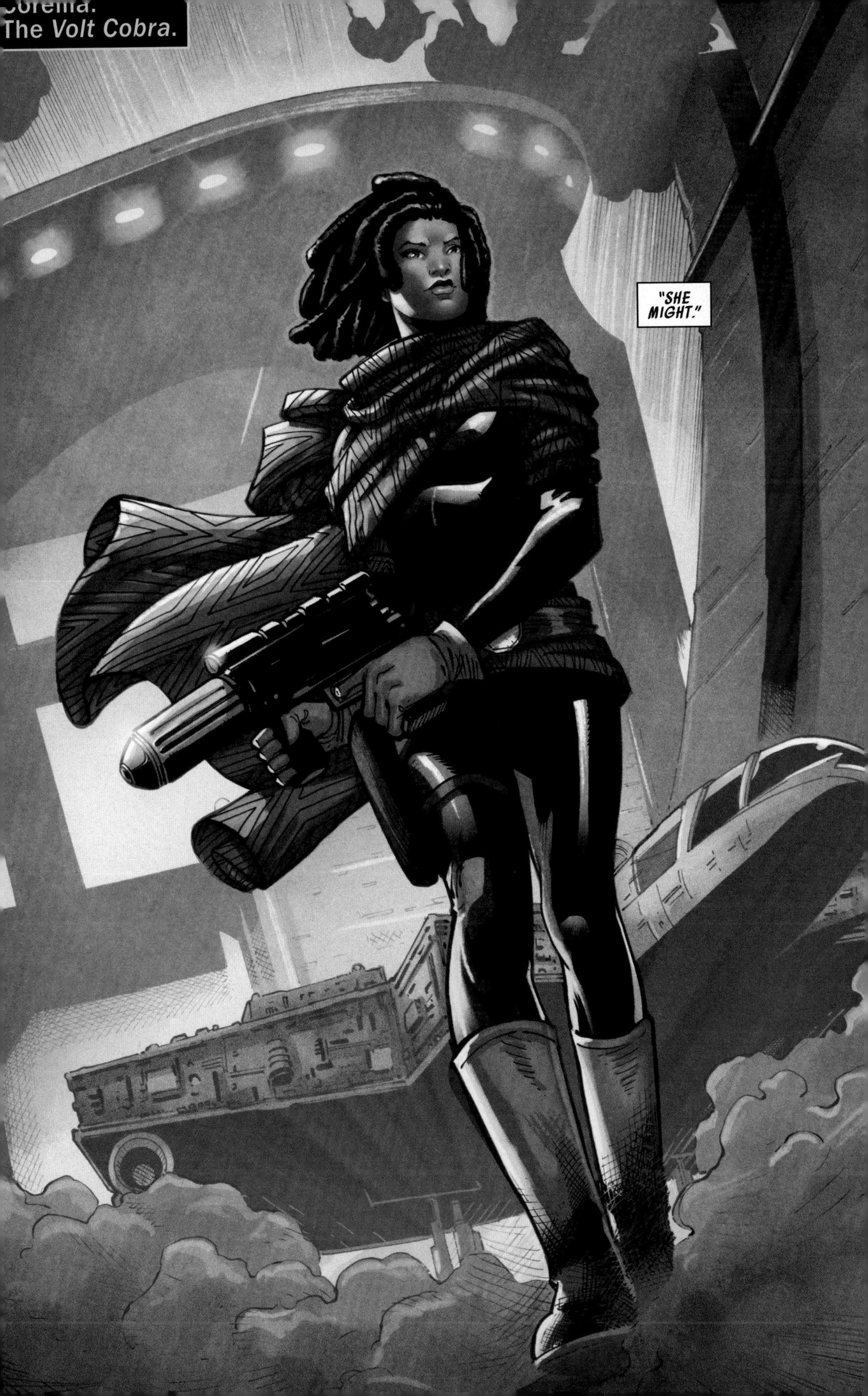
The Volt Cobra.
"SHE MIGHT."

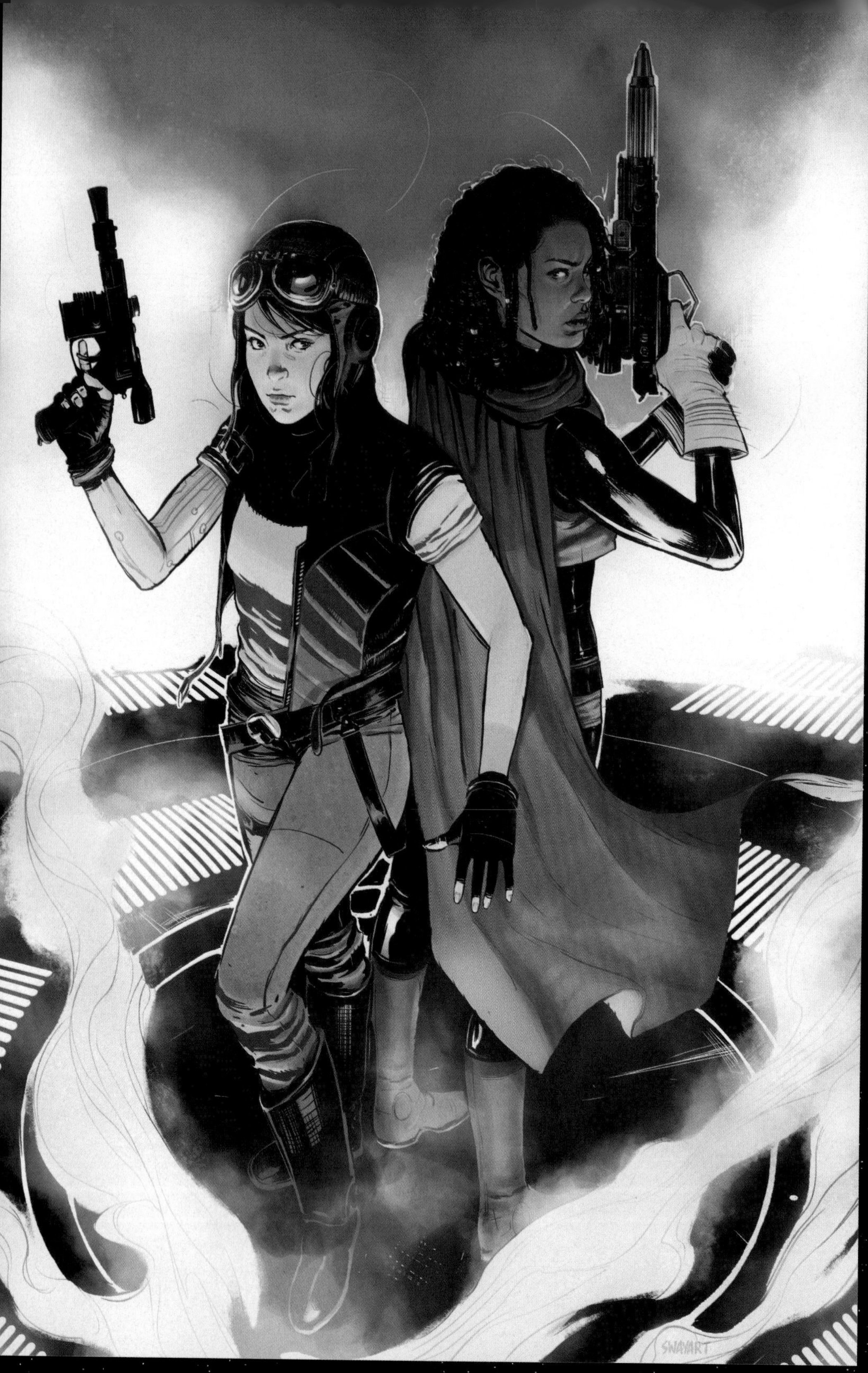
SWAYART

7 — THE OFFER

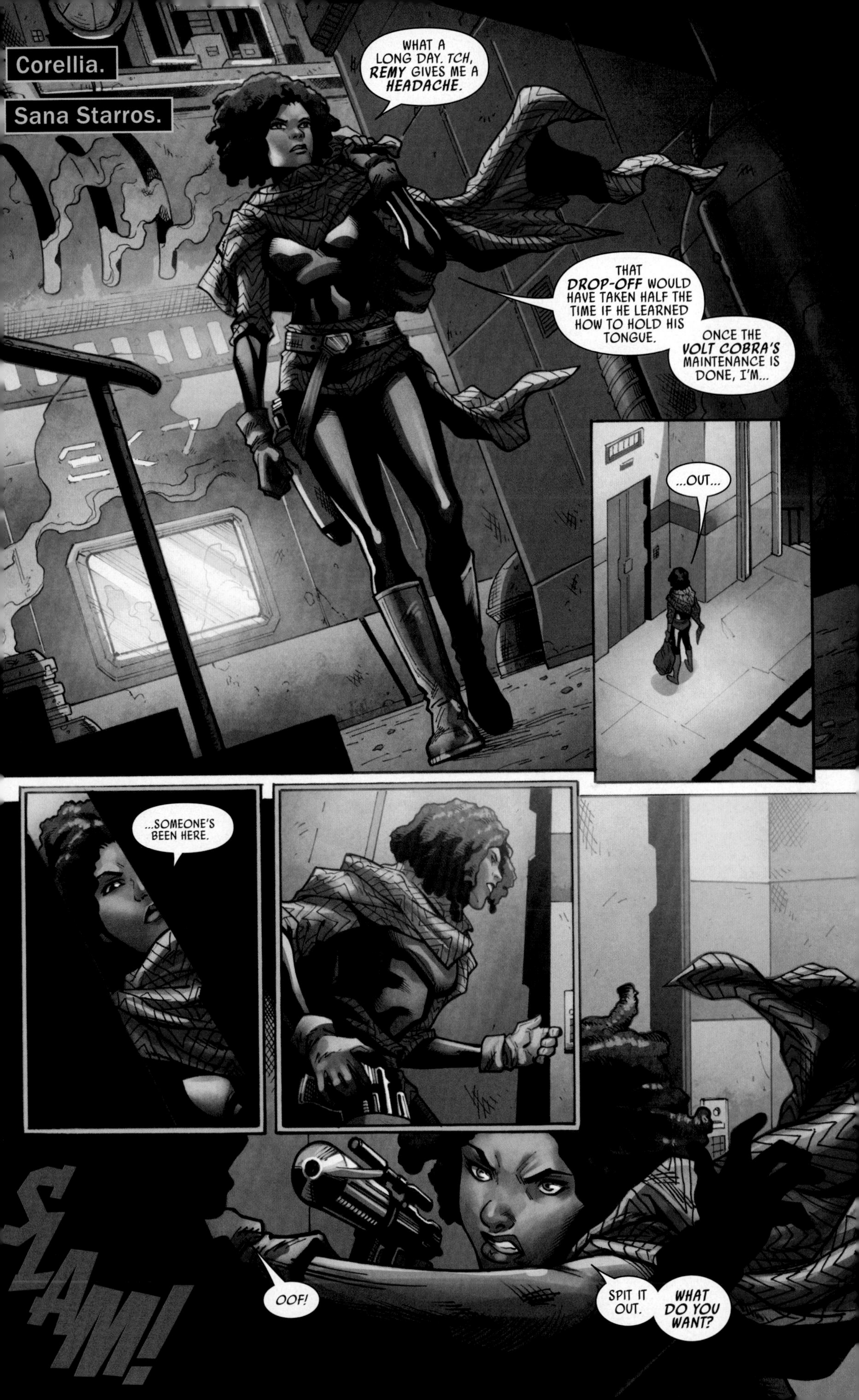
Corellia.
Sana Starros.
WHAT A LONG DAY. TCH, REMY GIVES ME A HEADACHE.
THAT DROP-OFF WOULD HAVE TAKEN HALF THE TIME IF HE LEARNED HOW TO HOLD HIS TONGUE.
ONCE THE VOLT COBRA'S MAINTENANCE IS DONE, I'M...
...OUT...
...SOMEONE'S BEEN HERE.
SLAM!
OOF!
SPIT IT OUT.
WHAT DO YOU WANT?

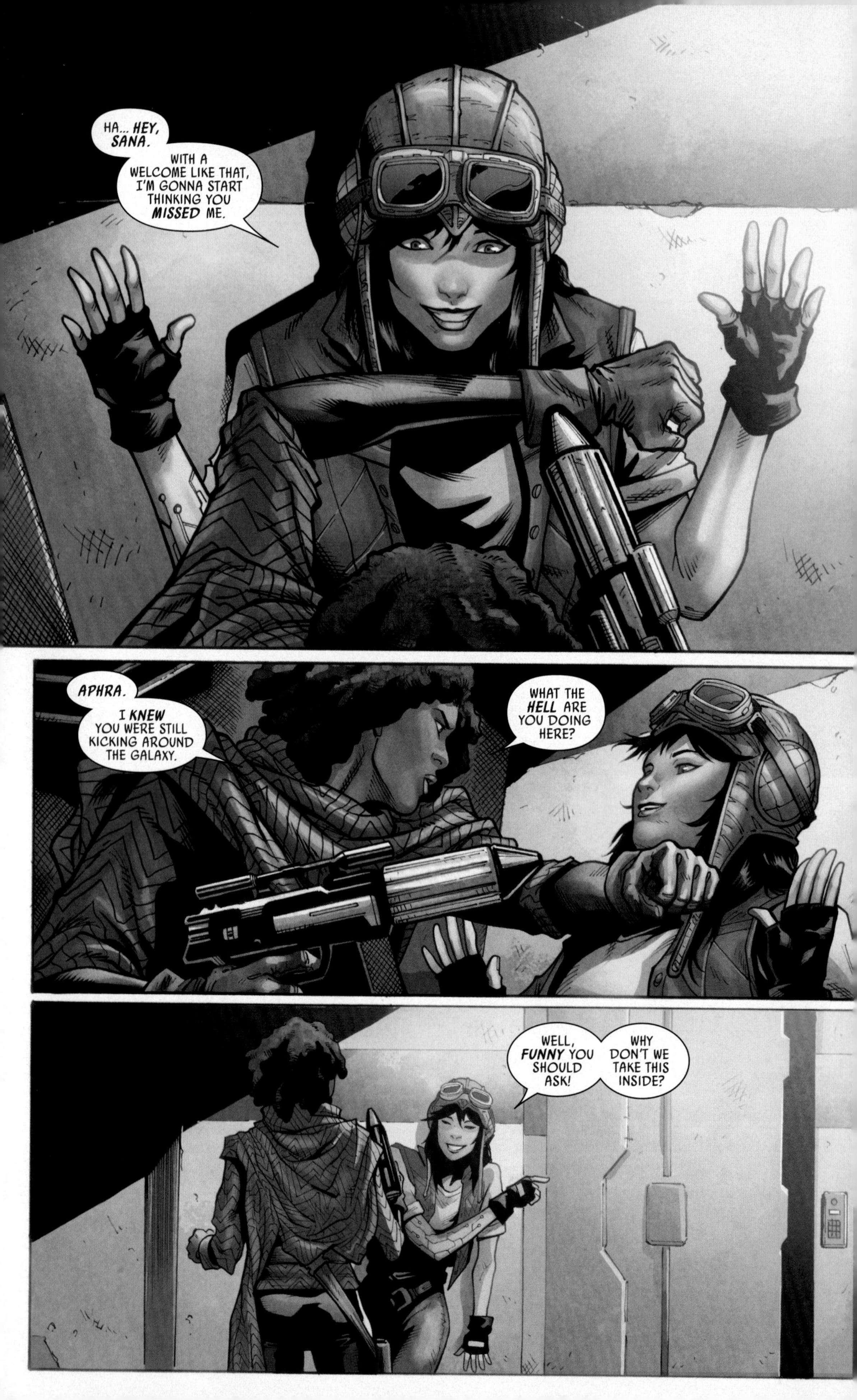

HA... HEY, SANA.
WITH A WELCOME LIKE THAT, I'M GONNA START THINKING YOU MISSED ME.
APHRA.
I KNEW YOU WERE STILL KICKING AROUND THE GALAXY.
WHAT THE HELL ARE YOU DOING HERE?
WELL, FUNNY YOU SHOULD ASK!
WHY DON'T WE TAKE THIS INSIDE?

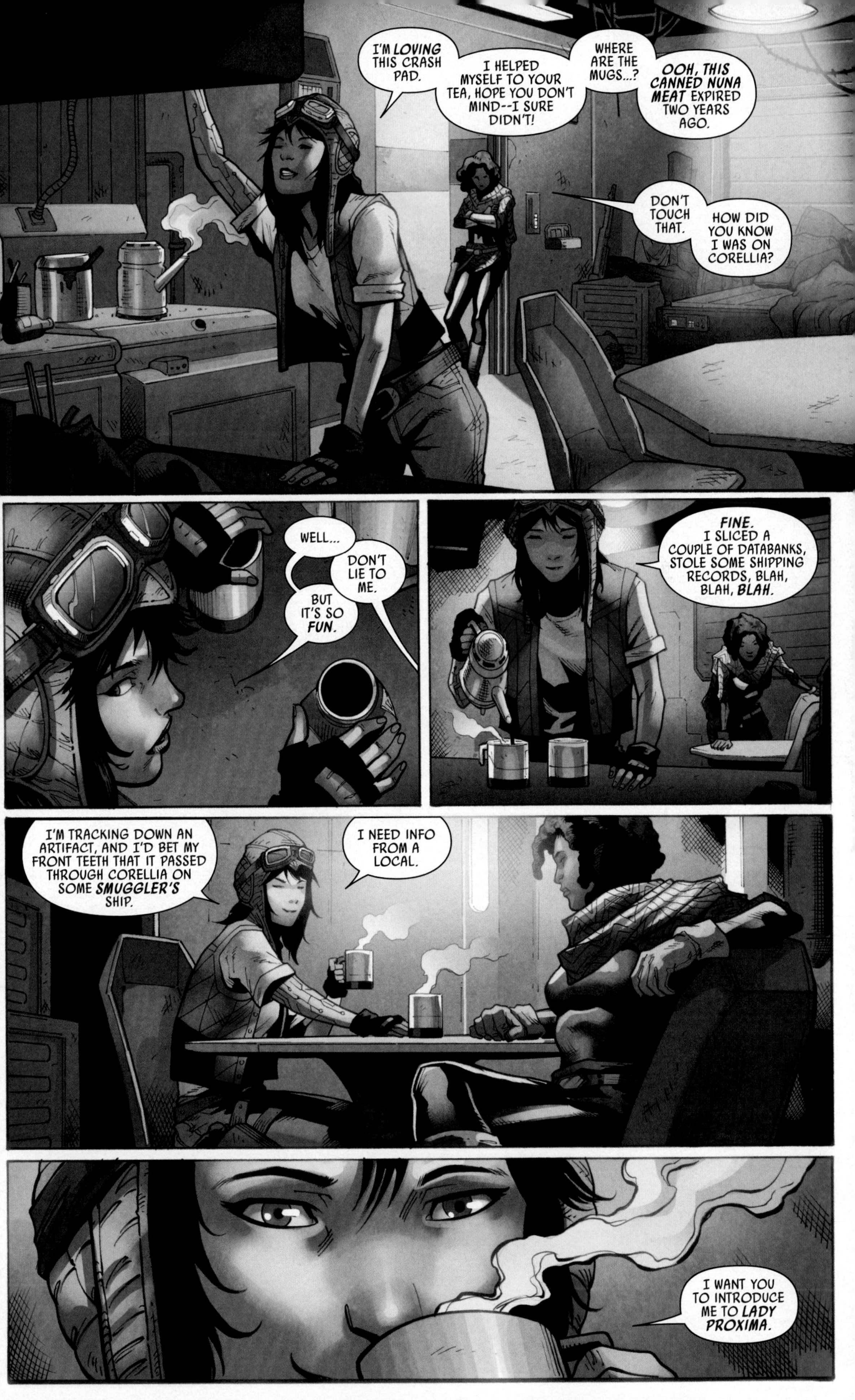
I'M LOVING THIS CRASH PAD.
I HELPED MYSELF TO YOUR TEA, HOPE YOU DON'T MIND--I SURE DIDN'T!
WHERE ARE THE MUGS...?
OOH, THIS CANNED NUNA MEAT EXPIRED TWO YEARS AGO.
DON'T TOUCH THAT.
HOW DID YOU KNOW I WAS ON CORELLIA?
WELL...
DON'T LIE TO ME.
BUT IT'S SO FUN.
FINE. I SLICED A COUPLE OF DATABANKS, STOLE SOME SHIPPING RECORDS, BLAH, BLAH, BLAH.
I'M TRACKING DOWN AN ARTIFACT, AND I'D BET MY FRONT TEETH THAT IT PASSED THROUGH CORELLIA ON SOME SMUGGLER'S SHIP.
I NEED INFO FROM A LOCAL.
I WANT YOU TO INTRODUCE ME TO LADY PROXIMA.

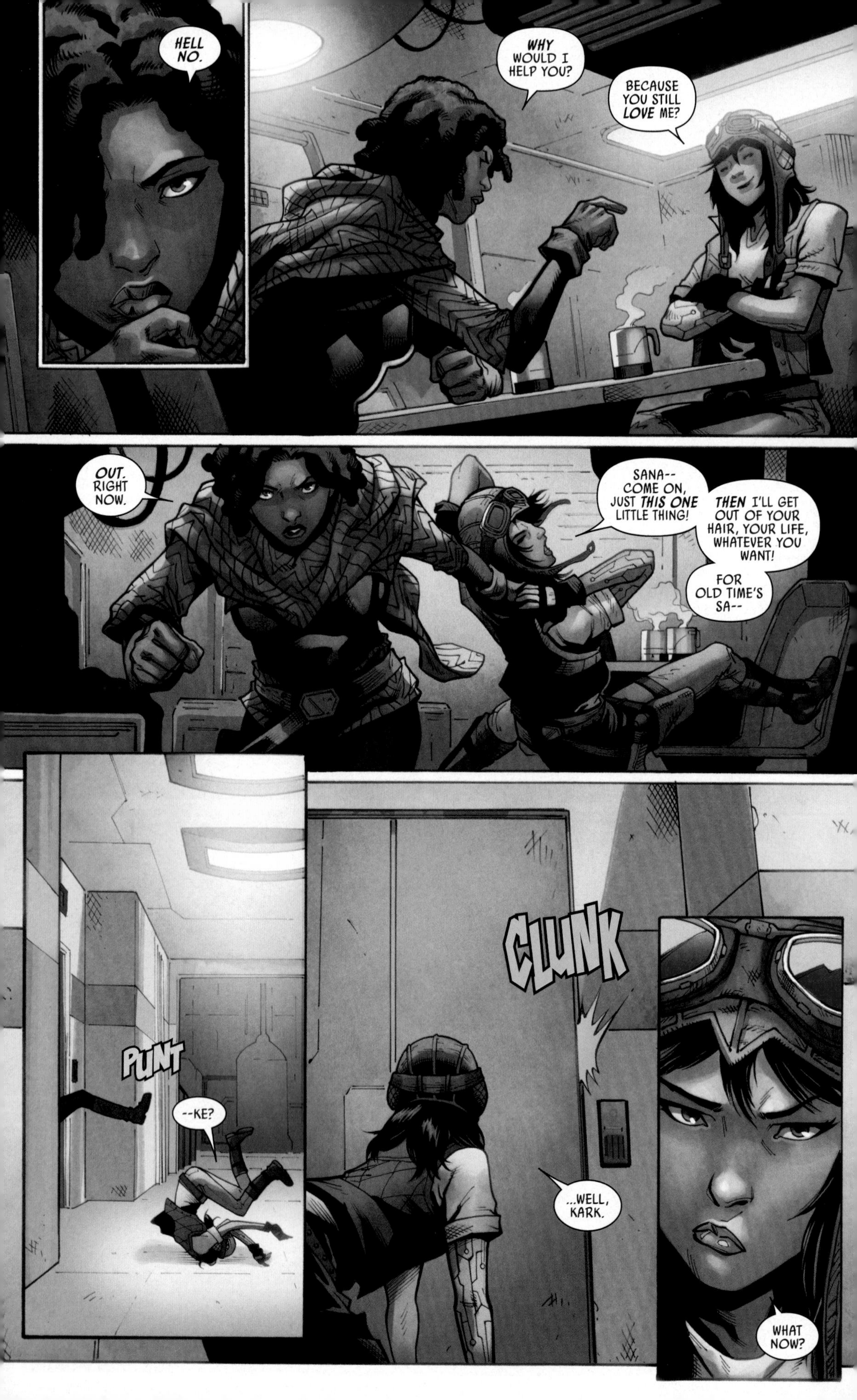
HELL NO.
WHY WOULD I HELP YOU?
BECAUSE YOU STILL LOVE ME?
OUT. RIGHT NOW.
SANA-- COME ON, JUST THIS ONE LITTLE THING!
THEN I'LL GET OUT OF YOUR HAIR, YOUR LIFE, WHATEVER YOU WANT!
FOR OLD TIME'S SA--
PUNT
--KE?
CLUNK
...WELL, KARK.
WHAT NOW?

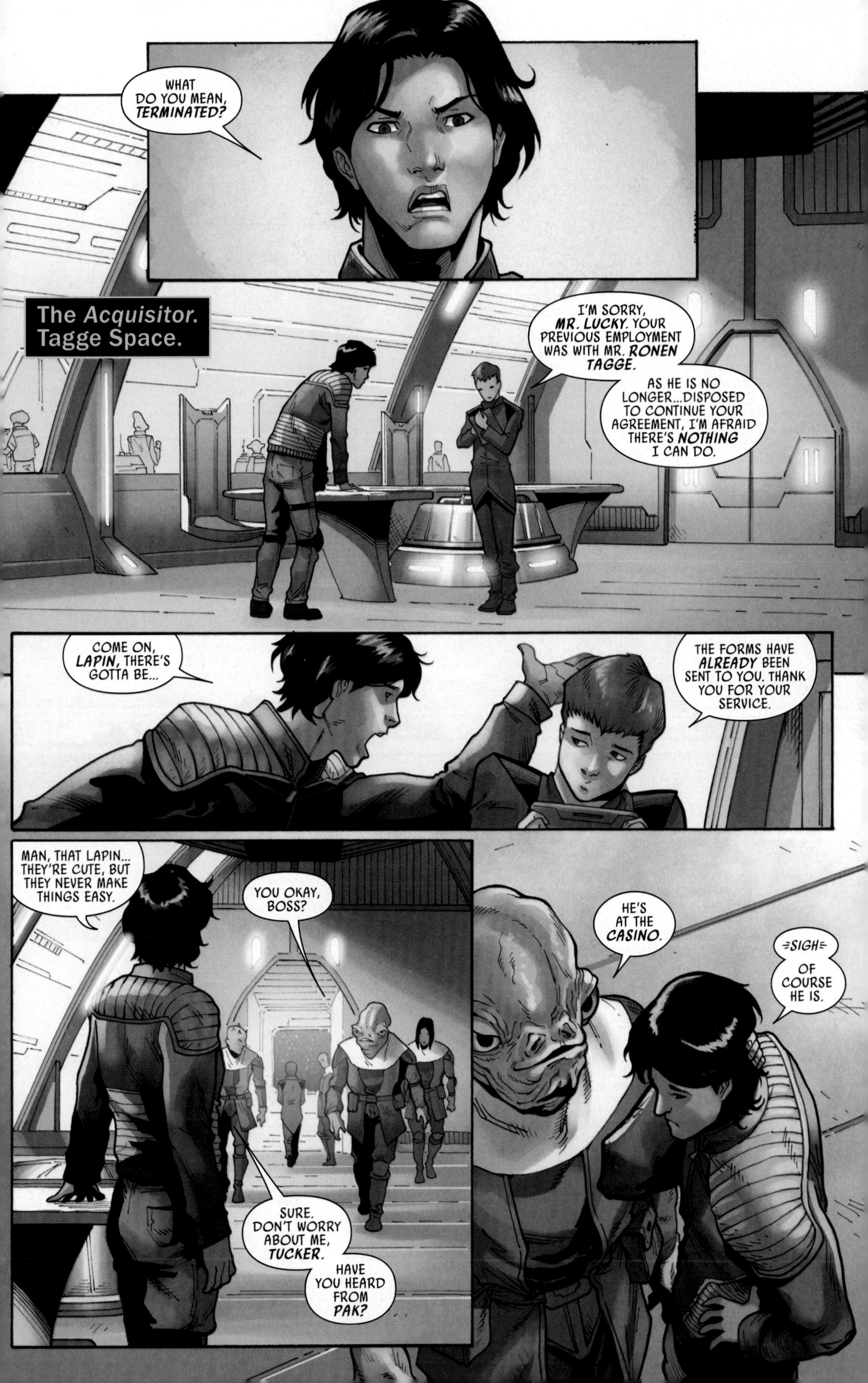
WHAT DO YOU MEAN, TERMINATED?
The Acquisitor. Tagge Space.
I'M SORRY, MR. LUCKY. YOUR PREVIOUS EMPLOYMENT WAS WITH MR. RONEN TAGGE.
AS HE IS NO LONGER...DISPOSED TO CONTINUE YOUR AGREEMENT, I'M AFRAID THERE'S NOTHING I CAN DO.
COME ON, LAPIN, THERE'S GOTTA BE...
THE FORMS HAVE ALREADY BEEN SENT TO YOU. THANK YOU FOR YOUR SERVICE.
MAN, THAT LAPIN... THEY'RE CUTE, BUT THEY NEVER MAKE THINGS EASY.
YOU OKAY, BOSS?
SURE. DON'T WORRY ABOUT ME, TUCKER.
HAVE YOU HEARD FROM PAK?
HE'S AT THE CASINO.
=SIGH=
OF COURSE HE IS.

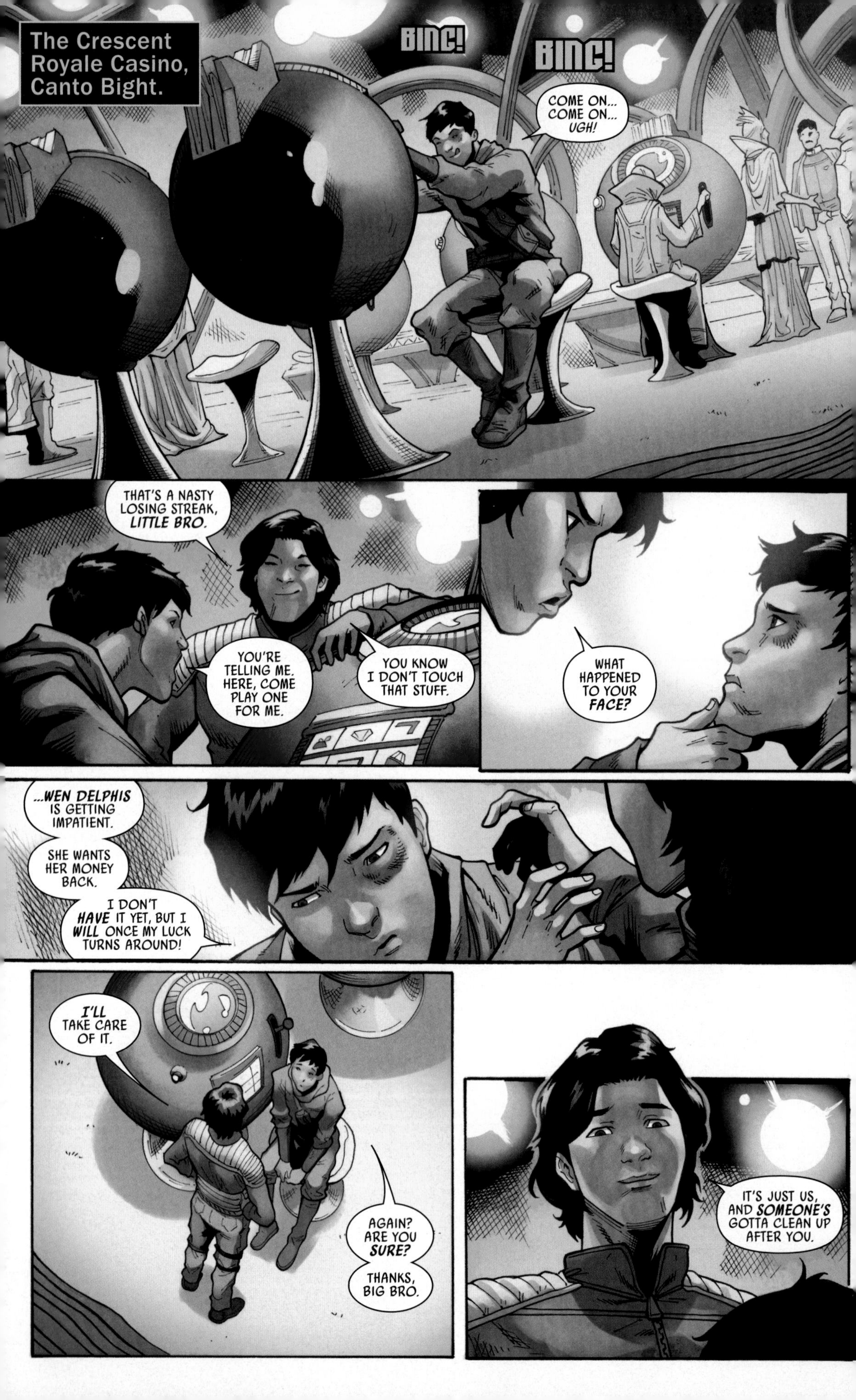
The Crescent Royale Casino, Canto Bight.
BINC!
BINC!
COME ON... COME ON... UGH!
THAT'S A NASTY LOSING STREAK, LITTLE BRO.
YOU'RE TELLING ME. HERE, COME PLAY ONE FOR ME.
YOU KNOW I DON'T TOUCH THAT STUFF.
WHAT HAPPENED TO YOUR FACE?
...WEN DELPHIS IS GETTING IMPATIENT.
SHE WANTS HER MONEY BACK.
I DON'T HAVE IT YET, BUT I WILL ONCE MY LUCK TURNS AROUND!
I'LL TAKE CARE OF IT.
AGAIN? ARE YOU SURE?
THANKS, BIG BRO.
IT'S JUST US, AND SOMEONE'S GOTTA CLEAN UP AFTER YOU.

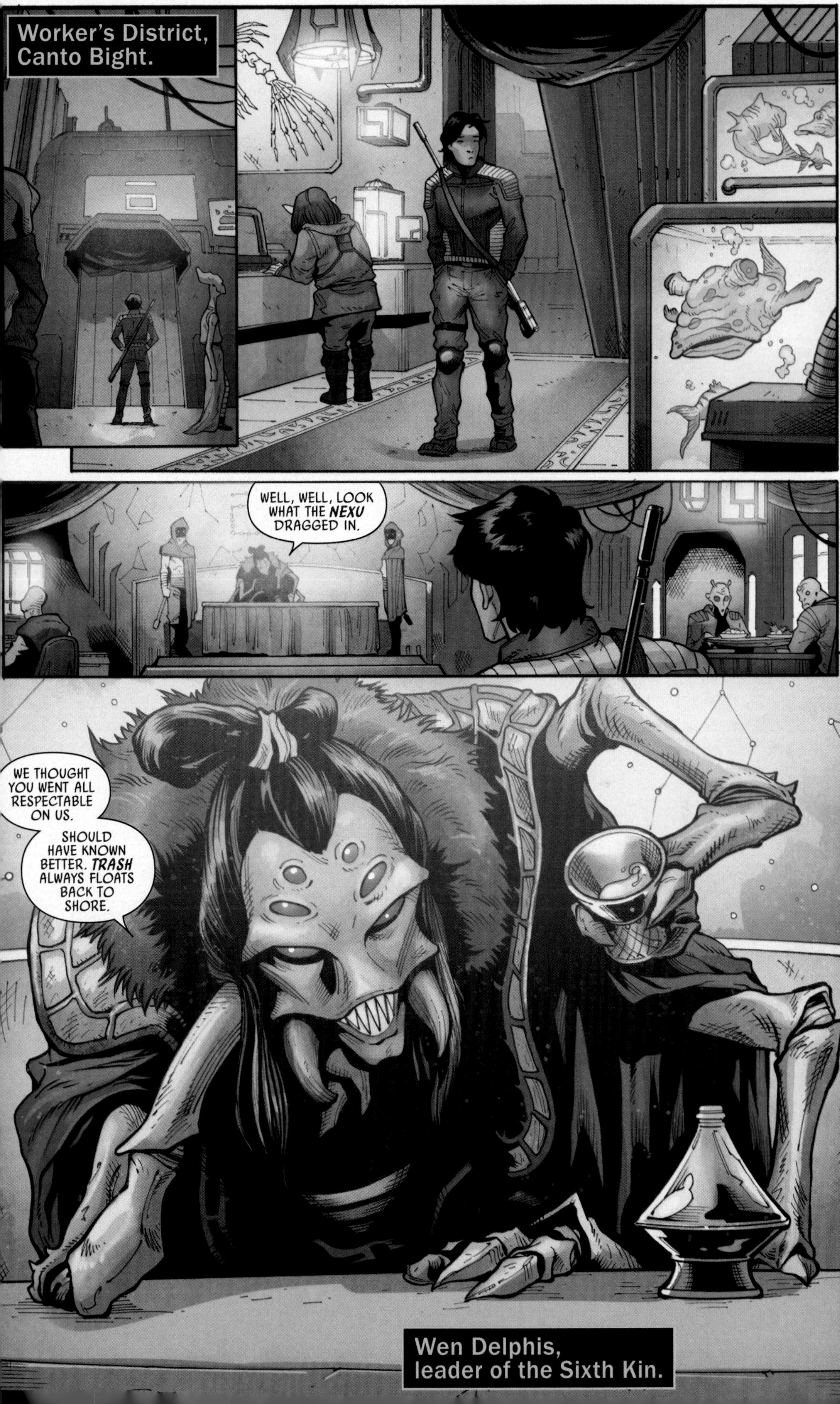

Worker's District, Canto Bight.
WELL, WELL, LOOK WHAT THE NEXU DRAGGED IN.
WE THOUGHT YOU WENT ALL RESPECTABLE ON US.
SHOULD HAVE KNOWN BETTER. TRASH ALWAYS FLOATS BACK TO SHORE.
Wen Delphis, leader of the Sixth Kin.

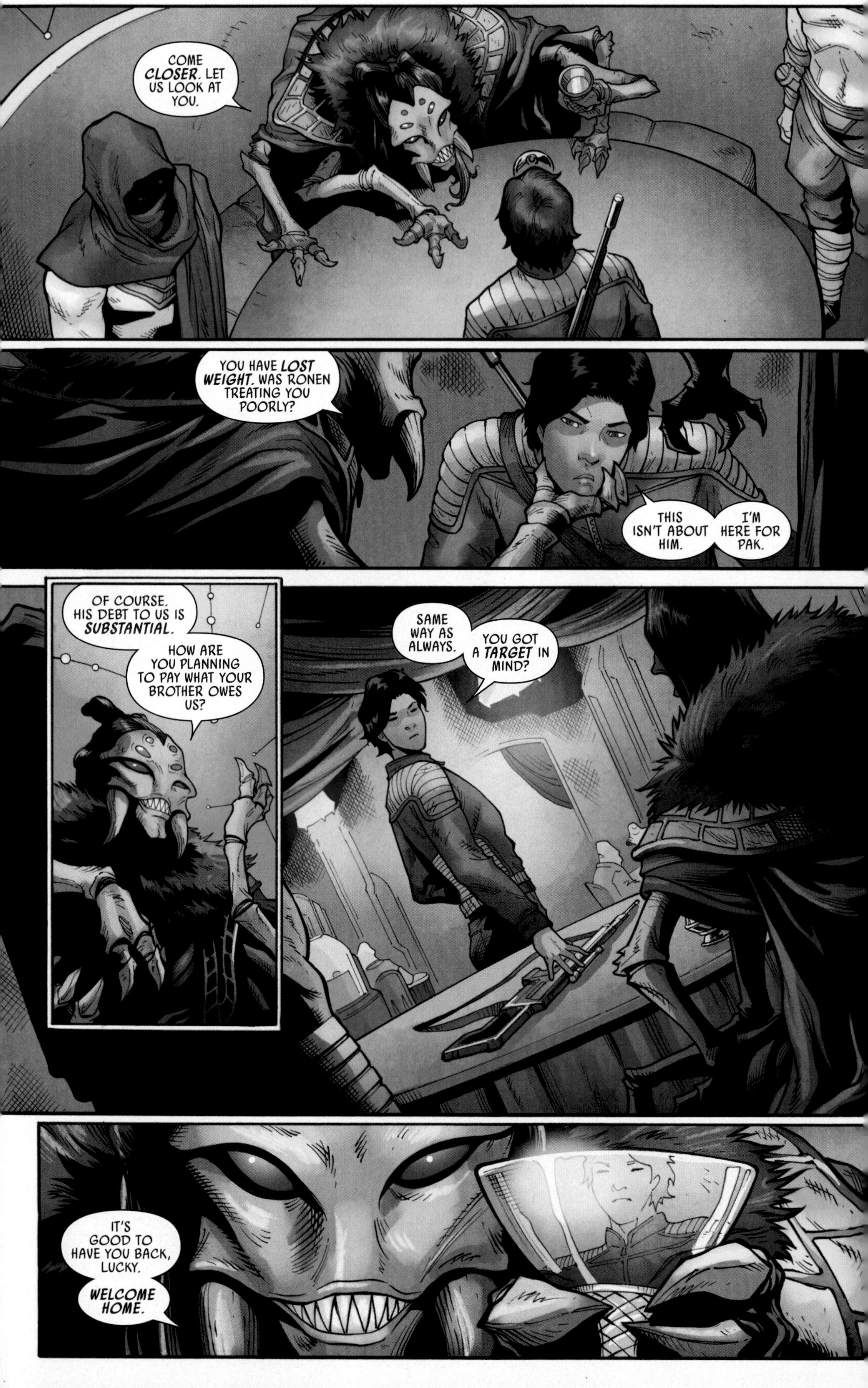
COME CLOSER. LET US LOOK AT YOU.
YOU HAVE LOST WEIGHT. WAS RONEN TREATING YOU POORLY?
THIS ISN'T ABOUT HIM.
I'M HERE FOR PAK.
OF COURSE. HIS DEBT TO US IS SUBSTANTIAL.
HOW ARE YOU PLANNING TO PAY WHAT YOUR BROTHER OWES US?
SAME WAY AS ALWAYS.
YOU GOT A TARGET IN MIND?
IT'S GOOD TO HAVE YOU BACK, LUCKY.
WELCOME HOME.

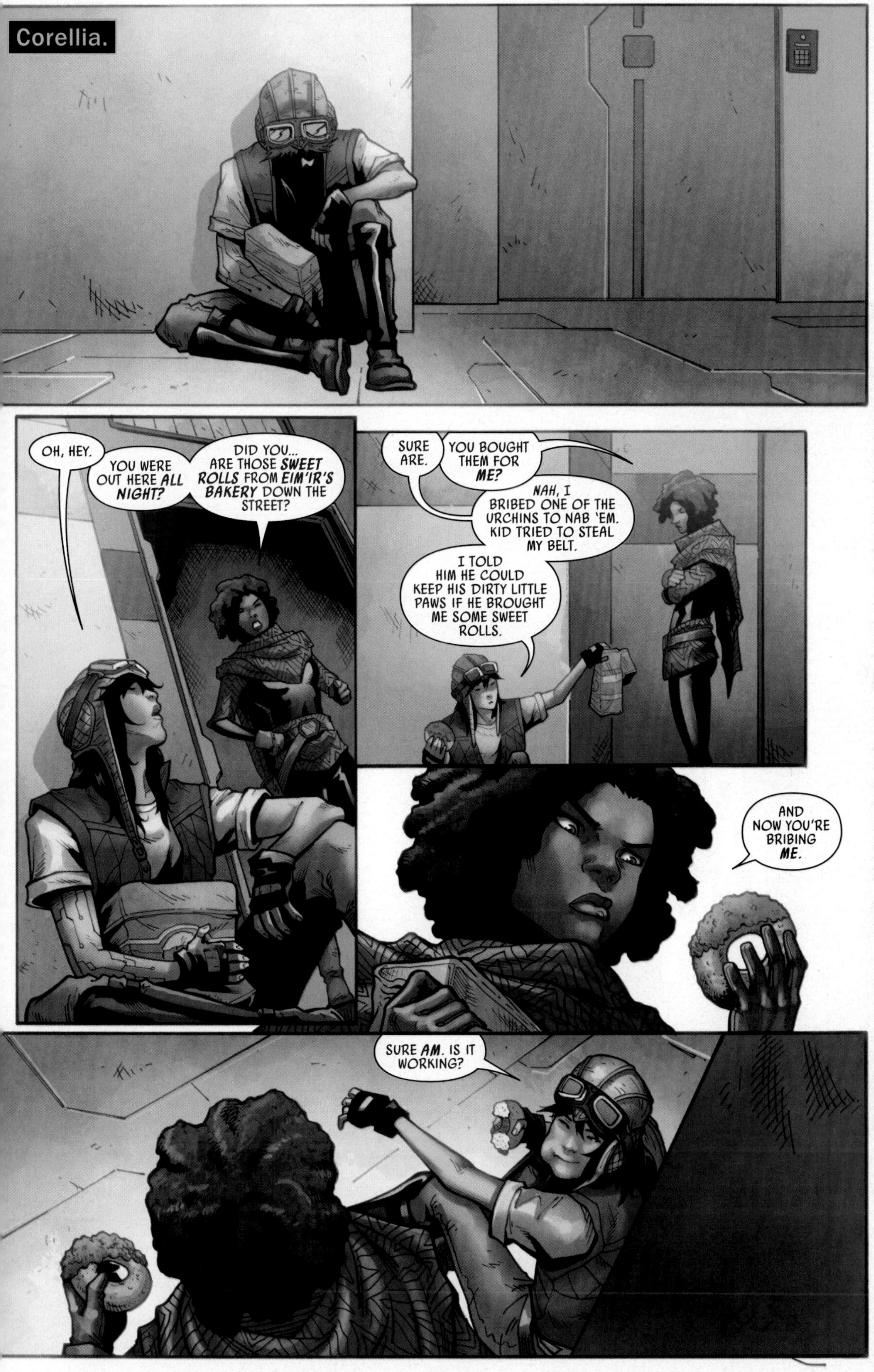
Corellia.
OH, HEY.
YOU WERE OUT HERE ALL NIGHT?
DID YOU... ARE THOSE SWEET ROLLS FROM EIM'IR'S BAKERY DOWN THE STREET?
SURE ARE.
YOU BOUGHT THEM FOR ME?
NAH, I BRIBED ONE OF THE URCHINS TO NAB 'EM. KID TRIED TO STEAL MY BELT.
I TOLD HIM HE COULD KEEP HIS DIRTY LITTLE PAWS IF HE BROUGHT ME SOME SWEET ROLLS.
AND NOW YOU'RE BRIBING ME.
SURE AM. IS IT WORKING?

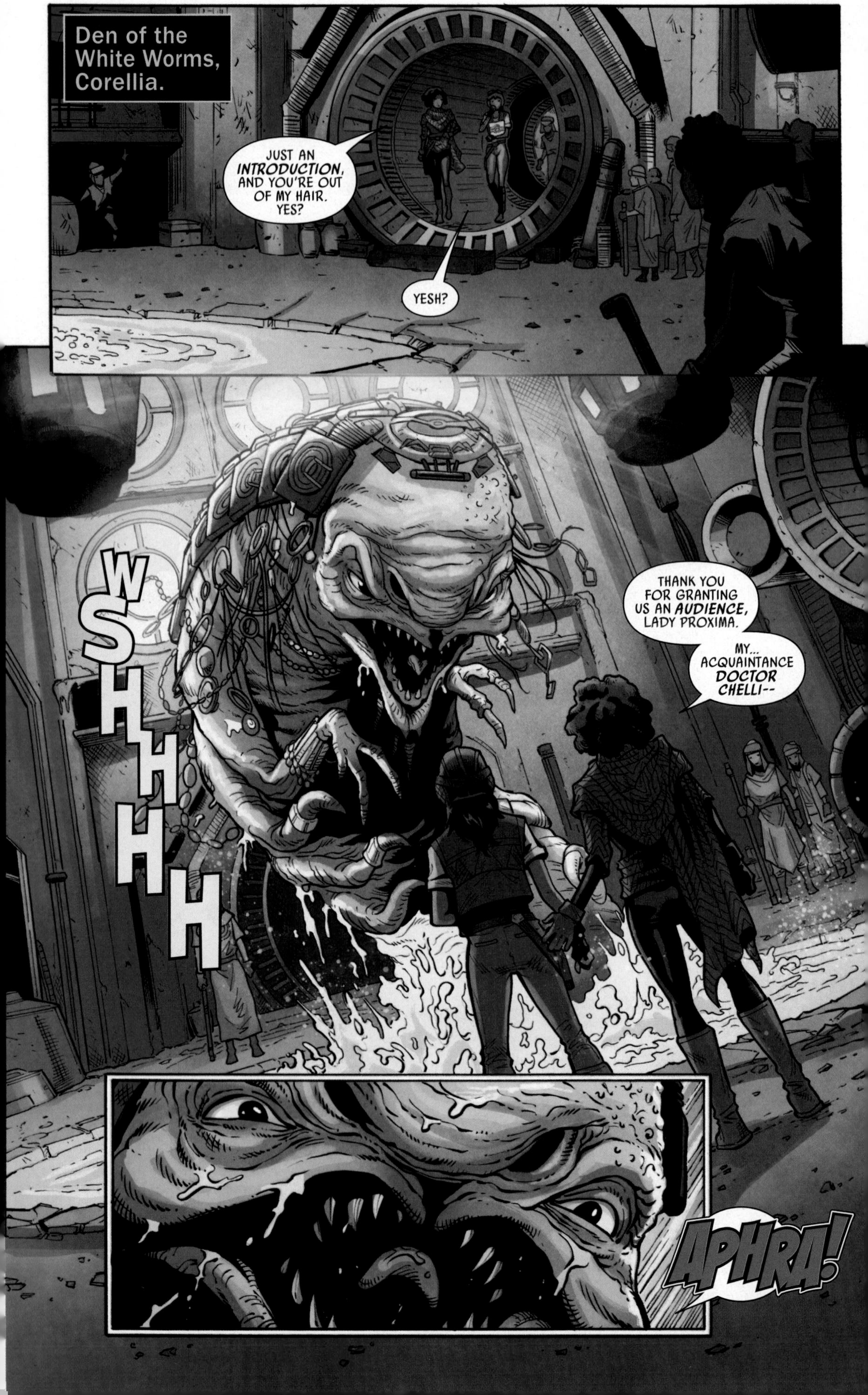
Den of the White Worms, Corellia.
JUST AN INTRODUCTION, AND YOU'RE OUT OF MY HAIR. YES?
YESH?
WSHHHHH
THANK YOU FOR GRANTING US AN AUDIENCE, LADY PROXIMA.
MY... ACQUAINTANCE DOCTOR CHELLI--
APHRA!

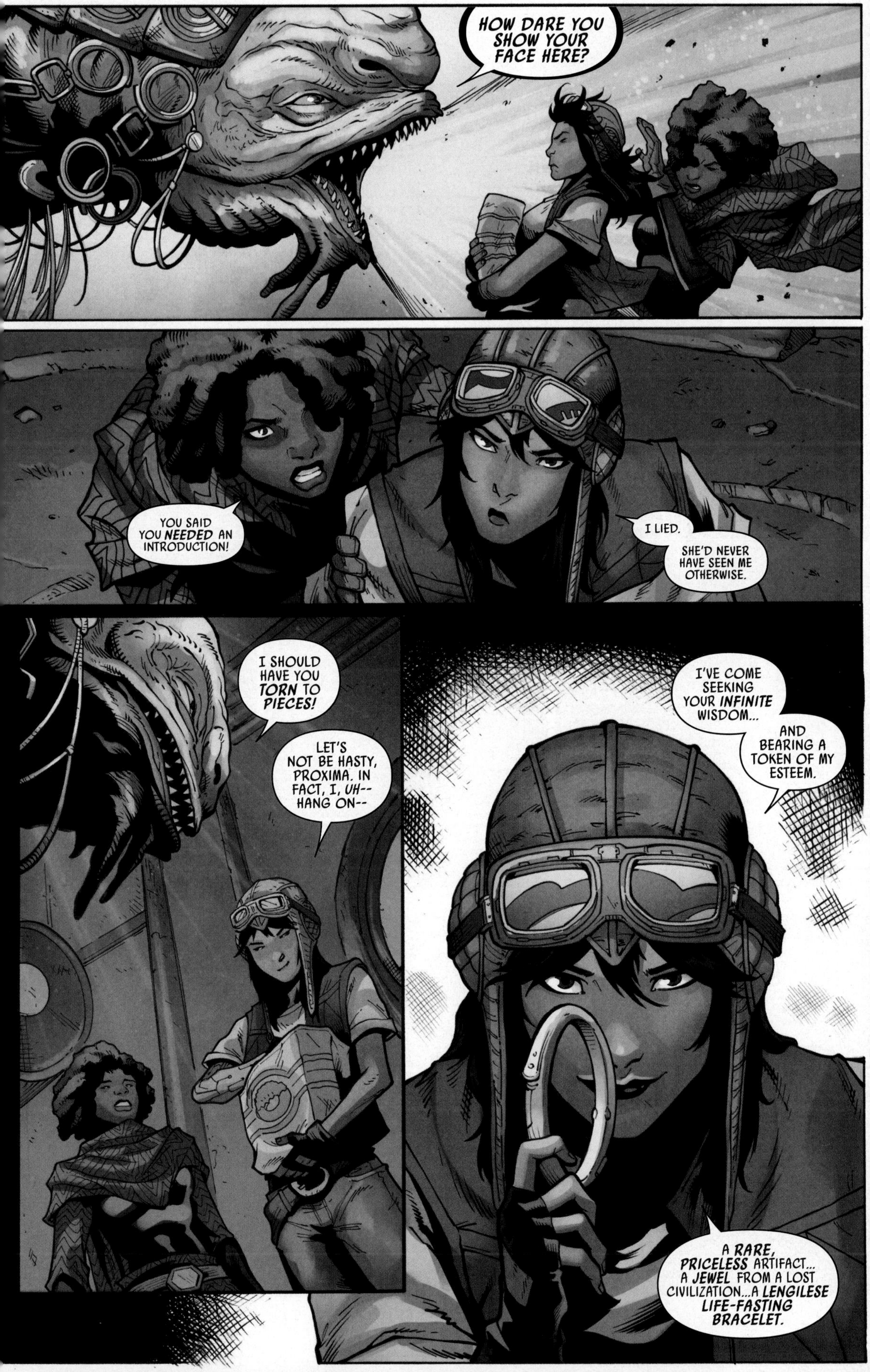
HOW DARE YOU SHOW YOUR FACE HERE?
YOU SAID YOU NEEDED AN INTRODUCTION!
I LIED.
SHE'D NEVER HAVE SEEN ME OTHERWISE.
I SHOULD HAVE YOU TORN TO PIECES!
LET'S NOT BE HASTY, PROXIMA. IN FACT, I, UH-- HANG ON--
I'VE COME SEEKING YOUR INFINITE WISDOM...
AND BEARING A TOKEN OF MY ESTEEM.
A RARE, PRICELESS ARTIFACT... A JEWEL FROM A LOST CIVILIZATION...A LENGILESE LIFE-FASTING BRACELET.

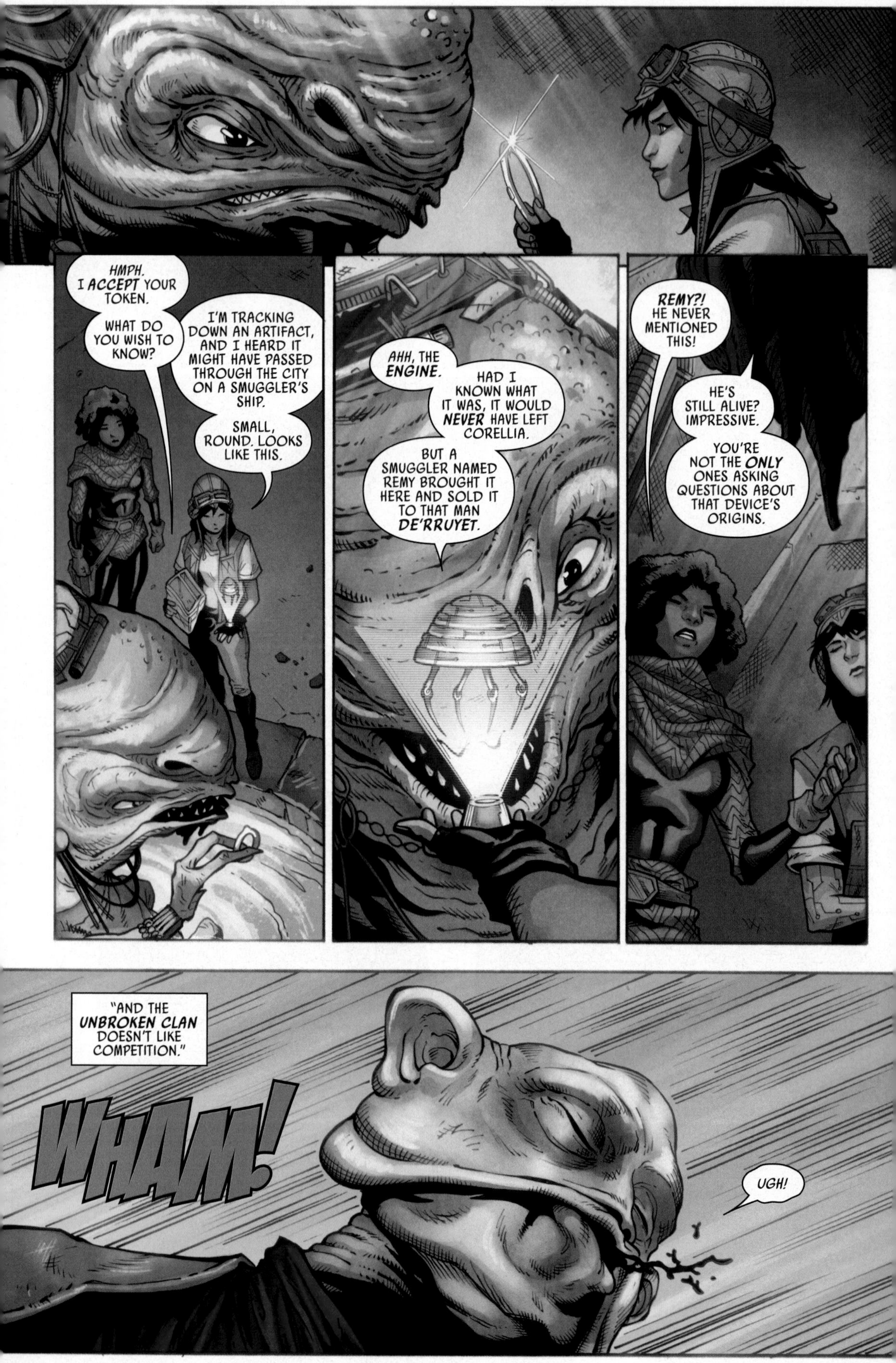
HMPH. I ACCEPT YOUR TOKEN.
WHAT DO YOU WISH TO KNOW?
I'M TRACKING DOWN AN ARTIFACT, AND I HEARD IT MIGHT HAVE PASSED THROUGH THE CITY ON A SMUGGLER'S SHIP.
SMALL, ROUND. LOOKS LIKE THIS.
AHH, THE ENGINE.
HAD I KNOWN WHAT IT WAS, IT WOULD NEVER HAVE LEFT CORELLIA.
BUT A SMUGGLER NAMED REMY BROUGHT IT HERE AND SOLD IT TO THAT MAN DE'RRUYET.
REMY?! HE NEVER MENTIONED THIS!
HE'S STILL ALIVE? IMPRESSIVE.
YOU'RE NOT THE ONLY ONES ASKING QUESTIONS ABOUT THAT DEVICE'S ORIGINS.
"AND THE UNBROKEN CLAN DOESN'T LIKE COMPETITION."
WHAM!
UGH!

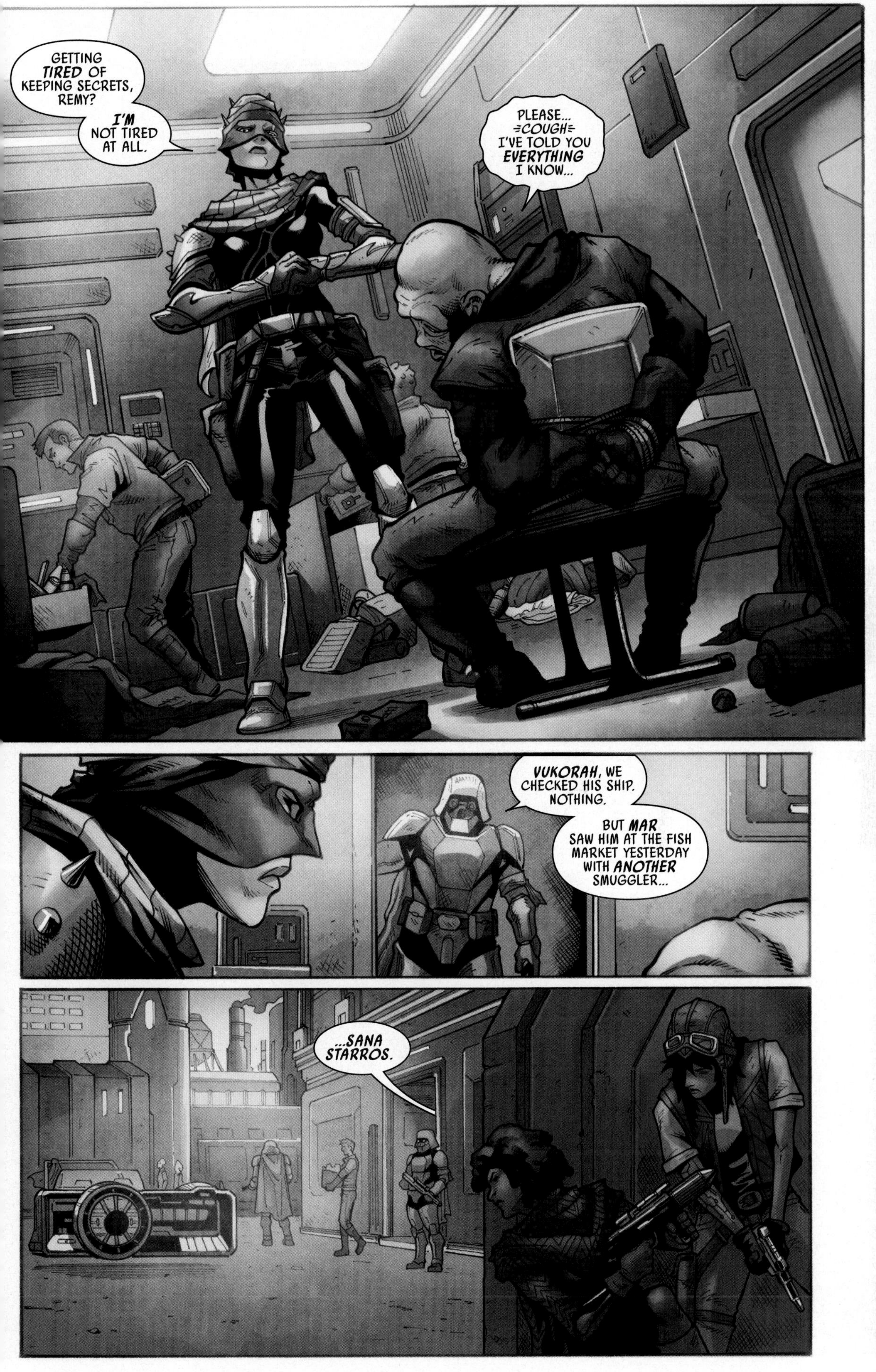
GETTING TIRED OF KEEPING SECRETS, REMY?
I'M NOT TIRED AT ALL.
PLEASE... =COUGH= I'VE TOLD YOU EVERYTHING I KNOW...
VUKORAH, WE CHECKED HIS SHIP. NOTHING.
BUT MAR SAW HIM AT THE FISH MARKET YESTERDAY WITH ANOTHER SMUGGLER...
...SANA STARROS.

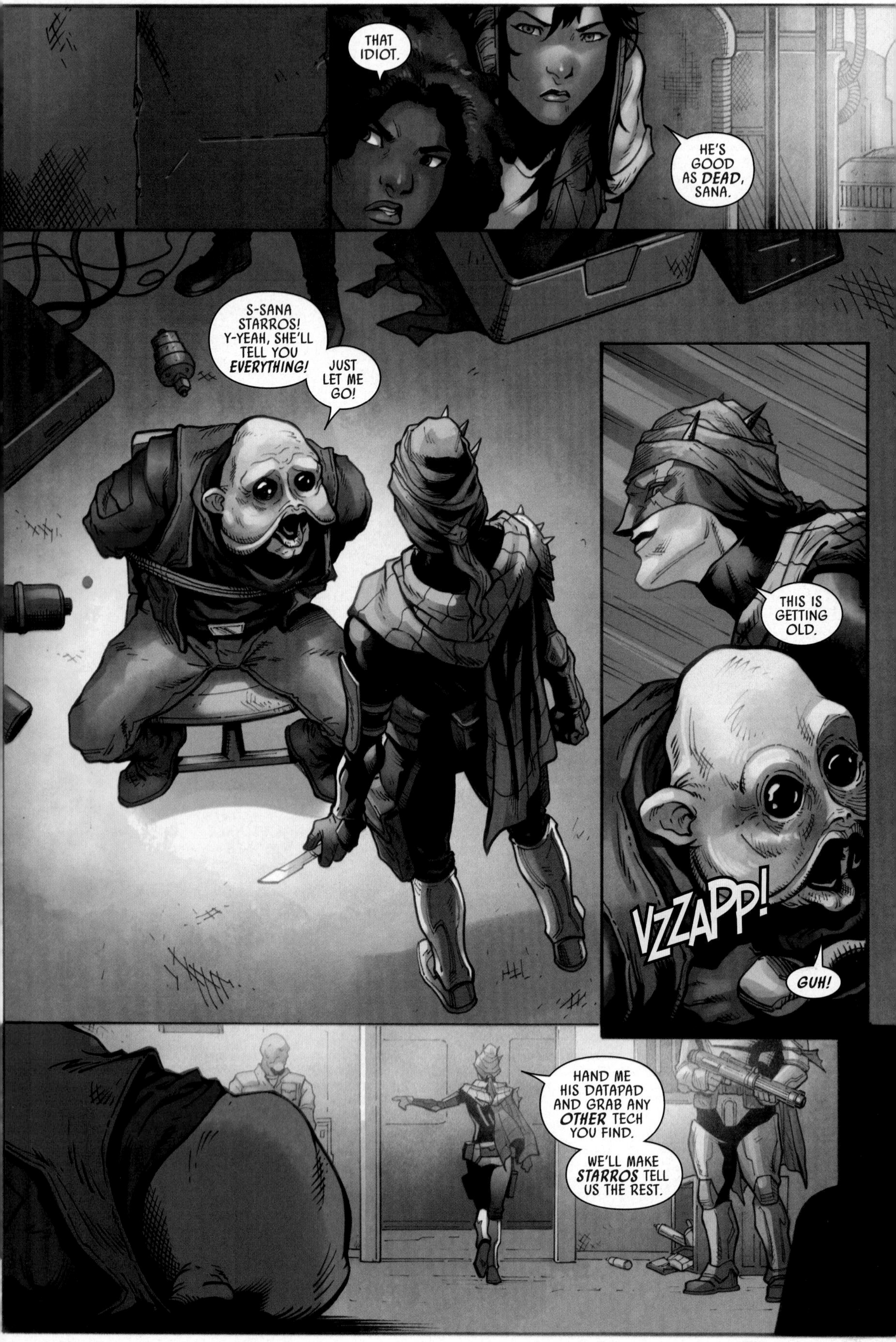
THAT IDIOT.
HE'S GOOD AS DEAD, SANA.
S-SANA STARROS! Y-YEAH, SHE'LL TELL YOU EVERYTHING!
JUST LET ME GO!
THIS IS GETTING OLD.
VZZAPP!
GUH!
HAND ME HIS DATAPAD AND GRAB ANY OTHER TECH YOU FIND.
WE'LL MAKE STARROS TELL US THE REST.

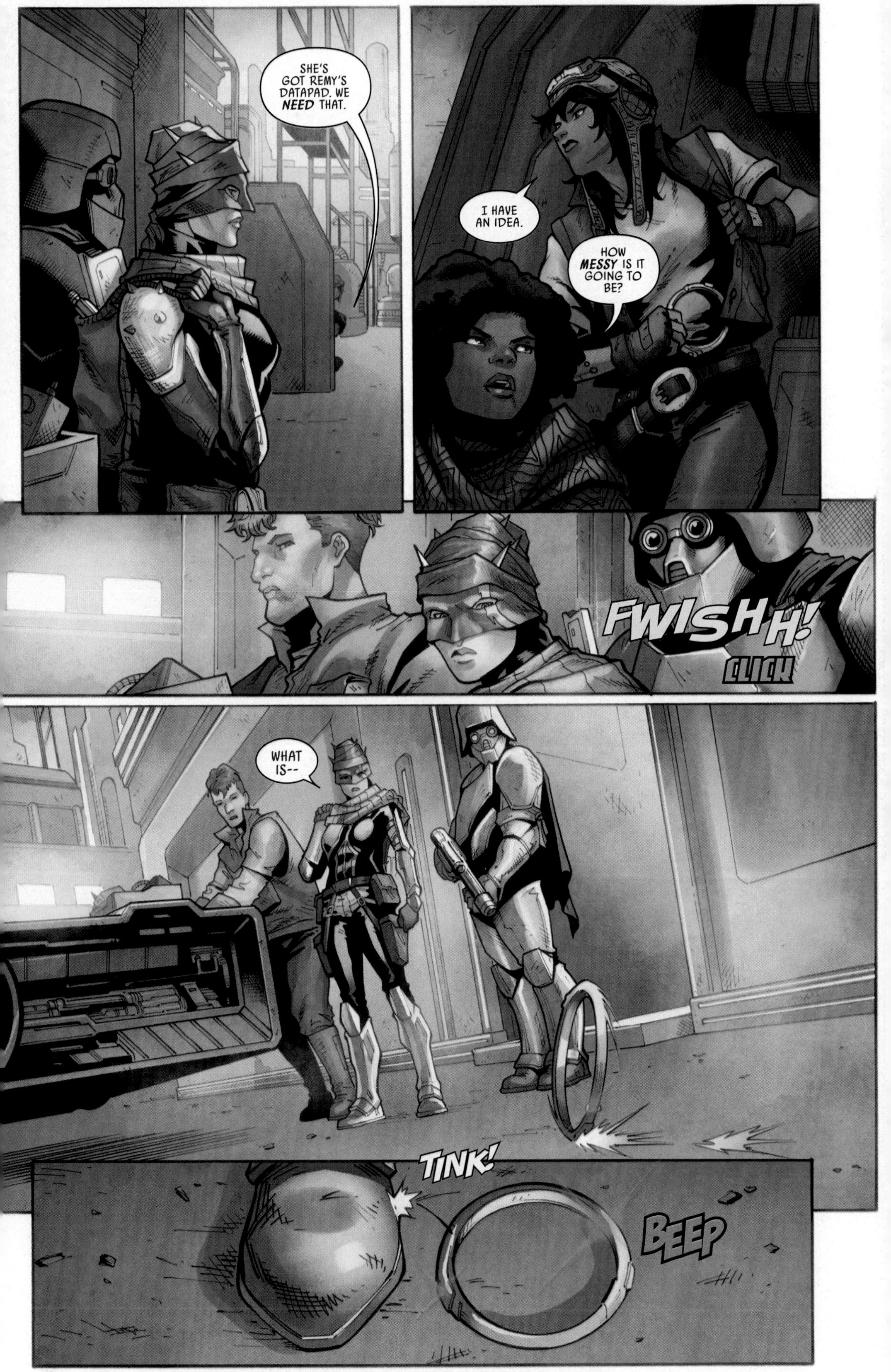
SHE'S GOT REMY'S DATAPAD. WE NEED THAT.
I HAVE AN IDEA.
HOW MESSY IS IT GOING TO BE?
FWISHH!
CLICK
WHAT IS--
TINK!
BEEP

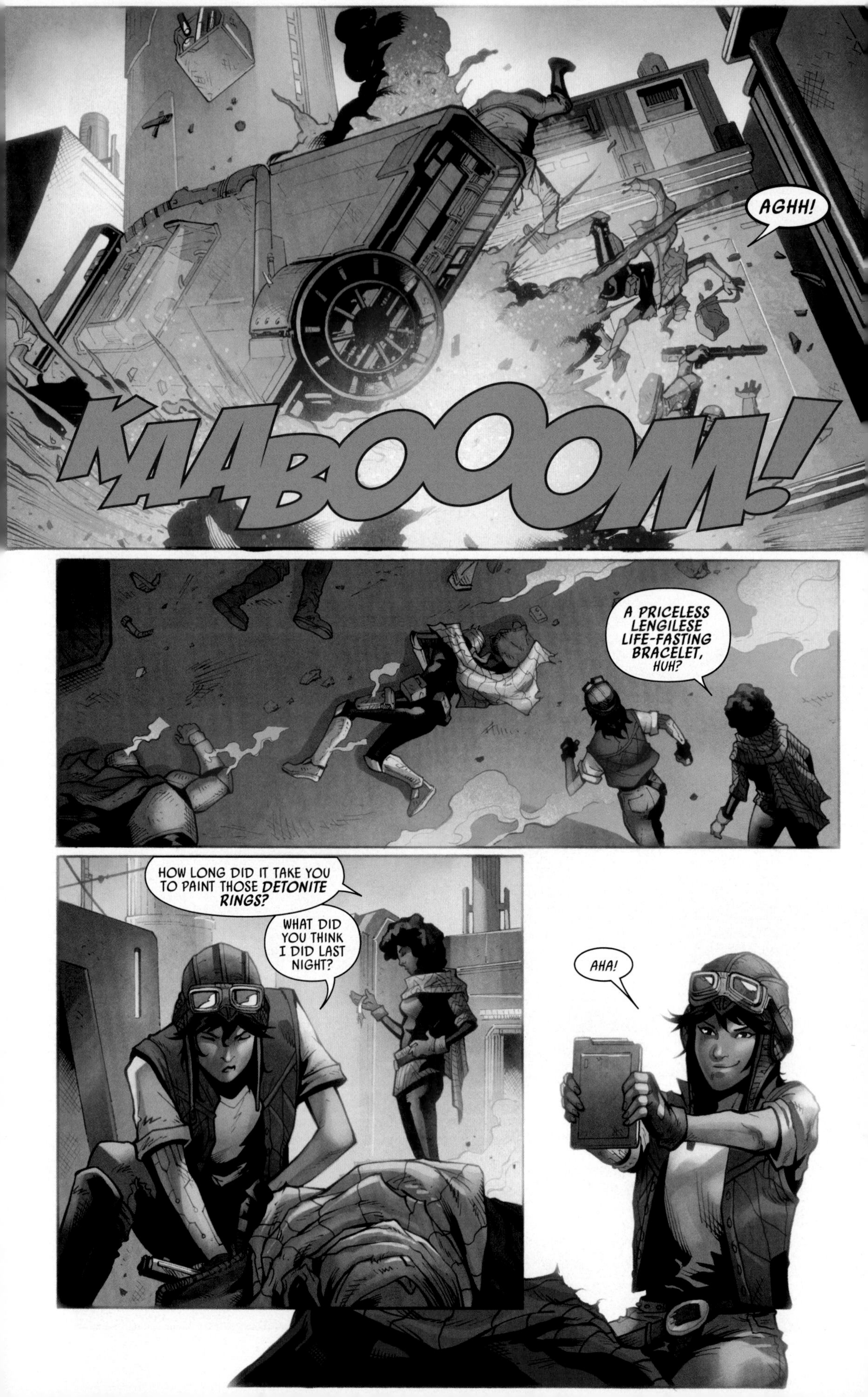
AGHH!
KAABOOOOM!
A PRICELESS LENGILESE LIFE-FASTING BRACELET, HUH?
HOW LONG DID IT TAKE YOU TO PAINT THOSE DETONITE RINGS?
WHAT DID YOU THINK I DID LAST NIGHT?
AHA!

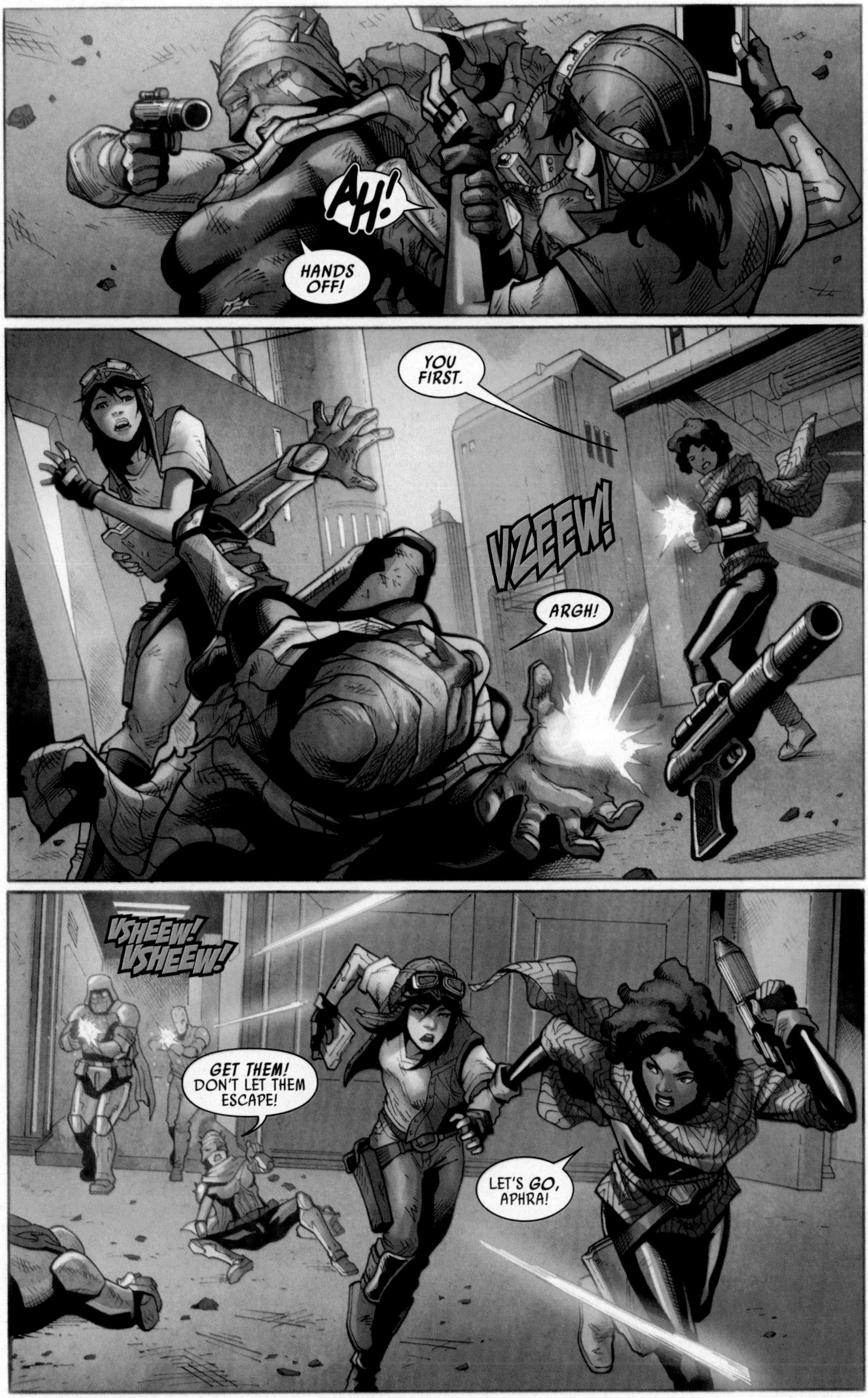
AH!
HANDS OFF!
YOU FIRST.
VZEEW!
ARGH!
VSHEEW! VSHEEW!
GET THEM! DON'T LET THEM ESCAPE!
LET'S GO, APHRA!

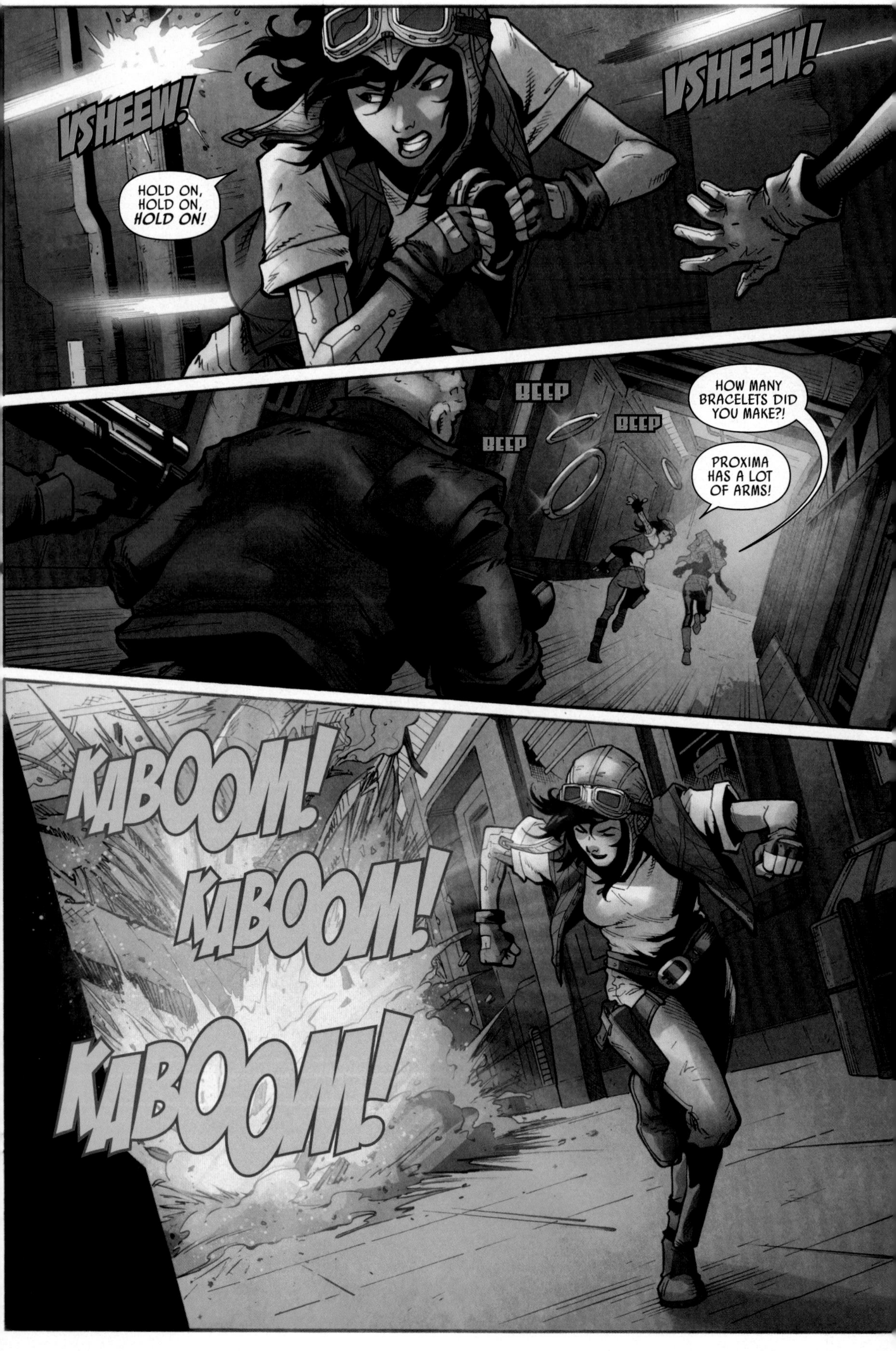
VSHEEW!
VSHEEW!
HOLD ON, HOLD ON, HOLD ON!
BEEP
BEEP
BEEP
HOW MANY BRACELETS DID YOU MAKE?!
PROXIMA HAS A LOT OF ARMS!
KABOOM!
KABOOM!
KABOOM!

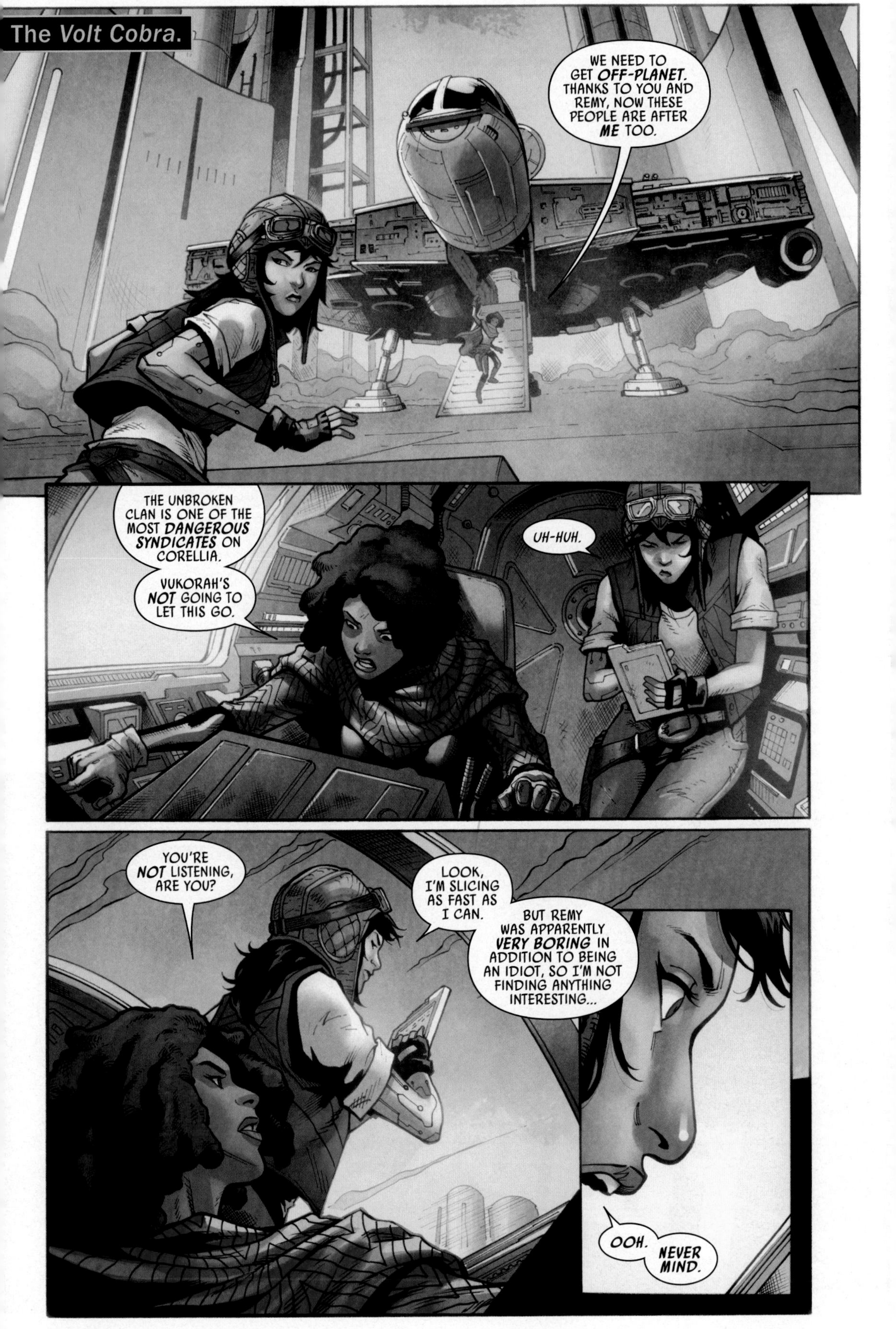
The Volt Cobra.
WE NEED TO GET OFF-PLANET. THANKS TO YOU AND REMY, NOW THESE PEOPLE ARE AFTER ME TOO.
THE UNBROKEN CLAN IS ONE OF THE MOST DANGEROUS SYNDICATES ON CORELLIA.
VUKORAH'S NOT GOING TO LET THIS GO.
UH-HUH.
YOU'RE NOT LISTENING, ARE YOU?
LOOK, I'M SLICING AS FAST AS I CAN.
BUT REMY WAS APPARENTLY VERY BORING IN ADDITION TO BEING AN IDIOT, SO I'M NOT FINDING ANYTHING INTERESTING...
OOH.
NEVER MIND.

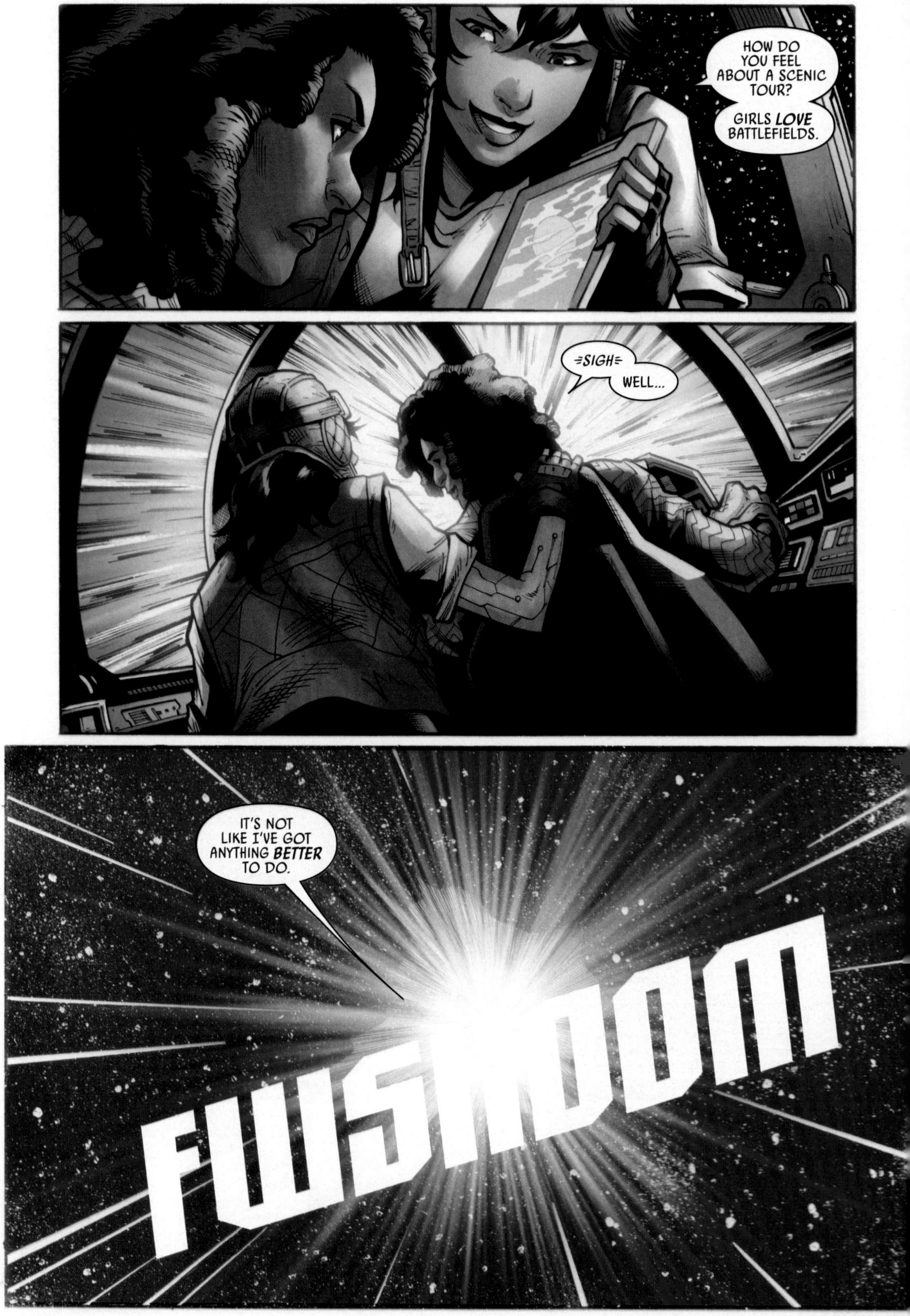
HOW DO YOU FEEL ABOUT A SCENIC TOUR?
GIRLS *LOVE* BATTLEFIELDS.
=*SIGH*=
WELL...
IT'S NOT LIKE I'VE GOT ANYTHING *BETTER* TO DO.
FWSHOOM

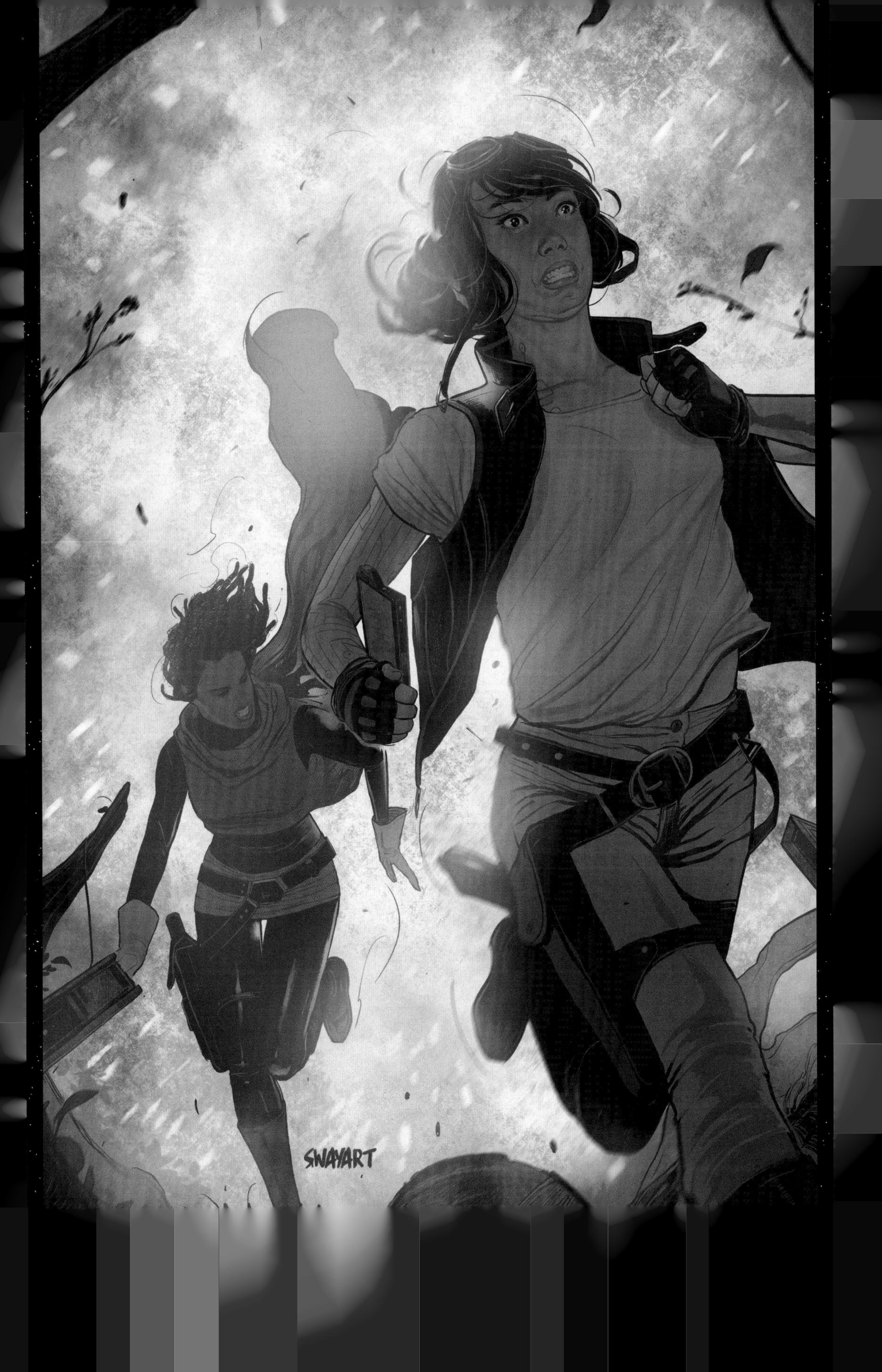
SWAYART

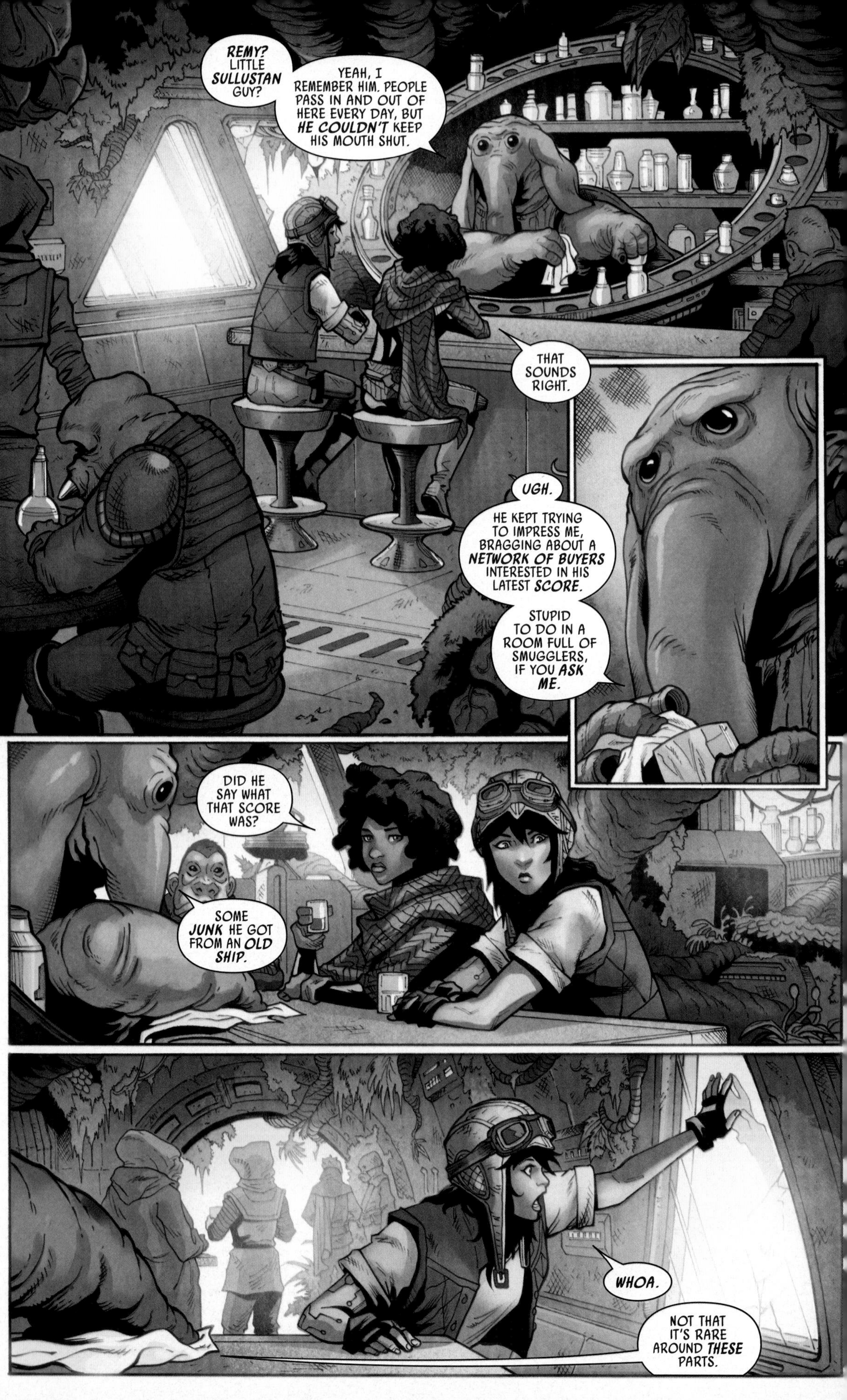
REMY? LITTLE SULLUSTAN GUY?
YEAH, I REMEMBER HIM. PEOPLE PASS IN AND OUT OF HERE EVERY DAY, BUT HE COULDN'T KEEP HIS MOUTH SHUT.
THAT SOUNDS RIGHT.
UGH.
HE KEPT TRYING TO IMPRESS ME, BRAGGING ABOUT A NETWORK OF BUYERS INTERESTED IN HIS LATEST SCORE.
STUPID TO DO IN A ROOM FULL OF SMUGGLERS, IF YOU ASK ME.
DID HE SAY WHAT THAT SCORE WAS?
SOME JUNK HE GOT FROM AN OLD SHIP.
WHOA.
NOT THAT IT'S RARE AROUND THESE PARTS.

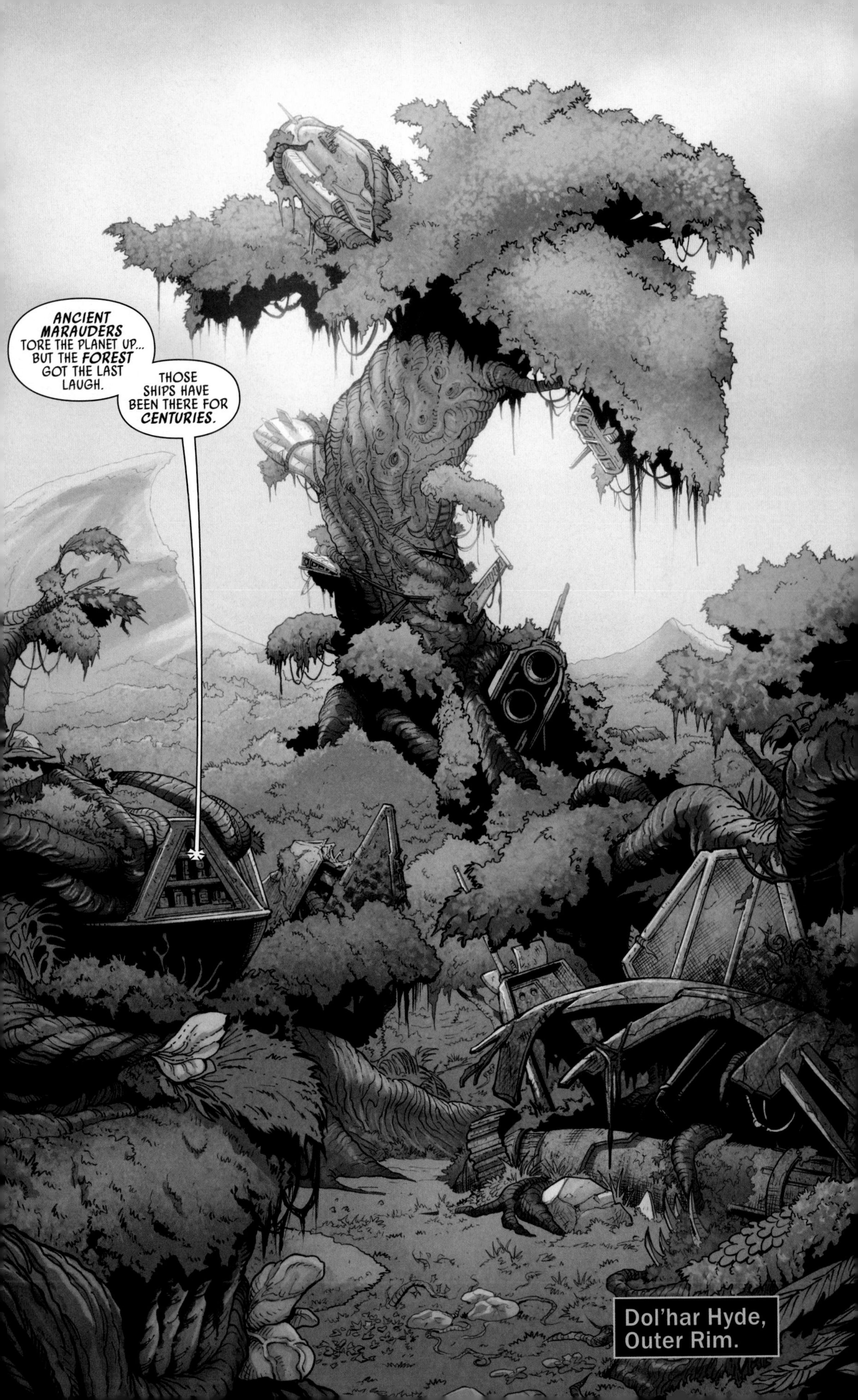
ANCIENT MARAUDERS TORE THE PLANET UP... BUT THE FOREST GOT THE LAST LAUGH.
THOSE SHIPS HAVE BEEN THERE FOR CENTURIES.
Dol'har Hyde, Outer Rim.

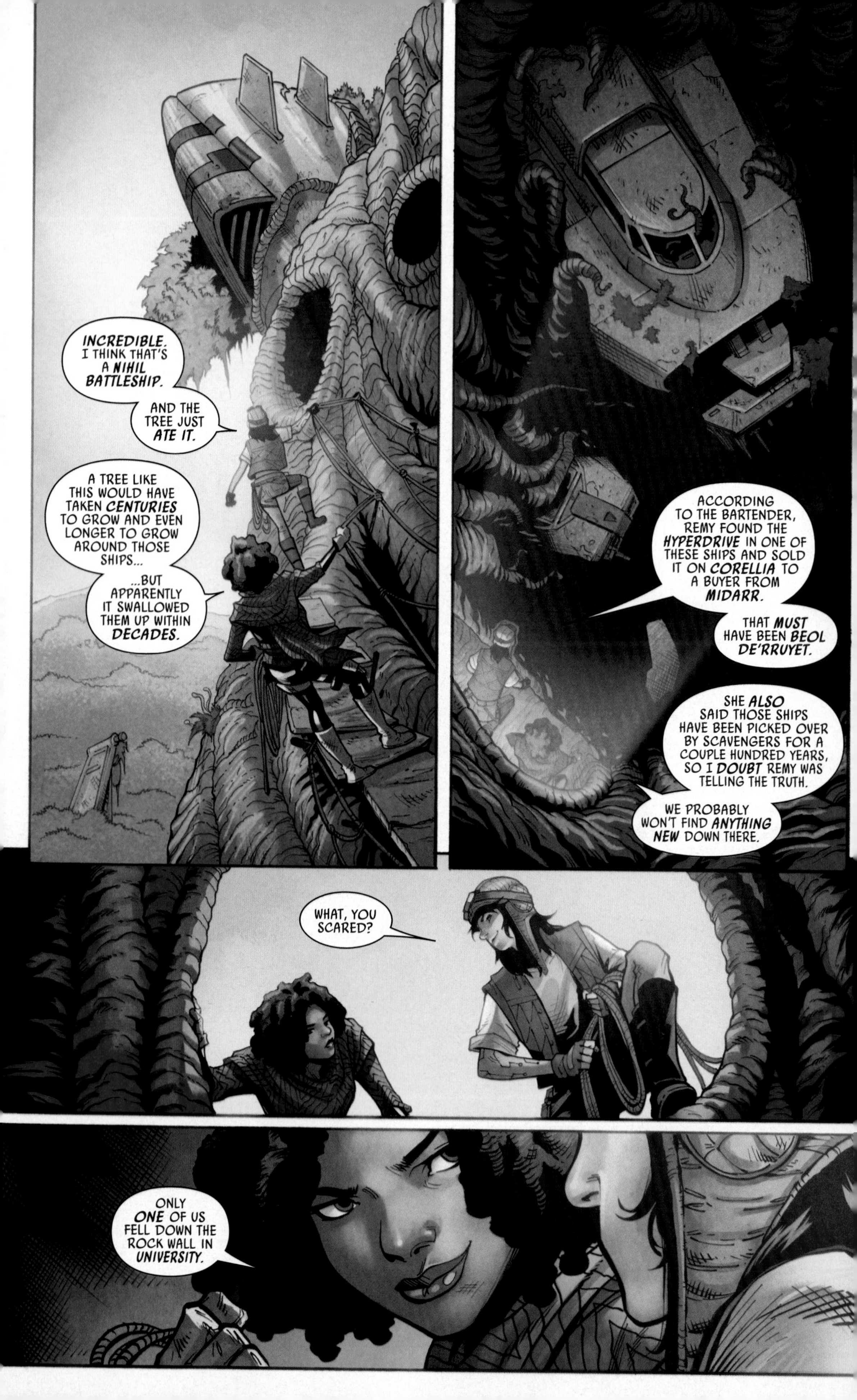
INCREDIBLE. I THINK THAT'S A NIHIL BATTLESHIP.
AND THE TREE JUST ATE IT.
A TREE LIKE THIS WOULD HAVE TAKEN CENTURIES TO GROW AND EVEN LONGER TO GROW AROUND THOSE SHIPS...
...BUT APPARENTLY IT SWALLOWED THEM UP WITHIN DECADES.
ACCORDING TO THE BARTENDER, REMY FOUND THE HYPERDRIVE IN ONE OF THESE SHIPS AND SOLD IT ON CORELLIA TO A BUYER FROM MIDARR.
THAT MUST HAVE BEEN BEOL DE'RRUYET.
SHE ALSO SAID THOSE SHIPS HAVE BEEN PICKED OVER BY SCAVENGERS FOR A COUPLE HUNDRED YEARS, SO I DOUBT REMY WAS TELLING THE TRUTH.
WE PROBABLY WON'T FIND ANYTHING NEW DOWN THERE.
WHAT, YOU SCARED?
ONLY ONE OF US FELL DOWN THE ROCK WALL IN UNIVERSITY.

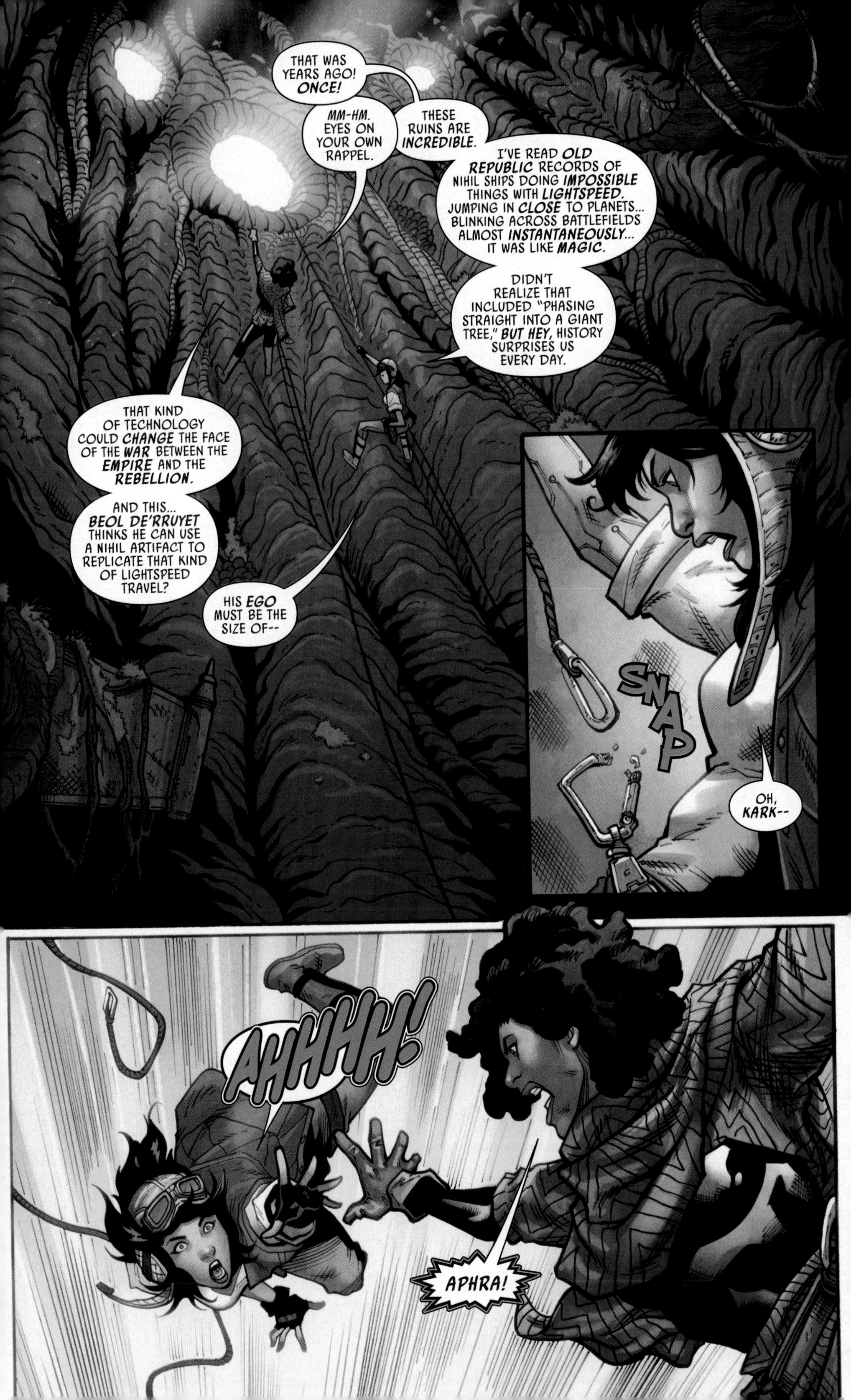
THAT WAS YEARS AGO! ONCE!
MM-HM. EYES ON YOUR OWN RAPPEL.
THESE RUINS ARE INCREDIBLE.
I'VE READ OLD REPUBLIC RECORDS OF NIHIL SHIPS DOING IMPOSSIBLE THINGS WITH LIGHTSPEED. JUMPING IN CLOSE TO PLANETS... BLINKING ACROSS BATTLEFIELDS ALMOST INSTANTANEOUSLY... IT WAS LIKE MAGIC.
DIDN'T REALIZE THAT INCLUDED "PHASING STRAIGHT INTO A GIANT TREE," BUT HEY, HISTORY SURPRISES US EVERY DAY.
THAT KIND OF TECHNOLOGY COULD CHANGE THE FACE OF THE WAR BETWEEN THE EMPIRE AND THE REBELLION.
AND THIS... BEOL DE'RRUYET THINKS HE CAN USE A NIHIL ARTIFACT TO REPLICATE THAT KIND OF LIGHTSPEED TRAVEL?
HIS EGO MUST BE THE SIZE OF--
SNAP
OH, KARK--
AHHHH!
APHRA!

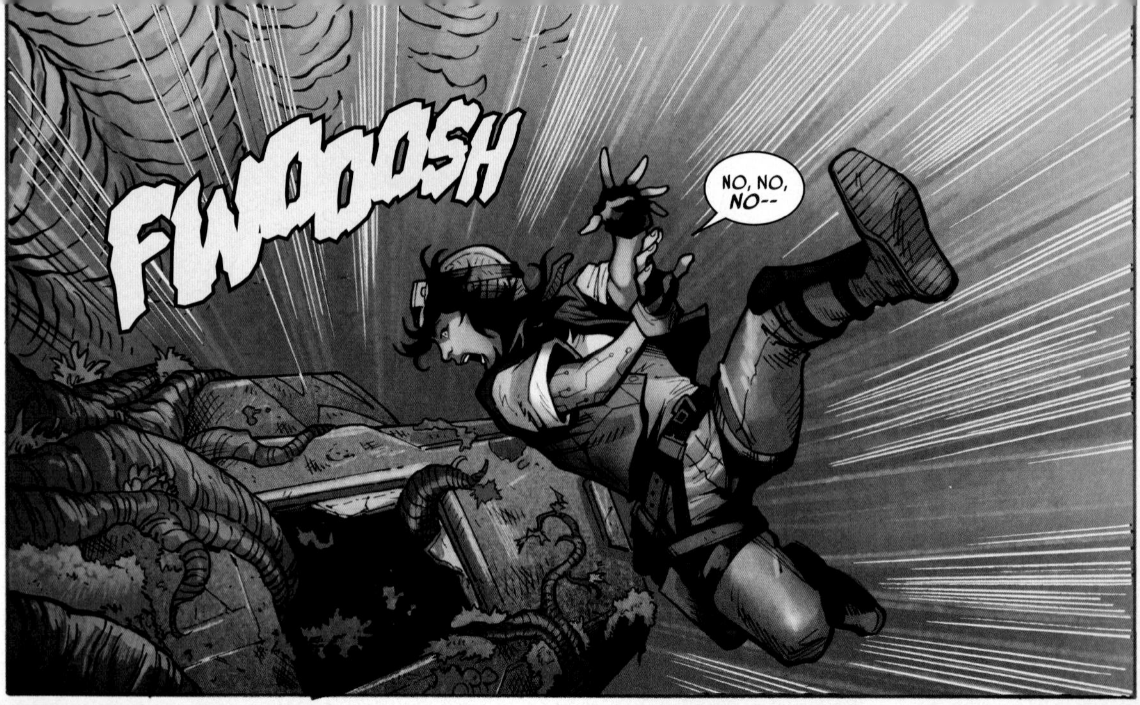
FWOOOSH
NO, NO, NO--

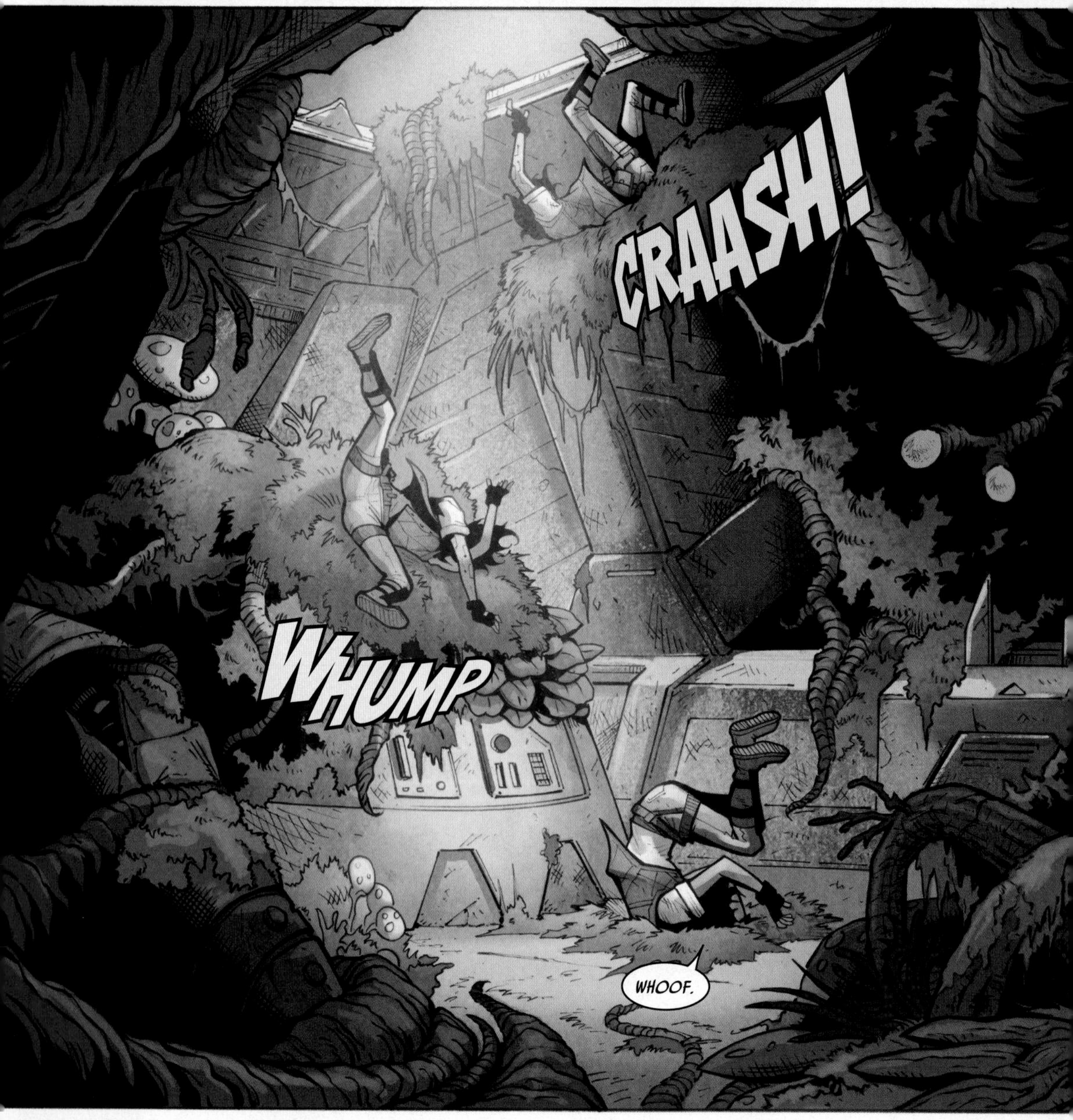
CRAASH!
WHUMP
WHOOF.

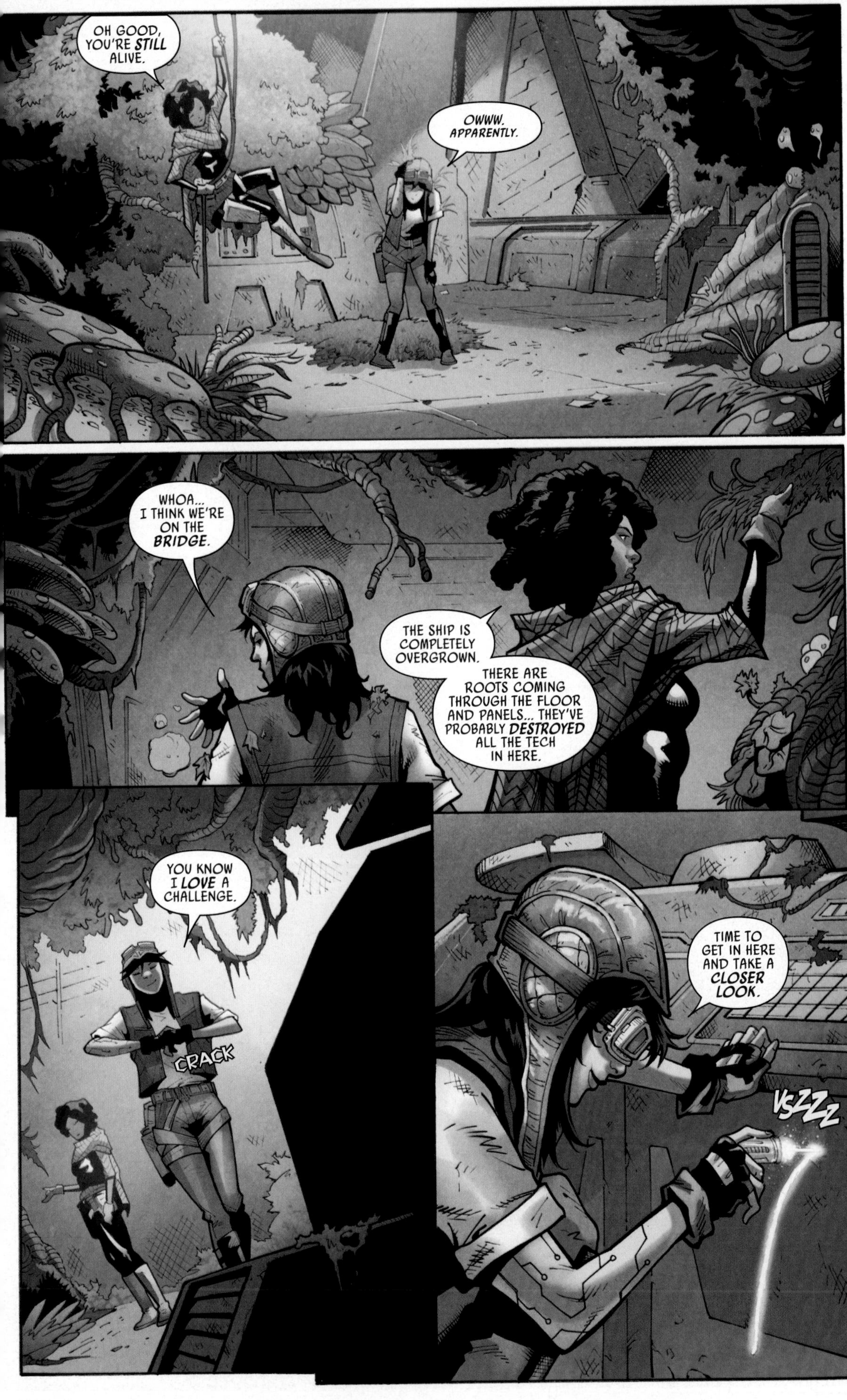
OH GOOD, YOU'RE STILL ALIVE.
OWWW. APPARENTLY.
WHOA... I THINK WE'RE ON THE BRIDGE.
THE SHIP IS COMPLETELY OVERGROWN.
THERE ARE ROOTS COMING THROUGH THE FLOOR AND PANELS... THEY'VE PROBABLY DESTROYED ALL THE TECH IN HERE.
YOU KNOW I LOVE A CHALLENGE.
CRACK
TIME TO GET IN HERE AND TAKE A CLOSER LOOK.
VSZZZ

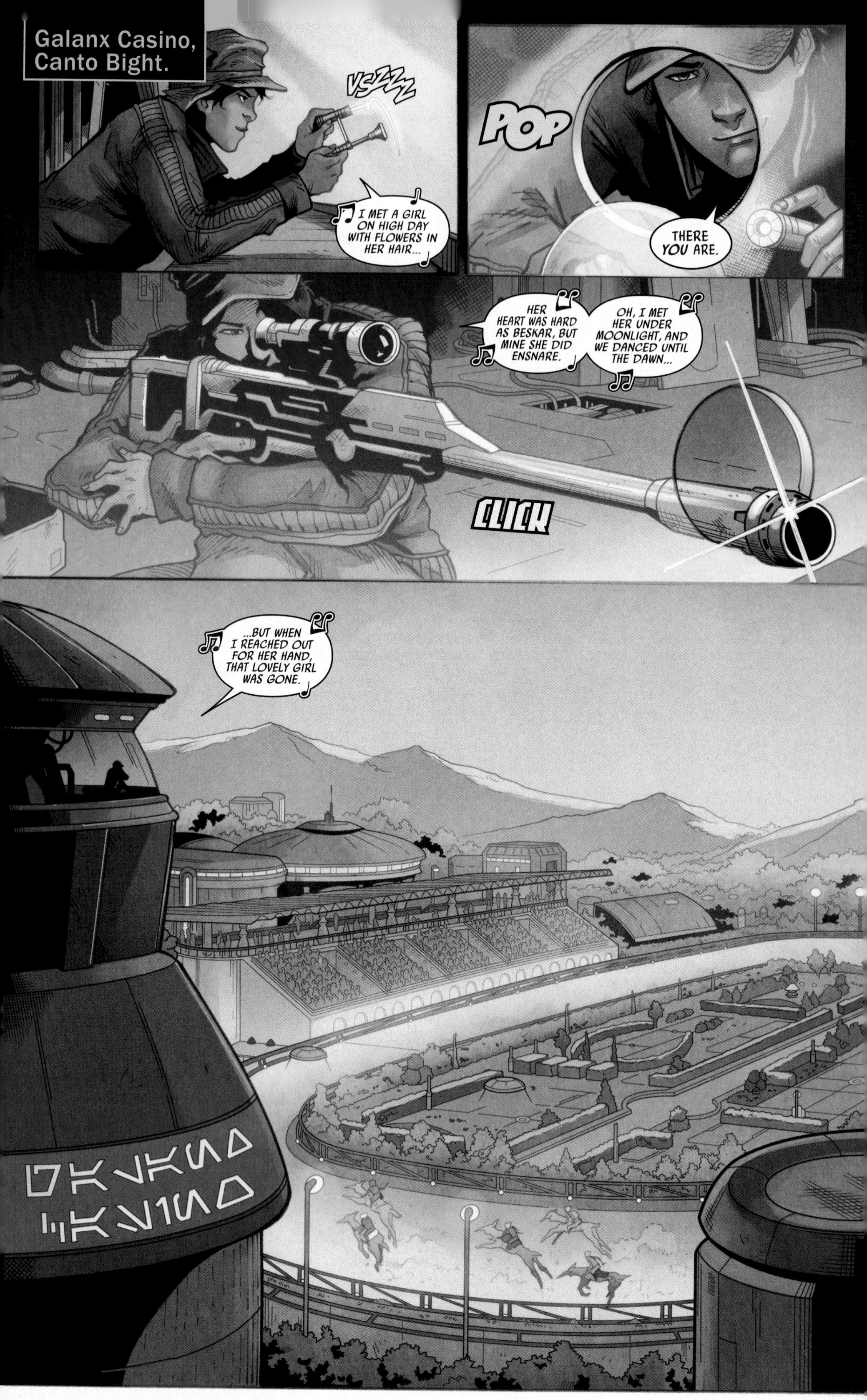

Galanx Casino, Canto Bight.
VSZZZ
I MET A GIRL ON HIGH DAY WITH FLOWERS IN HER HAIR...
POP
THERE YOU ARE.
HER HEART WAS HARD AS BESKAR, BUT MINE SHE DID ENSNARE.
OH, I MET HER UNDER MOONLIGHT, AND WE DANCED UNTIL THE DAWN...
CLICK
...BUT WHEN I REACHED OUT FOR HER HAND, THAT LOVELY GIRL WAS GONE.

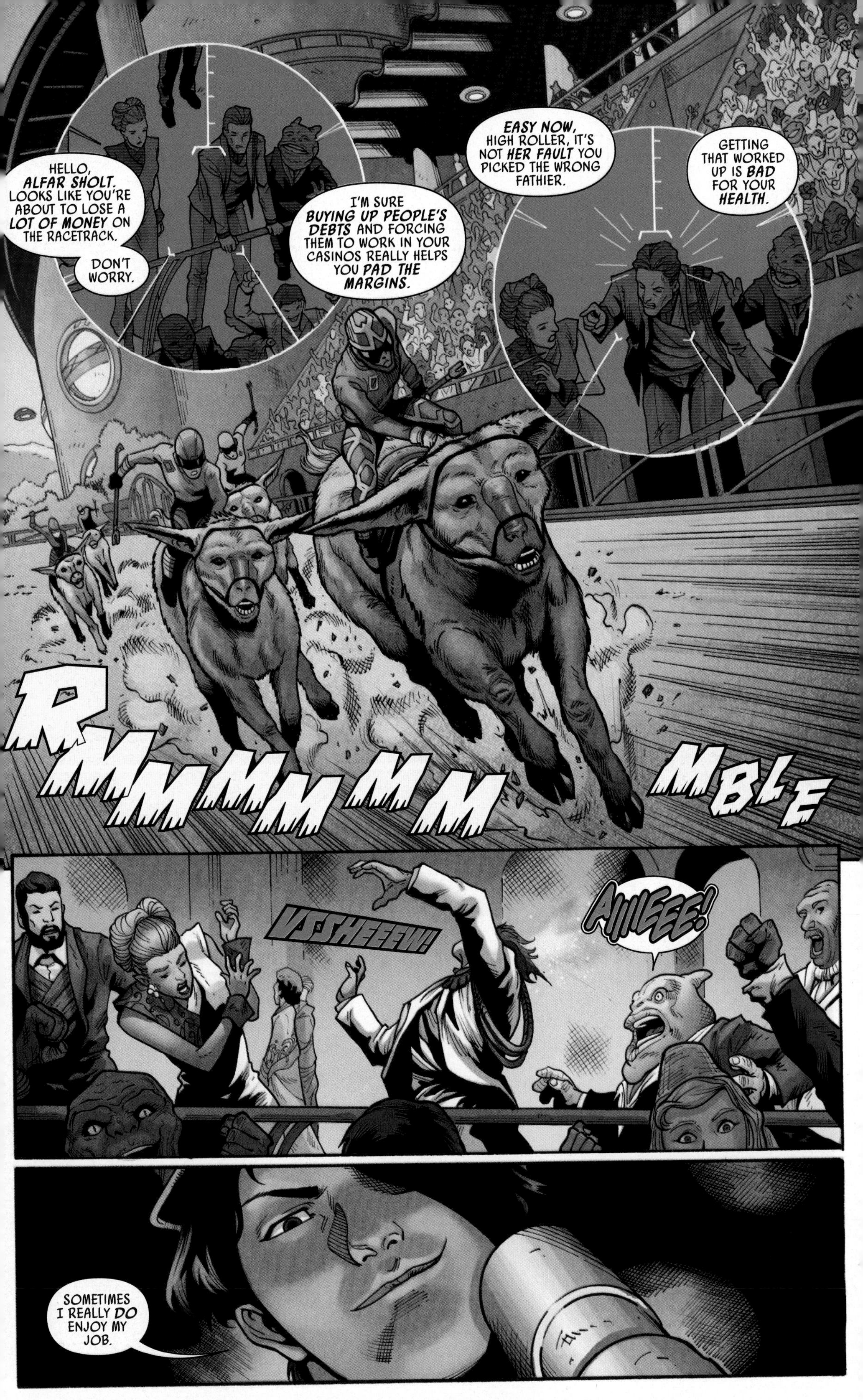
HELLO, ALFAR SHOLT. LOOKS LIKE YOU'RE ABOUT TO LOSE A LOT OF MONEY ON THE RACETRACK.
DON'T WORRY.
I'M SURE BUYING UP PEOPLE'S DEBTS AND FORCING THEM TO WORK IN YOUR CASINOS REALLY HELPS YOU PAD THE MARGINS.
EASY NOW, HIGH ROLLER, IT'S NOT HER FAULT YOU PICKED THE WRONG FATHIER.
GETTING THAT WORKED UP IS BAD FOR YOUR HEALTH.
RMMMMMMMM MBLE
VSSHEEEW!
AIIIEEE!
SOMETIMES I REALLY DO ENJOY MY JOB.

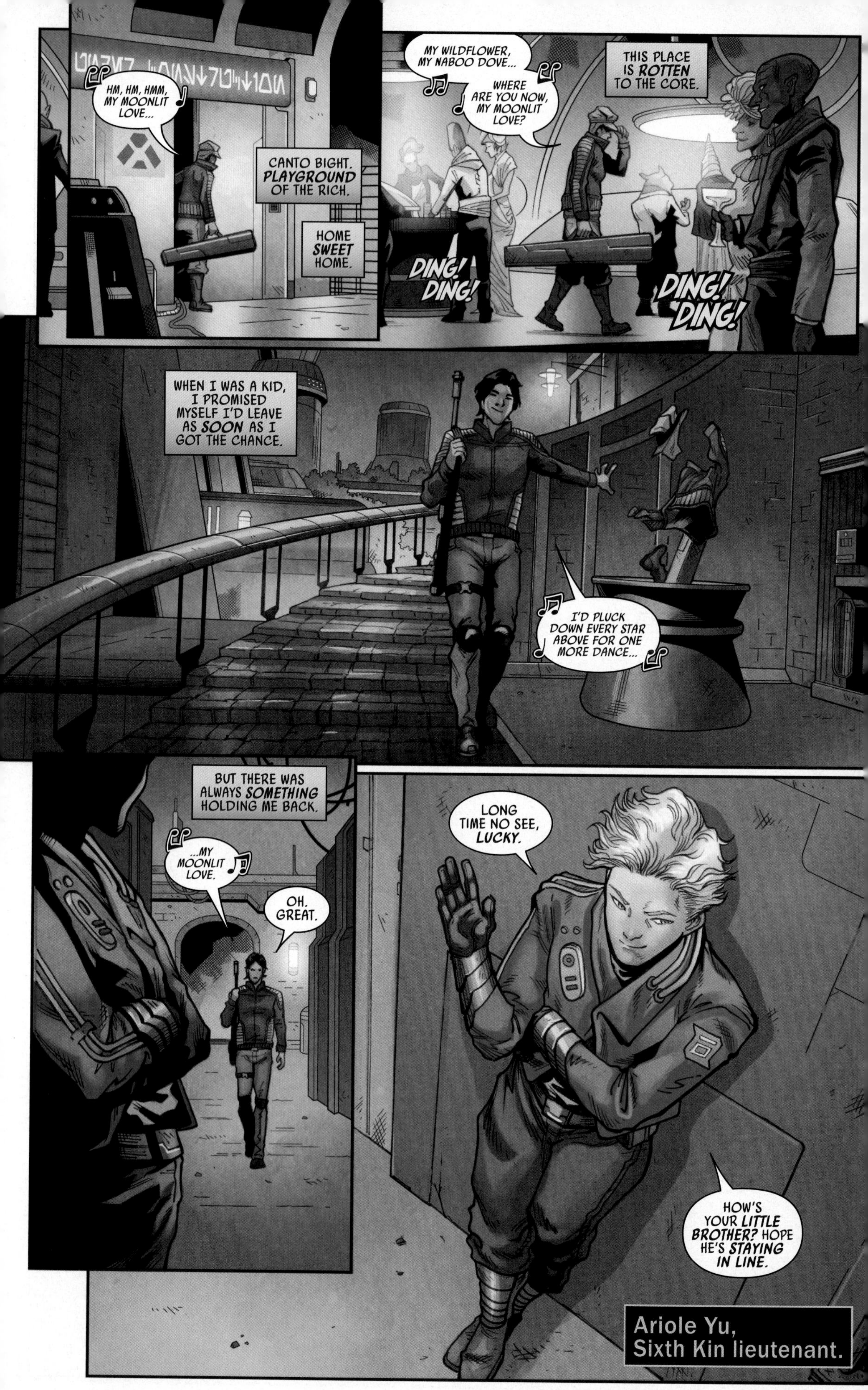
HM, HM, HMM, MY MOONLIT LOVE...
CANTO BIGHT. PLAYGROUND OF THE RICH.
HOME SWEET HOME.
MY WILDFLOWER, MY NABOO DOVE...
WHERE ARE YOU NOW, MY MOONLIT LOVE?
THIS PLACE IS ROTTEN TO THE CORE.
DING! DING!
DING! DING!
WHEN I WAS A KID, I PROMISED MYSELF I'D LEAVE AS SOON AS I GOT THE CHANCE.
I'D PLUCK DOWN EVERY STAR ABOVE FOR ONE MORE DANCE...
BUT THERE WAS ALWAYS SOMETHING HOLDING ME BACK.
...MY MOONLIT LOVE.
OH. GREAT.
LONG TIME NO SEE, LUCKY.
HOW'S YOUR LITTLE BROTHER? HOPE HE'S STAYING IN LINE.
Ariole Yu, Sixth Kin lieutenant.

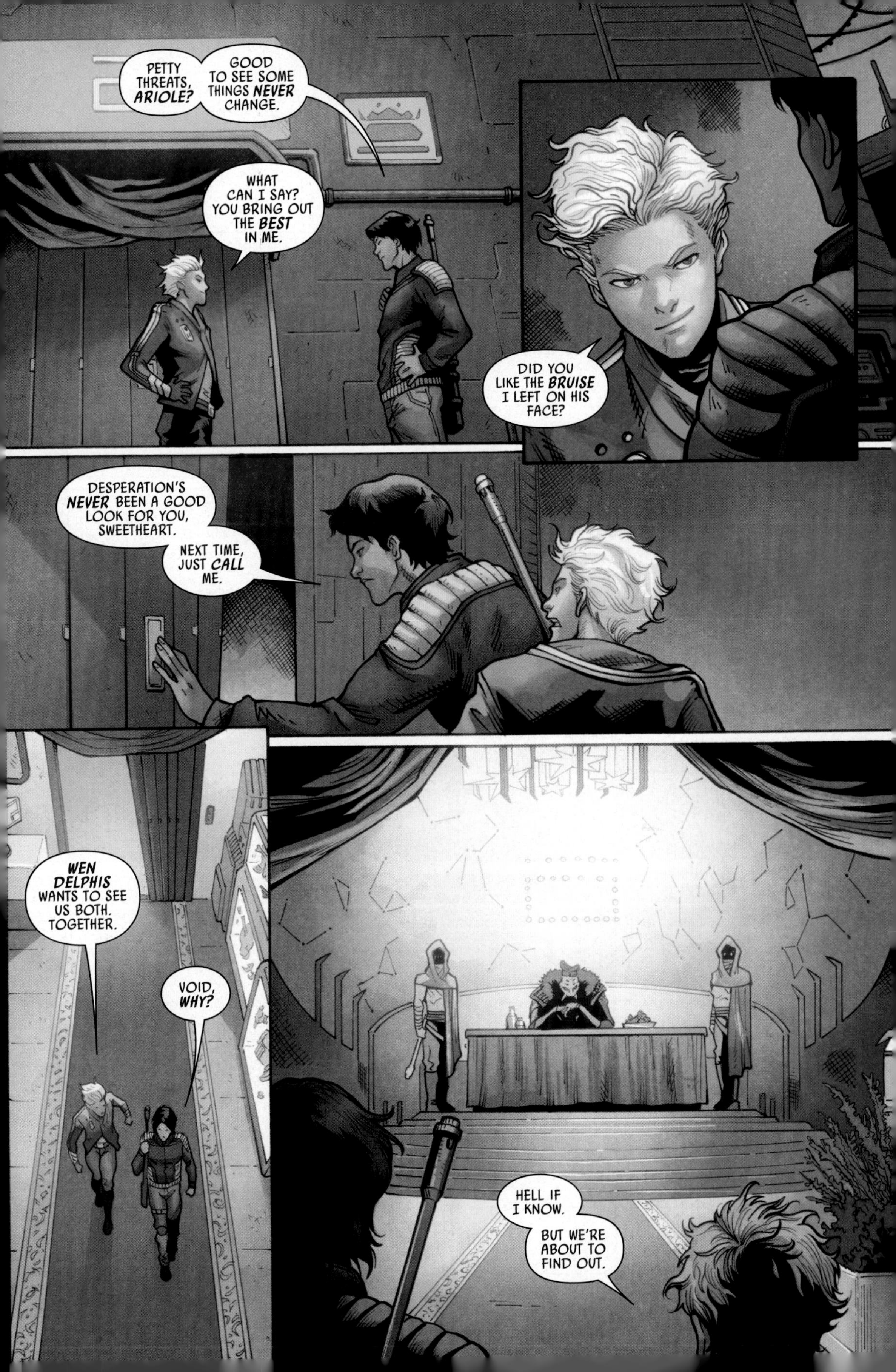
PETTY THREATS, ARIOLE?
GOOD TO SEE SOME THINGS NEVER CHANGE.
WHAT CAN I SAY? YOU BRING OUT THE BEST IN ME.
DID YOU LIKE THE BRUISE I LEFT ON HIS FACE?
DESPERATION'S NEVER BEEN A GOOD LOOK FOR YOU, SWEETHEART.
NEXT TIME, JUST CALL ME.
WEN DELPHIS WANTS TO SEE US BOTH. TOGETHER.
VOID, WHY?
HELL IF I KNOW.
BUT WE'RE ABOUT TO FIND OUT.

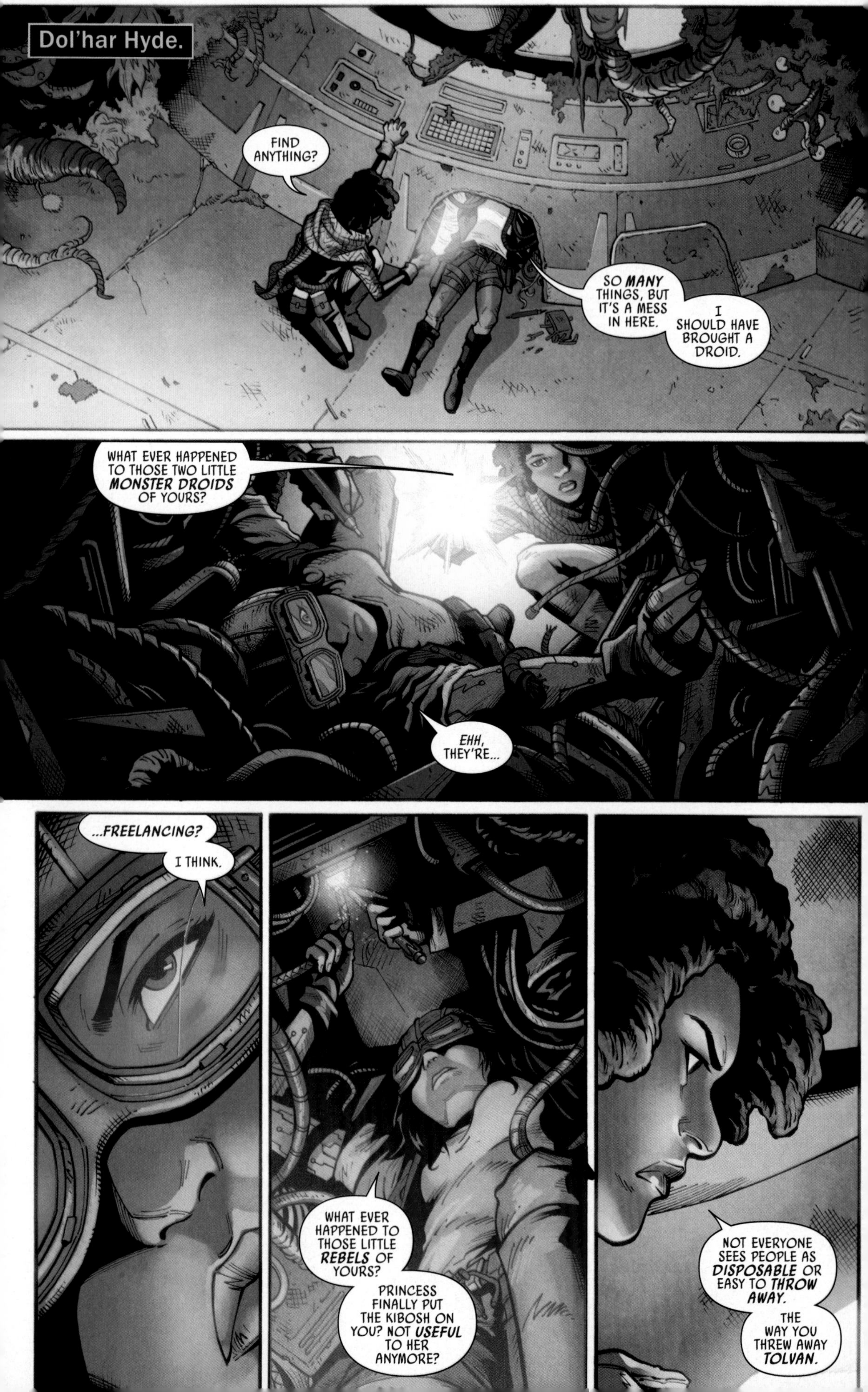
Dol'har Hyde.
FIND ANYTHING?
SO MANY THINGS, BUT IT'S A MESS IN HERE.
I SHOULD HAVE BROUGHT A DROID.
WHAT EVER HAPPENED TO THOSE TWO LITTLE MONSTER DROIDS OF YOURS?
EHH, THEY'RE...
...FREELANCING?
I THINK.
WHAT EVER HAPPENED TO THOSE LITTLE REBELS OF YOURS?
PRINCESS FINALLY PUT THE KIBOSH ON YOU? NOT USEFUL TO HER ANYMORE?
NOT EVERYONE SEES PEOPLE AS DISPOSABLE OR EASY TO THROW AWAY.
THE WAY YOU THREW AWAY TOLVAN.

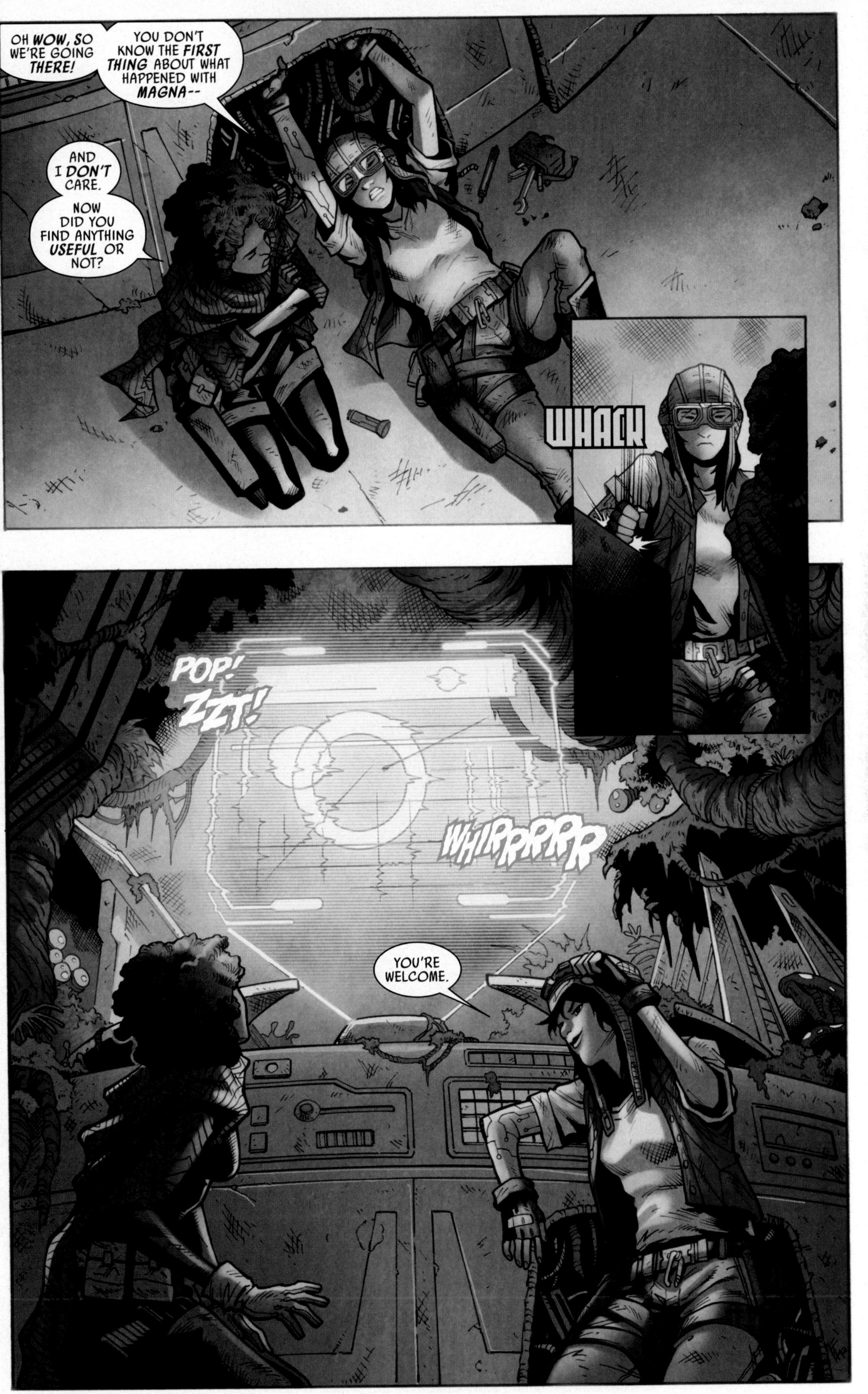
OH WOW, SO WE'RE GOING THERE!
YOU DON'T KNOW THE FIRST THING ABOUT WHAT HAPPENED WITH MAGNA--
AND I DON'T CARE.
NOW DID YOU FIND ANYTHING USEFUL OR NOT?
WHACK
POP! ZZT!
WHIRRRRR
YOU'RE WELCOME.

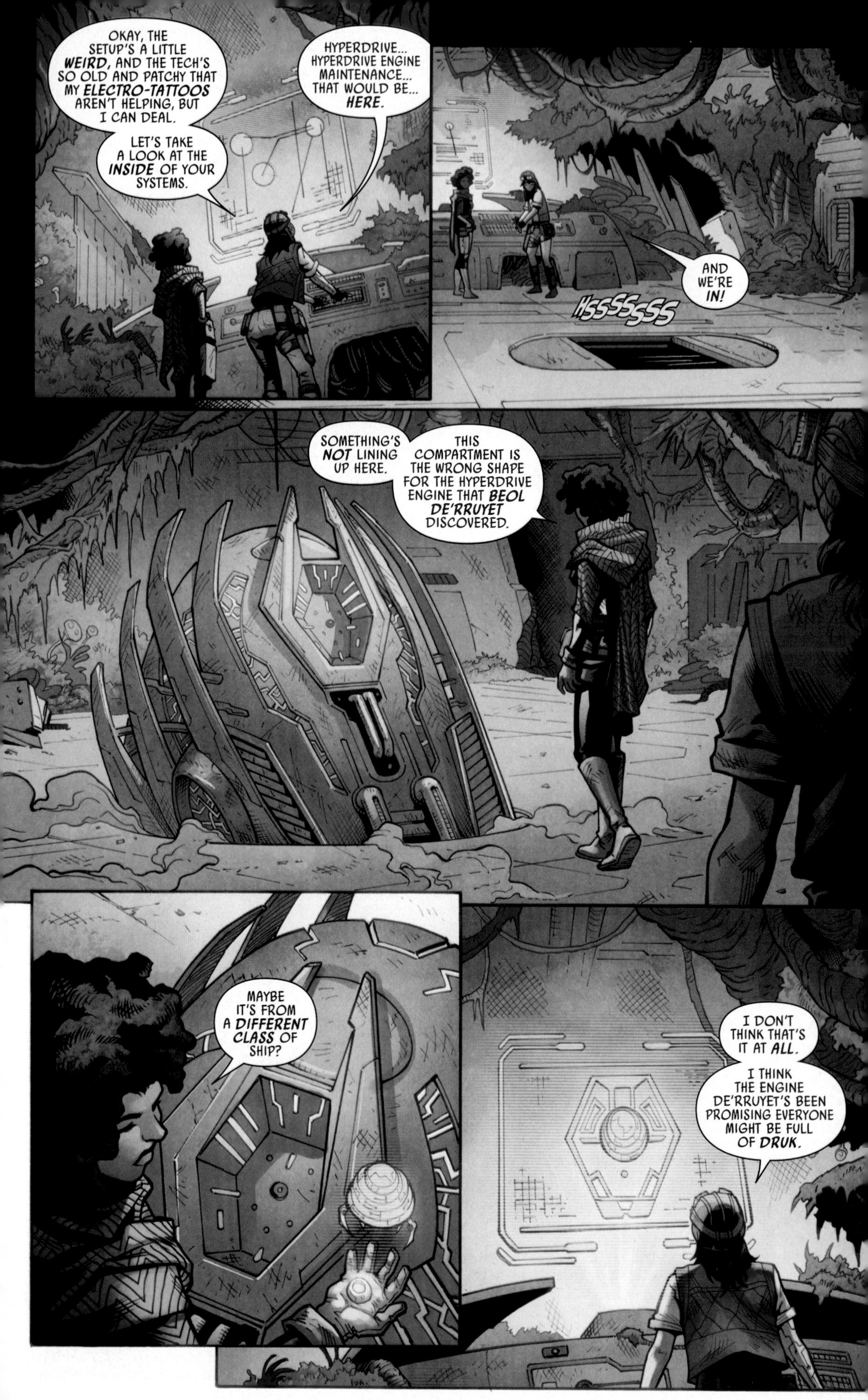

OKAY, THE SETUP'S A LITTLE **WEIRD**, AND THE TECH'S SO OLD AND PATCHY THAT MY **ELECTRO-TATTOOS** AREN'T HELPING, BUT I CAN DEAL.
LET'S TAKE A LOOK AT THE **INSIDE** OF YOUR SYSTEMS.
HYPERDRIVE... HYPERDRIVE ENGINE MAINTENANCE... THAT WOULD BE... **HERE.**
HSSSSSSS
AND WE'RE **IN!**
SOMETHING'S **NOT** LINING UP HERE.
THIS COMPARTMENT IS THE WRONG SHAPE FOR THE HYPERDRIVE ENGINE THAT **BEOL DE'RRUYET** DISCOVERED.
MAYBE IT'S FROM A **DIFFERENT CLASS** OF SHIP?
I DON'T THINK THAT'S IT AT **ALL.**
I THINK THE ENGINE DE'RRUYET'S BEEN PROMISING EVERYONE MIGHT BE FULL OF **DRUK.**

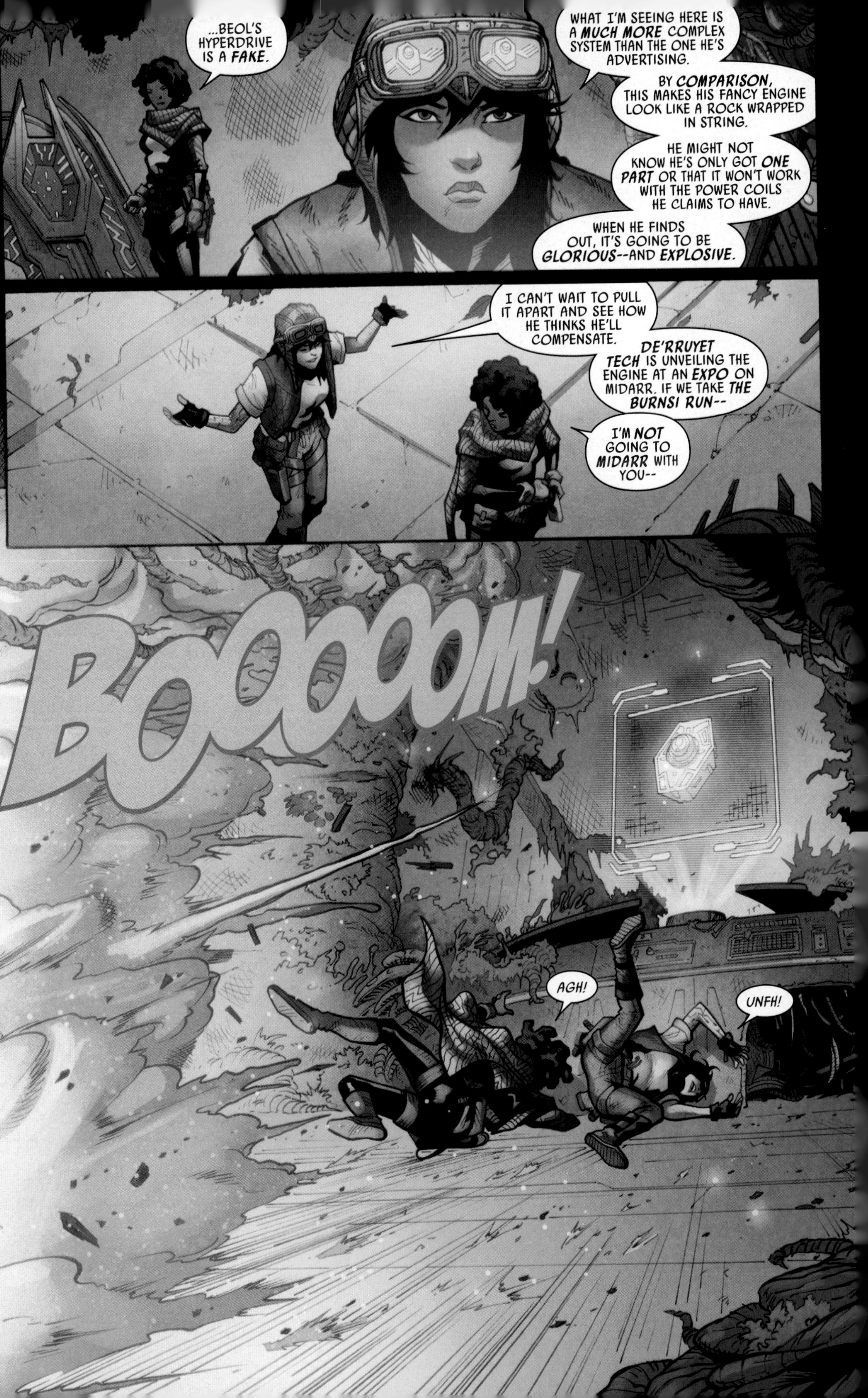
...BEOL'S HYPERDRIVE IS A FAKE.
WHAT I'M SEEING HERE IS A MUCH MORE COMPLEX SYSTEM THAN THE ONE HE'S ADVERTISING.
BY COMPARISON, THIS MAKES HIS FANCY ENGINE LOOK LIKE A ROCK WRAPPED IN STRING.
HE MIGHT NOT KNOW HE'S ONLY GOT ONE PART OR THAT IT WON'T WORK WITH THE POWER COILS HE CLAIMS TO HAVE.
WHEN HE FINDS OUT, IT'S GOING TO BE GLORIOUS--AND EXPLOSIVE.
I CAN'T WAIT TO PULL IT APART AND SEE HOW HE THINKS HE'LL COMPENSATE.
DE'RRUYET TECH IS UNVEILING THE ENGINE AT AN EXPO ON MIDARR. IF WE TAKE THE BURNSI RUN--
I'M NOT GOING TO MIDARR WITH YOU--
BOOOOOM!
AGH!
UNFH!

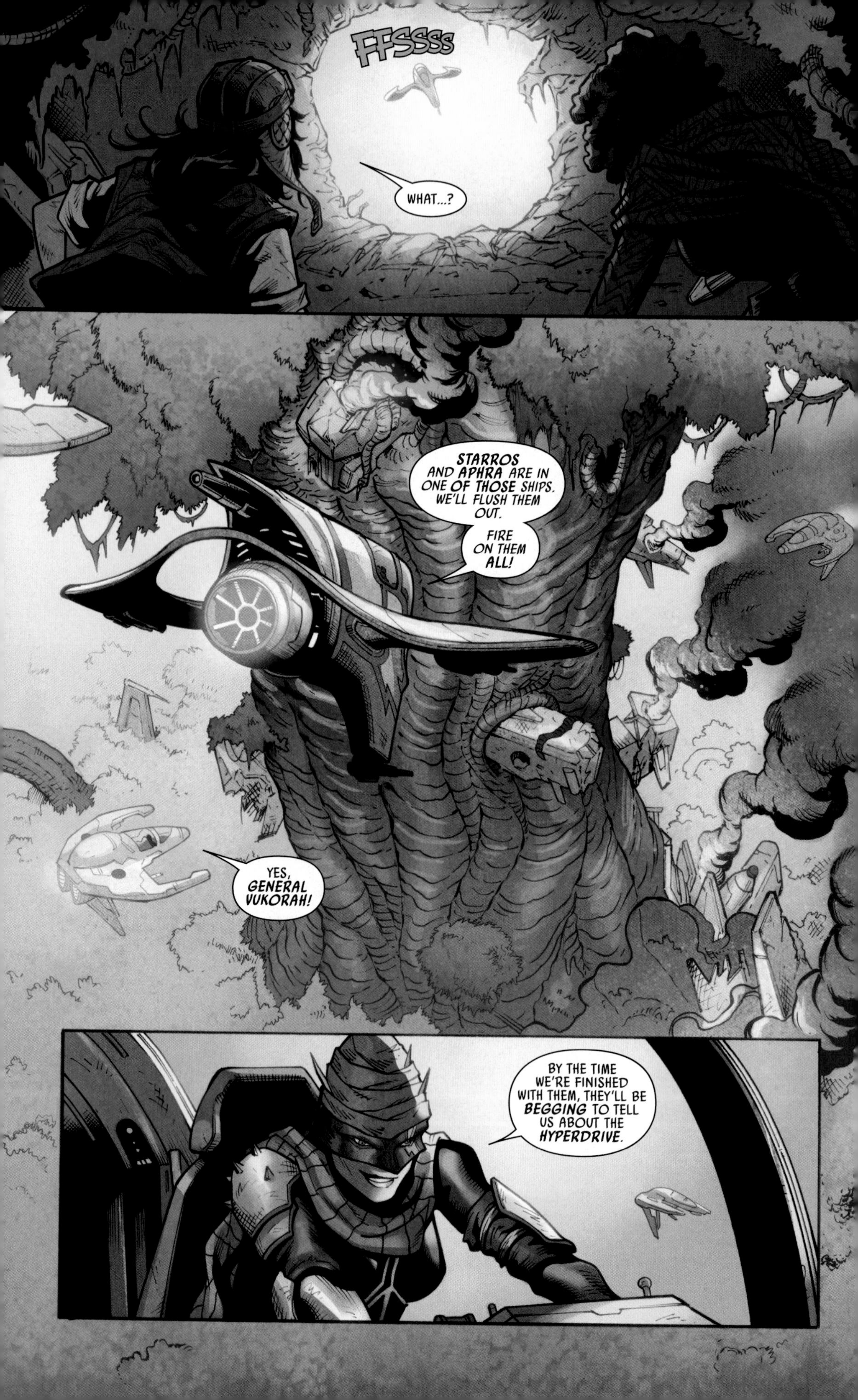
FFSSSS
WHAT...?
STARROS AND APHRA ARE IN ONE OF THOSE SHIPS. WE'LL FLUSH THEM OUT.
FIRE ON THEM ALL!
YES, GENERAL VUKORAH!
BY THE TIME WE'RE FINISHED WITH THEM, THEY'LL BE BEGGING TO TELL US ABOUT THE HYPERDRIVE.

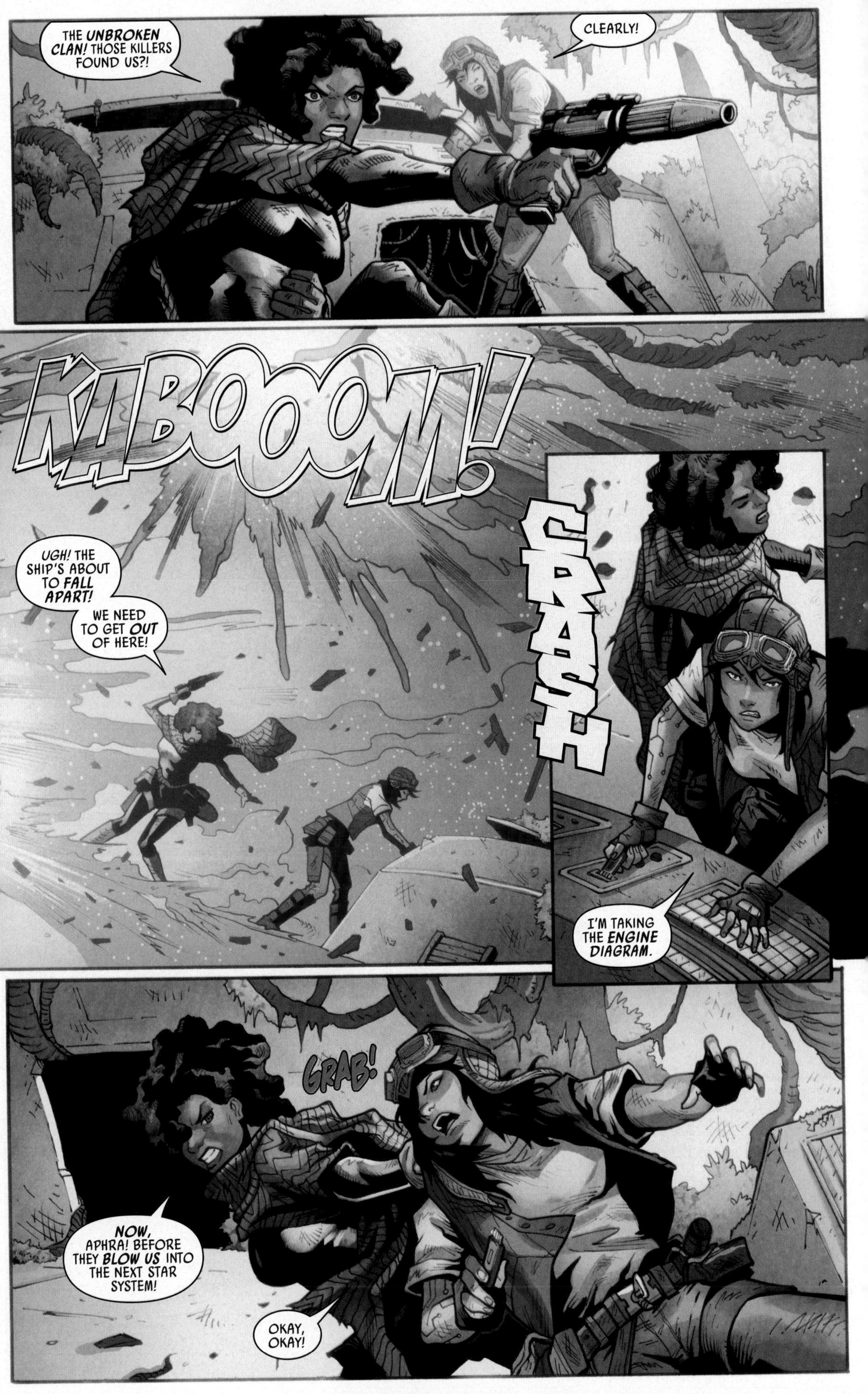
THE UNBROKEN CLAN! THOSE KILLERS FOUND US?!
CLEARLY!
KABOOOM!
UGH! THE SHIP'S ABOUT TO FALL APART!
WE NEED TO GET OUT OF HERE!
CRASH
I'M TAKING THE ENGINE DIAGRAM.
GRAB!
NOW, APHRA! BEFORE THEY BLOW US INTO THE NEXT STAR SYSTEM!
OKAY, OKAY!

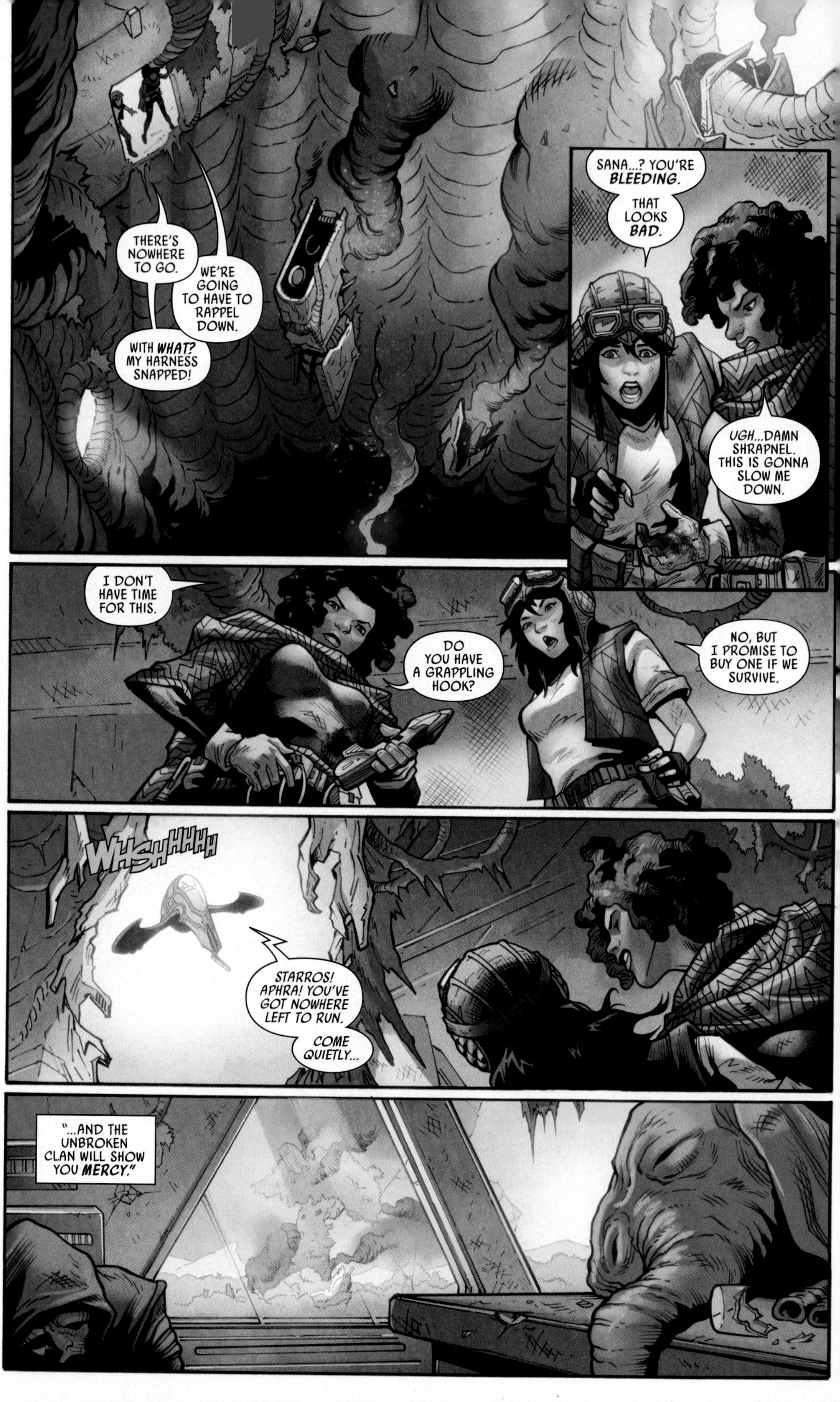

THERE'S NOWHERE TO GO.
WE'RE GOING TO HAVE TO RAPPEL DOWN.
WITH WHAT? MY HARNESS SNAPPED!
SANA...? YOU'RE BLEEDING.
THAT LOOKS BAD.
UGH...DAMN SHRAPNEL. THIS IS GONNA SLOW ME DOWN.
I DON'T HAVE TIME FOR THIS.
DO YOU HAVE A GRAPPLING HOOK?
NO, BUT I PROMISE TO BUY ONE IF WE SURVIVE.
WHSHHHHH
STARROS! APHRA! YOU'VE GOT NOWHERE LEFT TO RUN.
COME QUIETLY...
"...AND THE UNBROKEN CLAN WILL SHOW YOU MERCY."

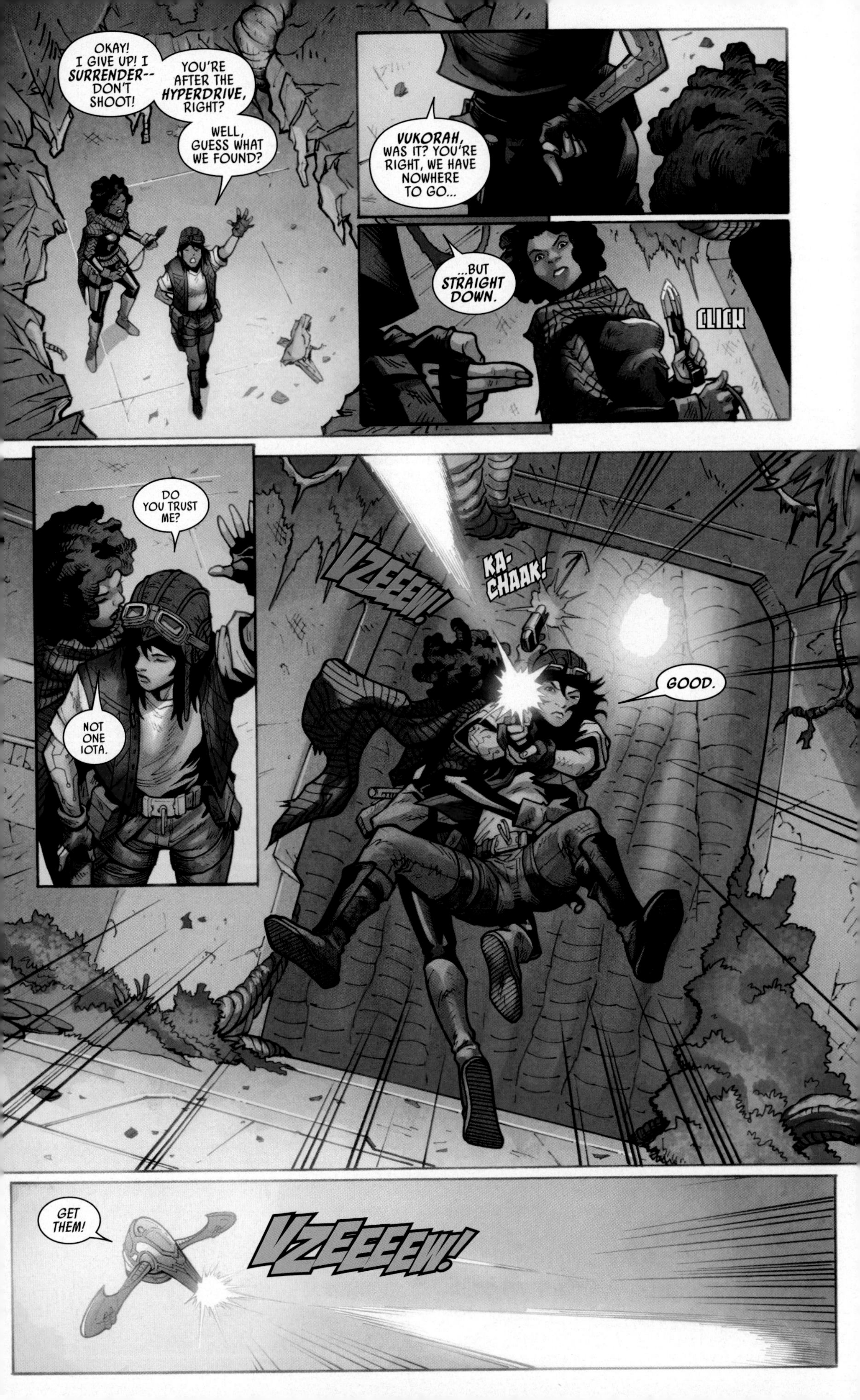
OKAY! I GIVE UP! I SURRENDER-- DON'T SHOOT!
YOU'RE AFTER THE HYPERDRIVE, RIGHT?
WELL, GUESS WHAT WE FOUND?
VUKORAH, WAS IT? YOU'RE RIGHT, WE HAVE NOWHERE TO GO...
...BUT STRAIGHT DOWN.
CLICK
DO YOU TRUST ME?
NOT ONE IOTA.
VZEEEW!
KA-CHAAK!
GOOD.
GET THEM!
VZEEEEW!

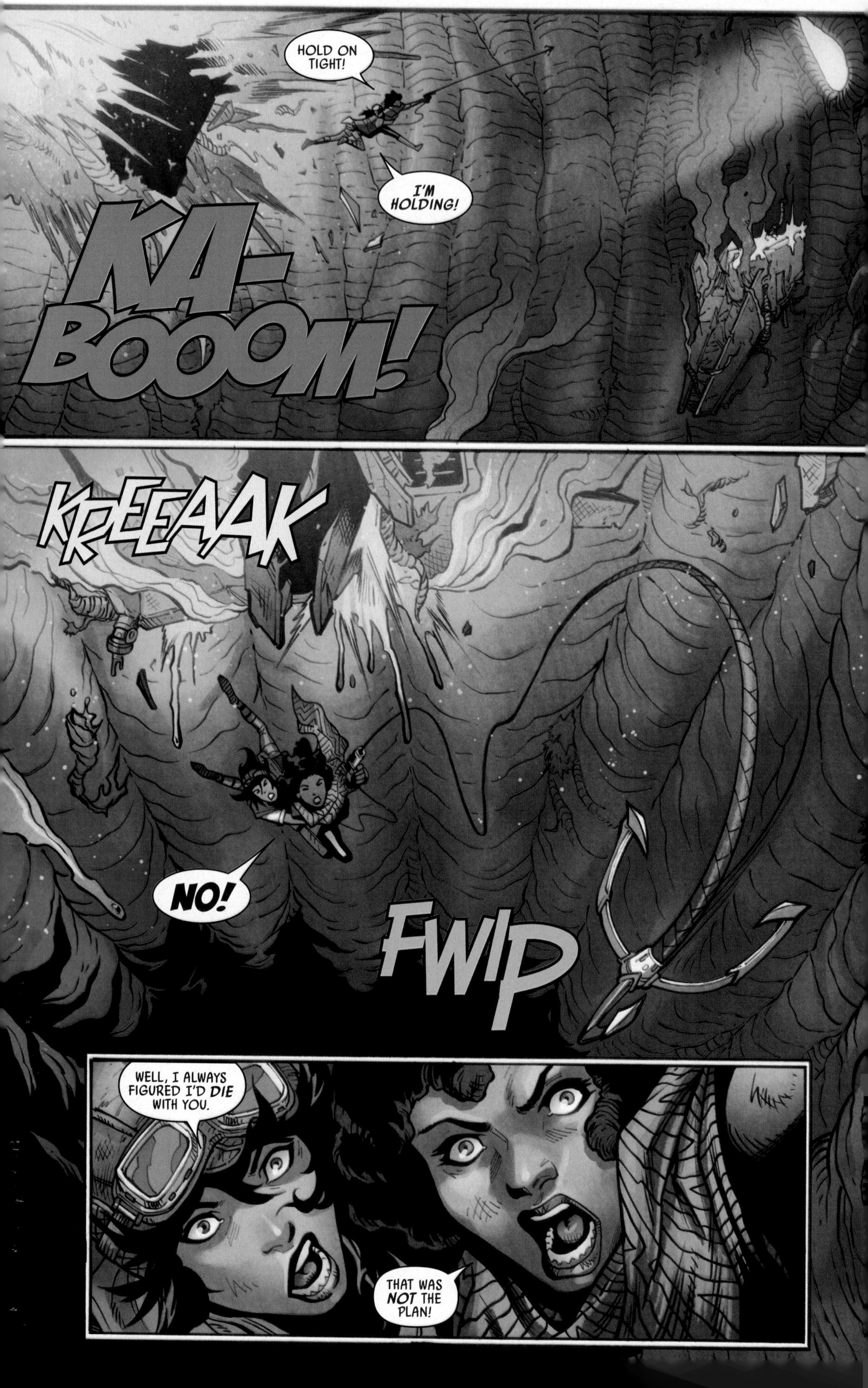
HOLD ON TIGHT!
I'M HOLDING!
KA-BOOOM!
KREEAAK
NO!
FWIP
WELL, I ALWAYS FIGURED I'D DIE WITH YOU.
THAT WAS NOT THE PLAN!

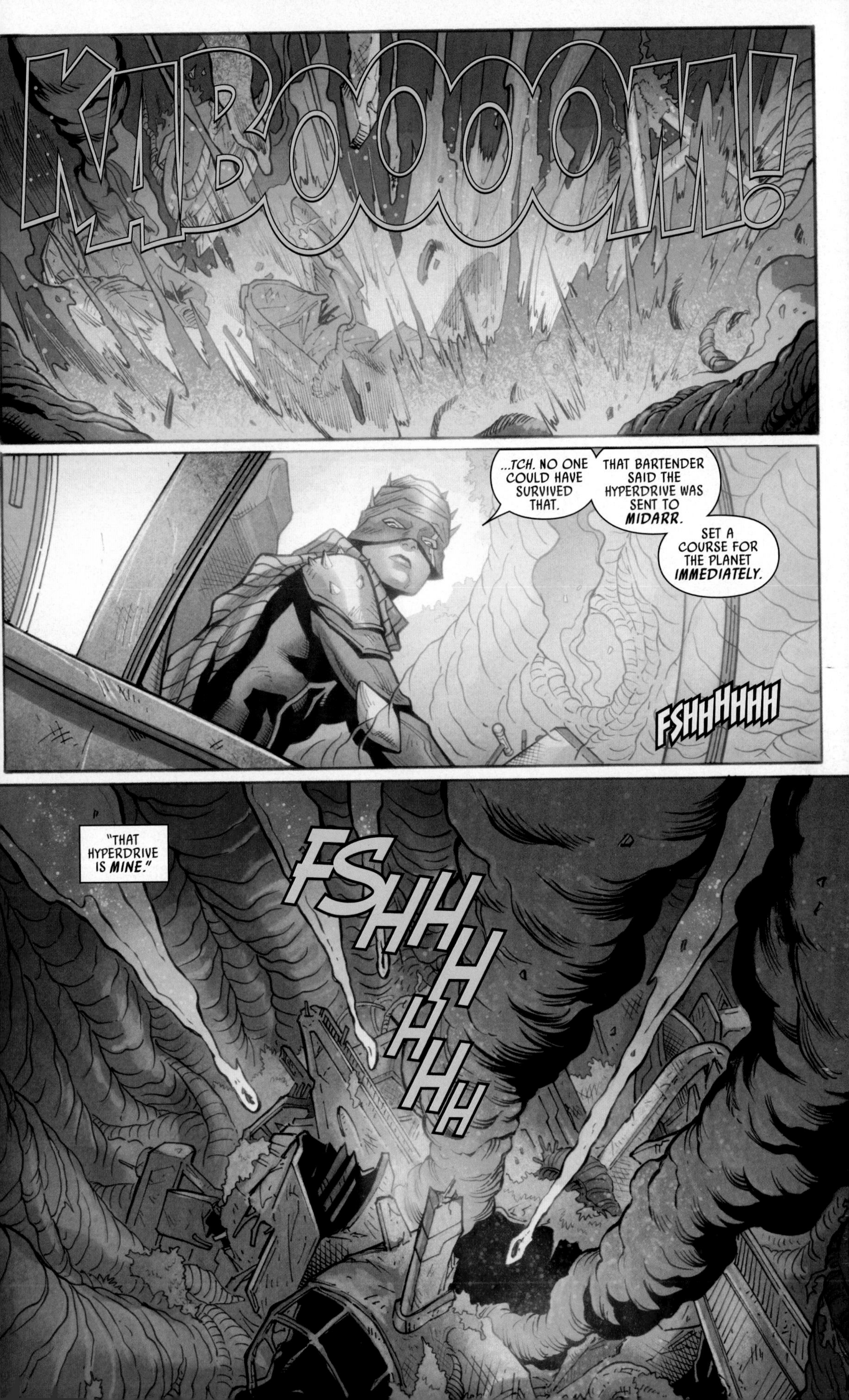
KABOOOOM!
...TCH. NO ONE COULD HAVE SURVIVED THAT.
THAT BARTENDER SAID THE HYPERDRIVE WAS SENT TO MIDARR.
SET A COURSE FOR THE PLANET IMMEDIATELY.
FSHHHHHH
"THAT HYPERDRIVE IS MINE."
FSHHHHHHH

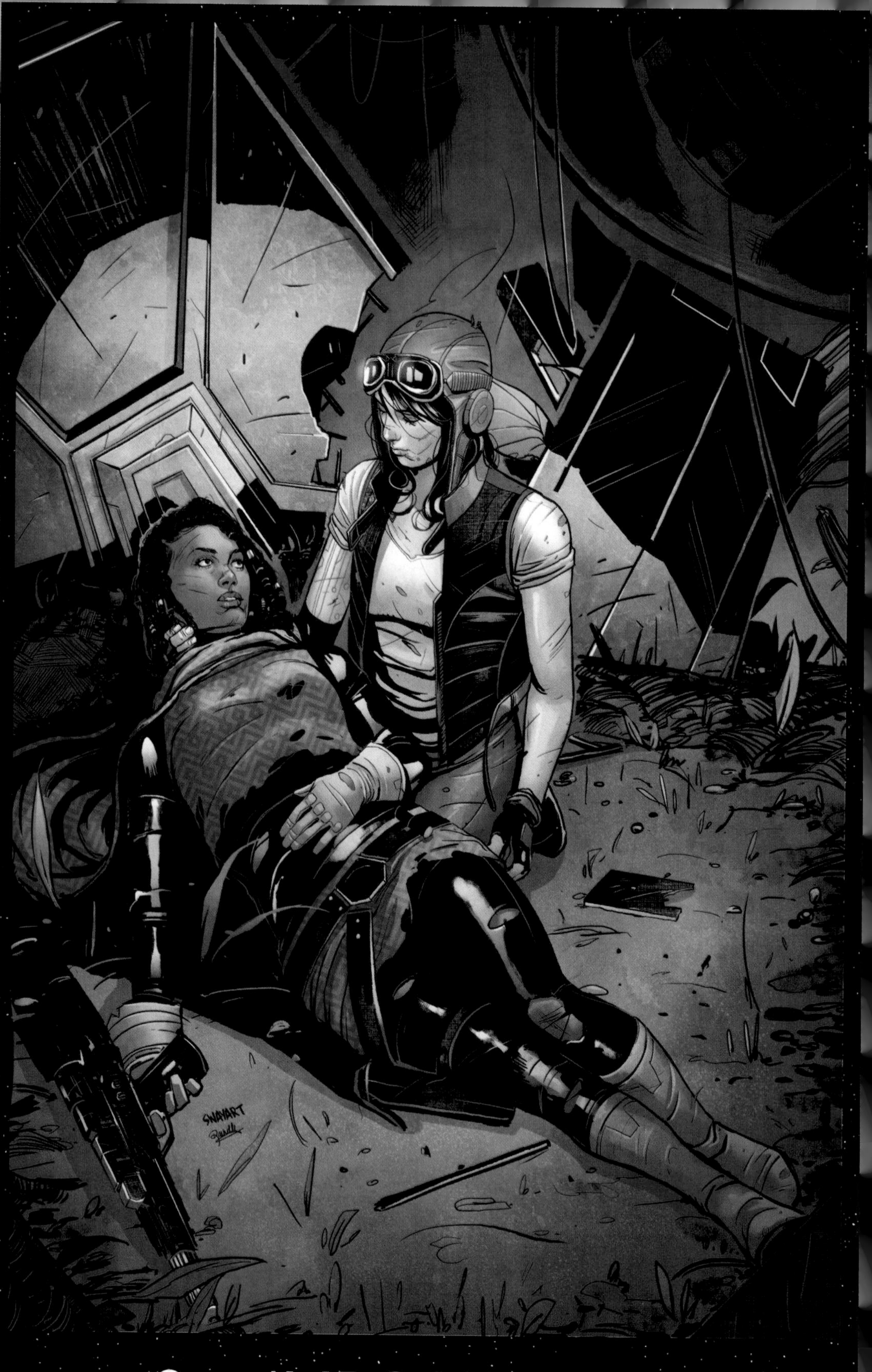

9 — IMPOSSIBILITIES

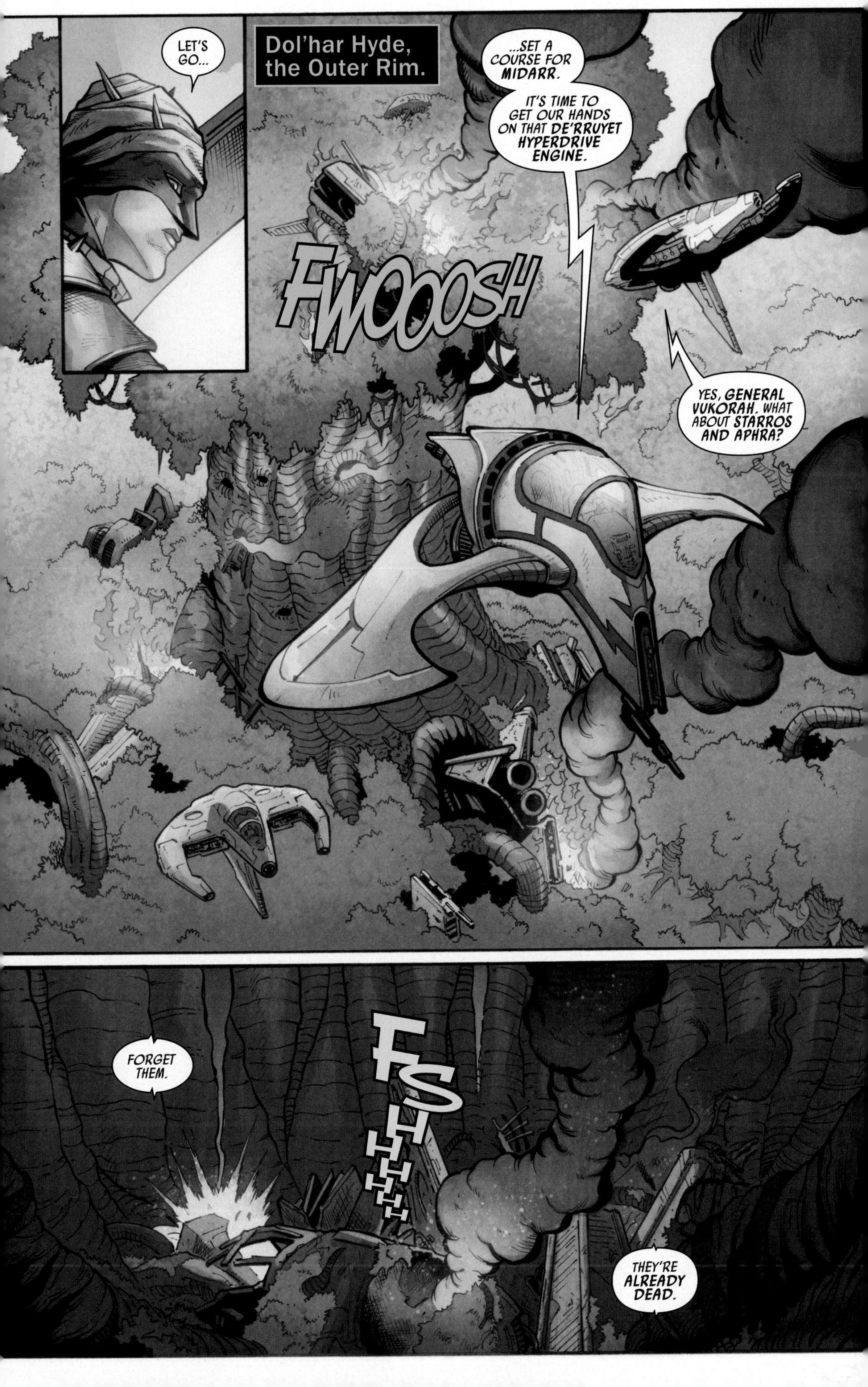
LET'S GO...
Dol'har Hyde, the Outer Rim.
...SET A COURSE FOR MIDARR.
IT'S TIME TO GET OUR HANDS ON THAT DE'RRUYET HYPERDRIVE ENGINE.
FWOOOSH
YES, GENERAL VUKORAH. WHAT ABOUT STARROS AND APHRA?
FORGET THEM.
FSHHHHHH
THEY'RE ALREADY DEAD.

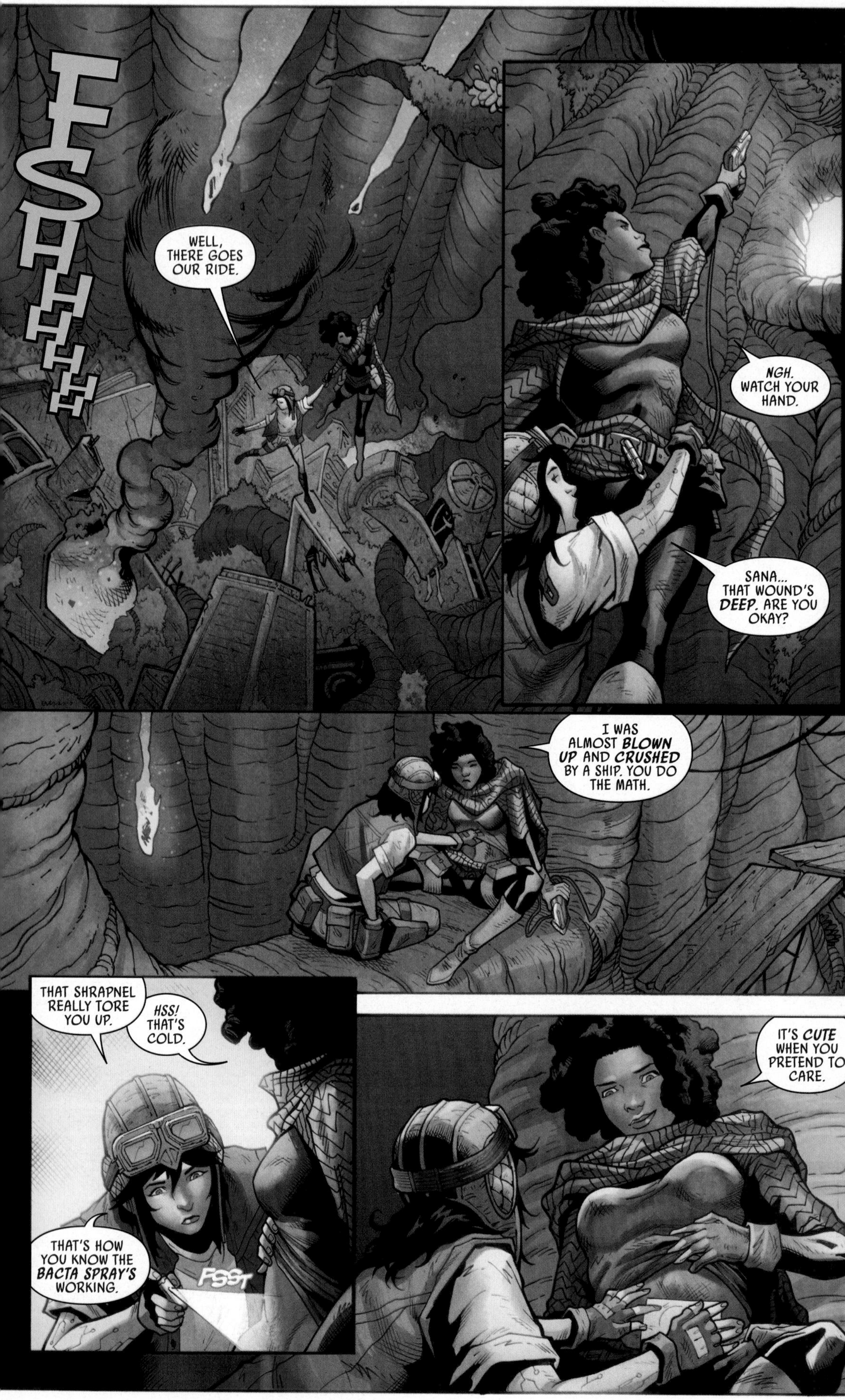
FSHHHHH
WELL, THERE GOES OUR RIDE.
NGH. WATCH YOUR HAND.
SANA... THAT WOUND'S DEEP. ARE YOU OKAY?
I WAS ALMOST BLOWN UP AND CRUSHED BY A SHIP. YOU DO THE MATH.
THAT SHRAPNEL REALLY TORE YOU UP.
HSS! THAT'S COLD.
THAT'S HOW YOU KNOW THE BACTA SPRAY'S WORKING.
FSST
IT'S CUTE WHEN YOU PRETEND TO CARE.

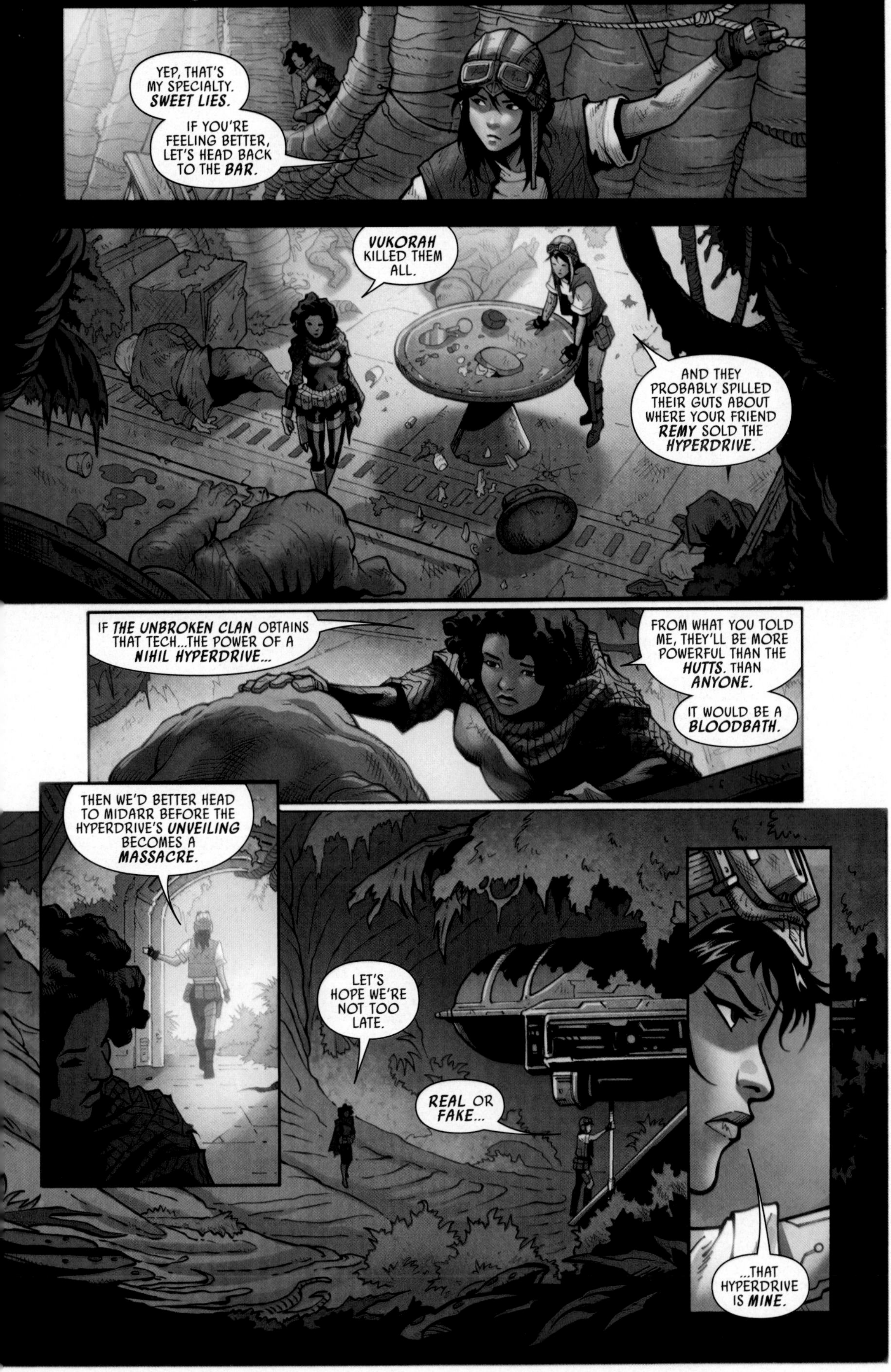

YEP, THAT'S MY SPECIALTY. SWEET LIES.
IF YOU'RE FEELING BETTER, LET'S HEAD BACK TO THE BAR.
VUKORAH KILLED THEM ALL.
AND THEY PROBABLY SPILLED THEIR GUTS ABOUT WHERE YOUR FRIEND REMY SOLD THE HYPERDRIVE.
IF THE UNBROKEN CLAN OBTAINS THAT TECH...THE POWER OF A NIHIL HYPERDRIVE...
FROM WHAT YOU TOLD ME, THEY'LL BE MORE POWERFUL THAN THE HUTTS. THAN ANYONE.
IT WOULD BE A BLOODBATH.
THEN WE'D BETTER HEAD TO MIDARR BEFORE THE HYPERDRIVE'S UNVEILING BECOMES A MASSACRE.
LET'S HOPE WE'RE NOT TOO LATE.
REAL OR FAKE...
...THAT HYPERDRIVE IS MINE.

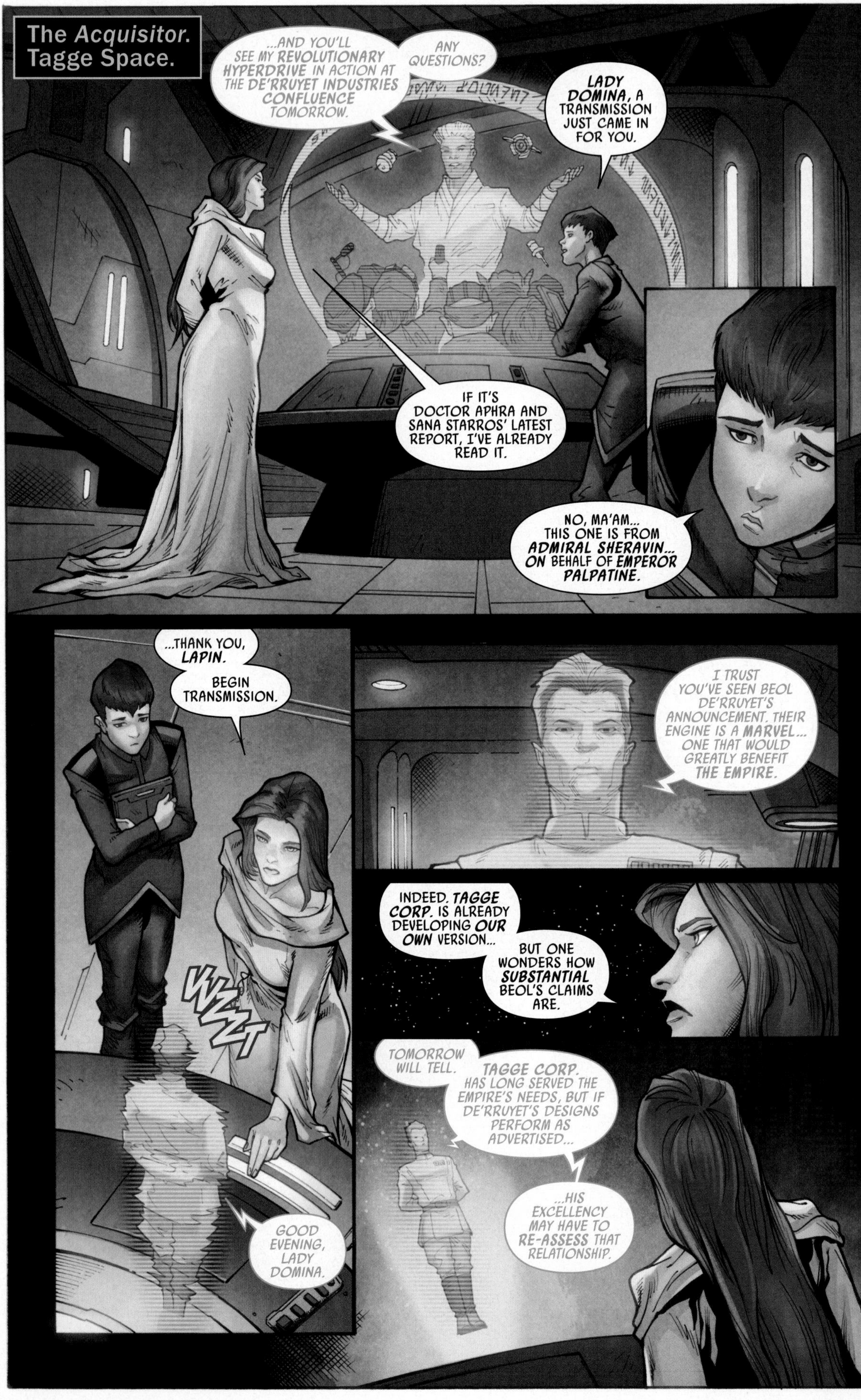
The Acquisitor. Tagge Space.
...AND YOU'LL SEE MY REVOLUTIONARY HYPERDRIVE IN ACTION AT THE DE'RRUYET INDUSTRIES CONFLUENCE TOMORROW.
ANY QUESTIONS?
LADY DOMINA, A TRANSMISSION JUST CAME IN FOR YOU.
IF IT'S DOCTOR APHRA AND SANA STARROS' LATEST REPORT, I'VE ALREADY READ IT.
NO, MA'AM... THIS ONE IS FROM ADMIRAL SHERAVIN... ON BEHALF OF EMPEROR PALPATINE.
...THANK YOU, LAPIN.
BEGIN TRANSMISSION.
WMT
GOOD EVENING, LADY DOMINA.
I TRUST YOU'VE SEEN BEOL DE'RRUYET'S ANNOUNCEMENT. THEIR ENGINE IS A MARVEL... ONE THAT WOULD GREATLY BENEFIT THE EMPIRE.
INDEED. TAGGE CORP. IS ALREADY DEVELOPING OUR OWN VERSION...
BUT ONE WONDERS HOW SUBSTANTIAL BEOL'S CLAIMS ARE.
TOMORROW WILL TELL.
TAGGE CORP. HAS LONG SERVED THE EMPIRE'S NEEDS, BUT IF DE'RRUYET'S DESIGNS PERFORM AS ADVERTISED...
...HIS EXCELLENCY MAY HAVE TO RE-ASSESS THAT RELATIONSHIP.

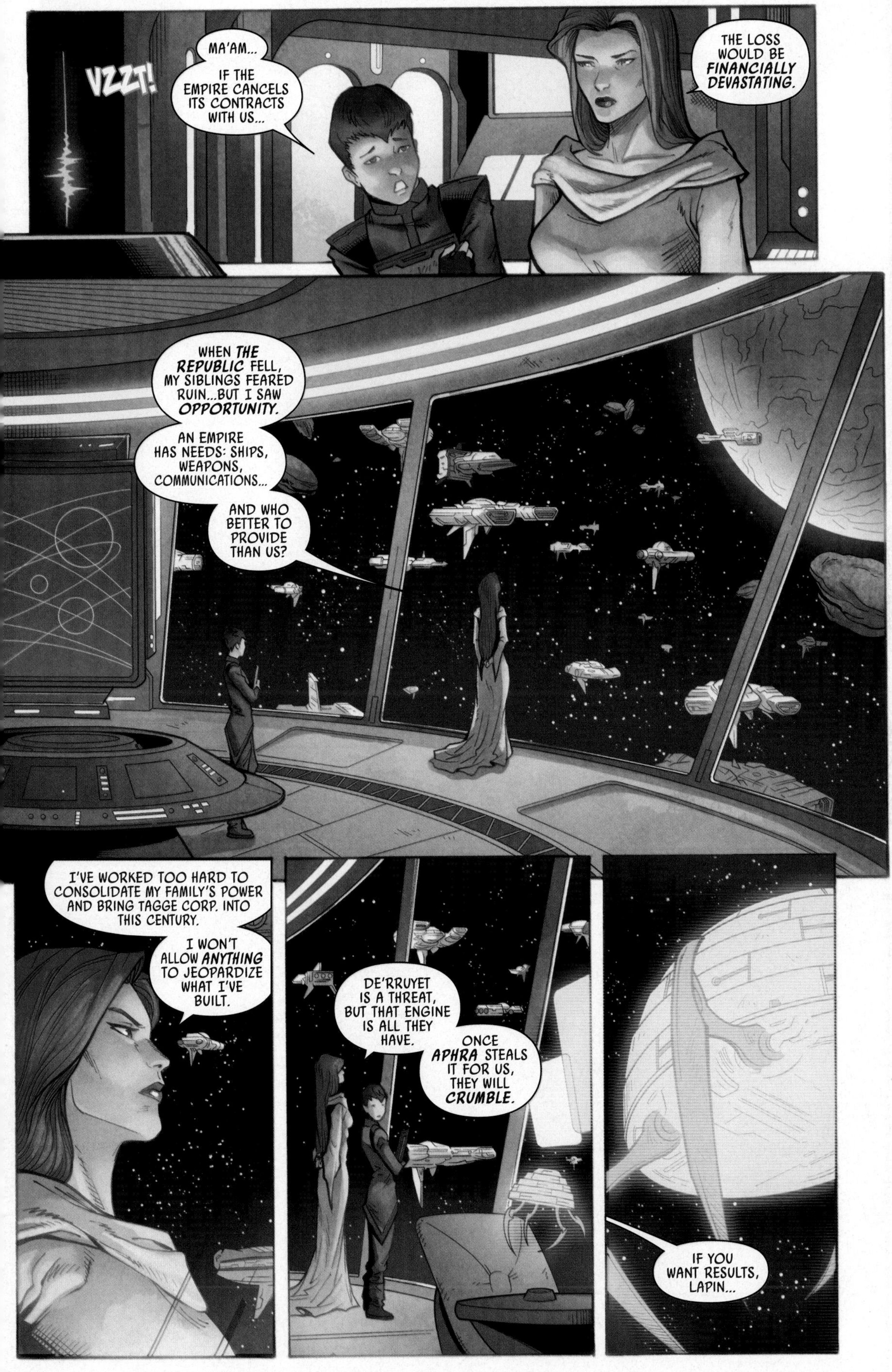
VZZT!
MA'AM...
IF THE EMPIRE CANCELS ITS CONTRACTS WITH US...
THE LOSS WOULD BE FINANCIALLY DEVASTATING.
WHEN THE REPUBLIC FELL, MY SIBLINGS FEARED RUIN...BUT I SAW OPPORTUNITY.
AN EMPIRE HAS NEEDS: SHIPS, WEAPONS, COMMUNICATIONS...
AND WHO BETTER TO PROVIDE THAN US?
I'VE WORKED TOO HARD TO CONSOLIDATE MY FAMILY'S POWER AND BRING TAGGE CORP. INTO THIS CENTURY.
I WON'T ALLOW ANYTHING TO JEOPARDIZE WHAT I'VE BUILT.
DE'RRUYET IS A THREAT, BUT THAT ENGINE IS ALL THEY HAVE.
ONCE APHRA STEALS IT FOR US, THEY WILL CRUMBLE.
IF YOU WANT RESULTS, LAPIN...

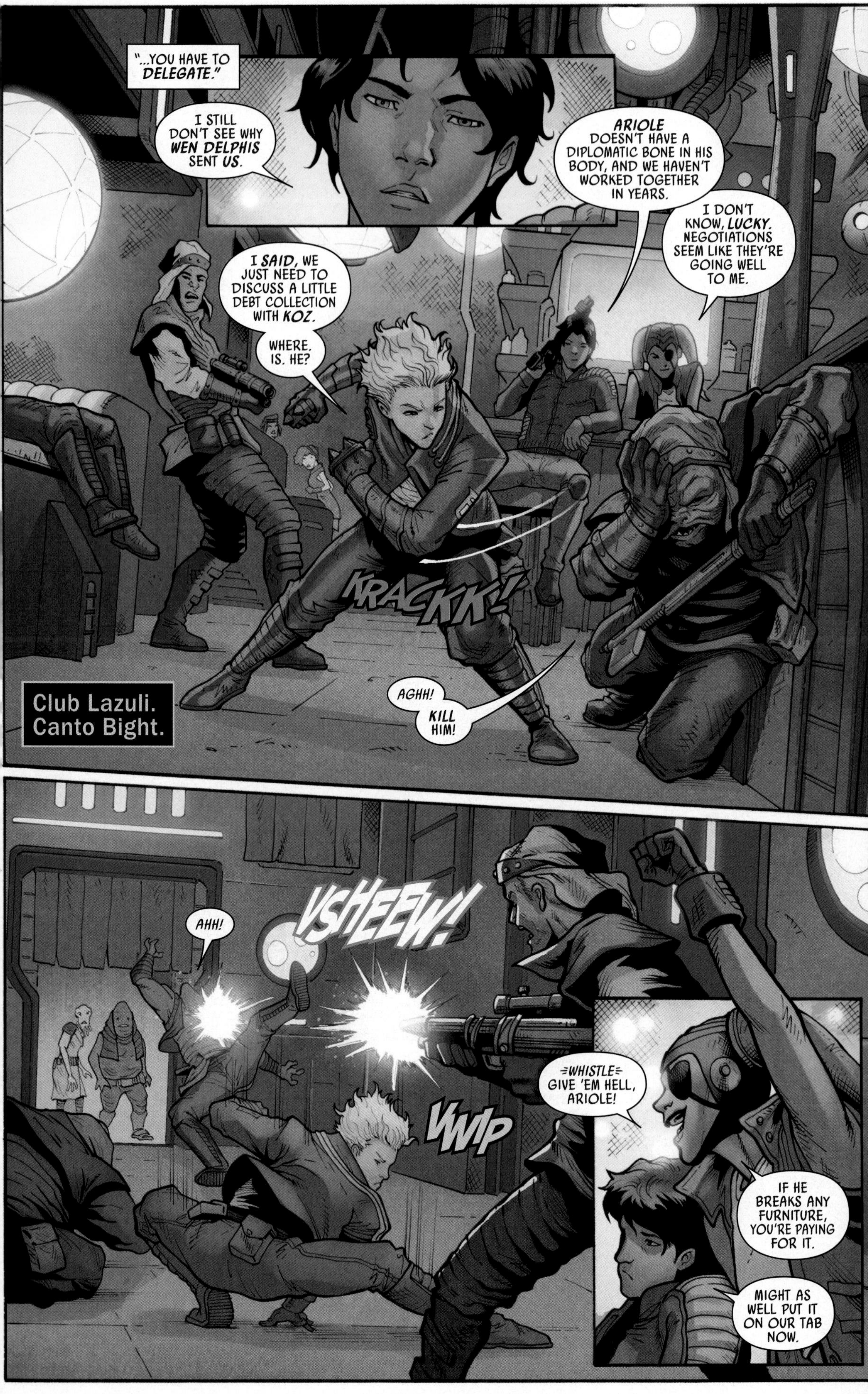
"...YOU HAVE TO DELEGATE."
I STILL DON'T SEE WHY WEN DELPHIS SENT US.
ARIOLE DOESN'T HAVE A DIPLOMATIC BONE IN HIS BODY, AND WE HAVEN'T WORKED TOGETHER IN YEARS.
I DON'T KNOW, LUCKY. NEGOTIATIONS SEEM LIKE THEY'RE GOING WELL TO ME.
I SAID, WE JUST NEED TO DISCUSS A LITTLE DEBT COLLECTION WITH KOZ.
WHERE. IS. HE?
KRACKK!
Club Lazuli. Canto Bight.
AGHH!
KILL HIM!
AHH!
VSHEEW!
VWIP
=WHISTLE= GIVE 'EM HELL, ARIOLE!
IF HE BREAKS ANY FURNITURE, YOU'RE PAYING FOR IT.
MIGHT AS WELL PUT IT ON OUR TAB NOW.

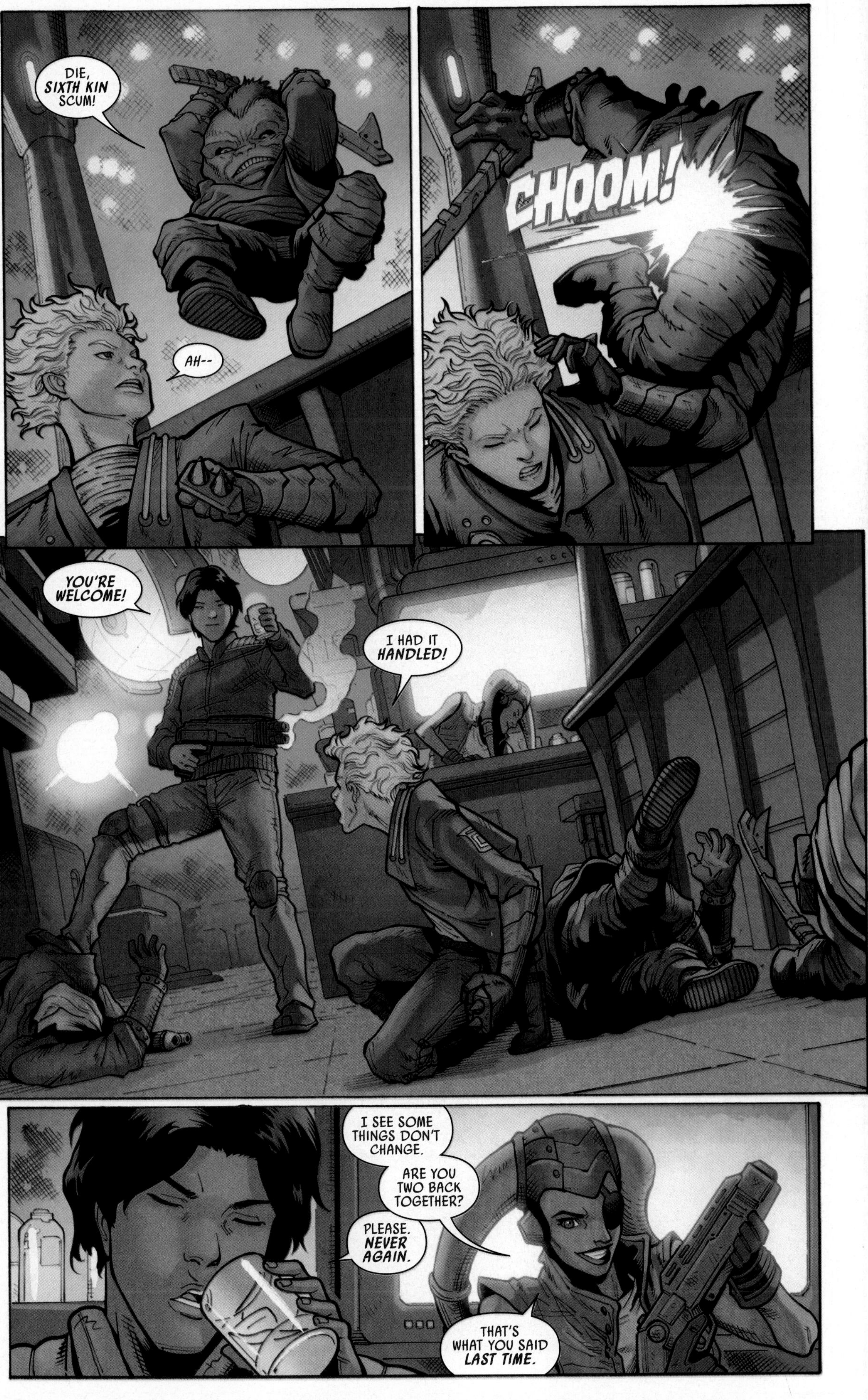
DIE, SIXTH KIN SCUM!
AH--
CHOOM!
YOU'RE WELCOME!
I HAD IT HANDLED!
I SEE SOME THINGS DON'T CHANGE.
ARE YOU TWO BACK TOGETHER?
PLEASE. NEVER AGAIN.
THAT'S WHAT YOU SAID LAST TIME.

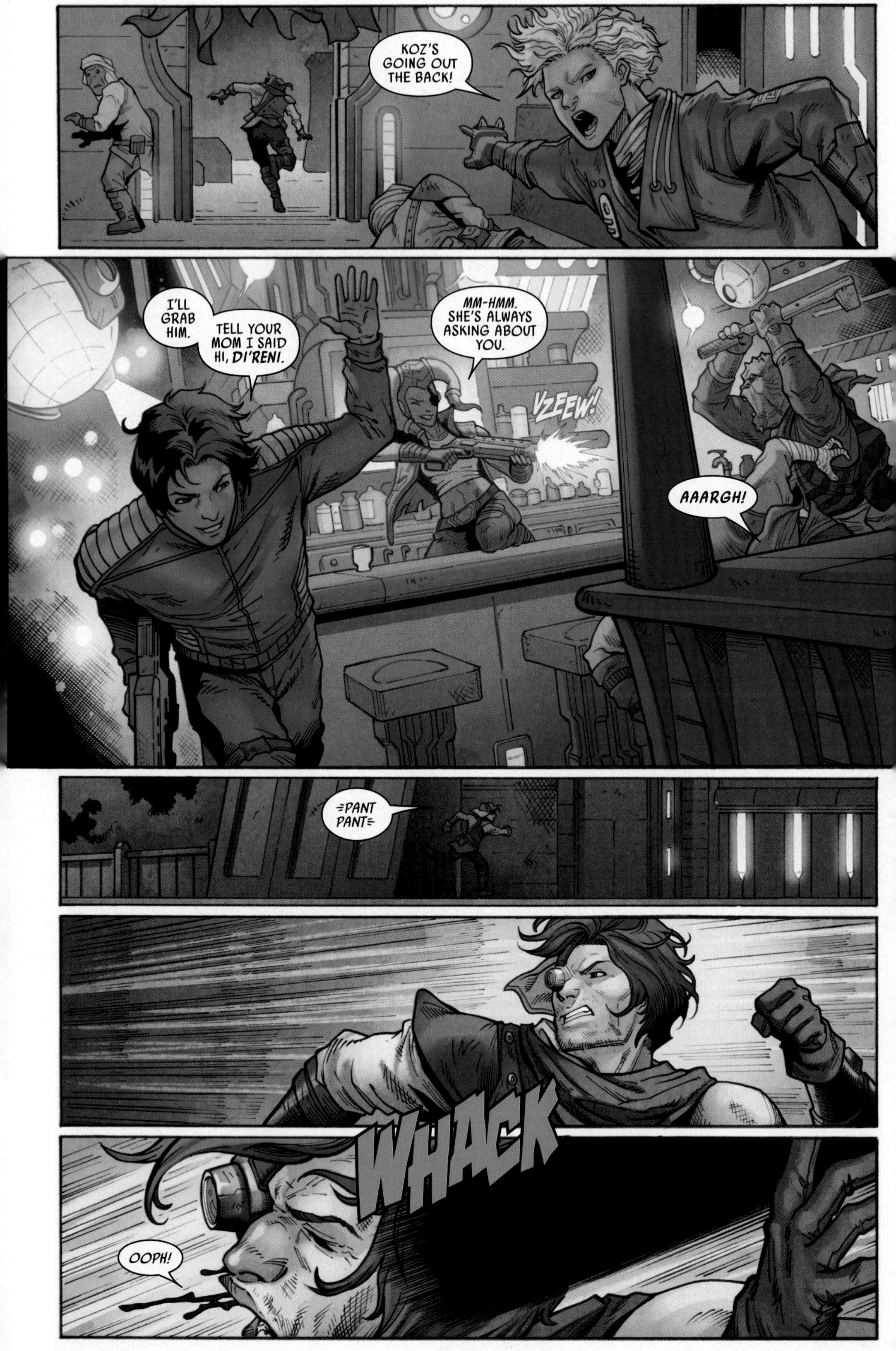
KOZ'S GOING OUT THE BACK!
I'LL GRAB HIM.
TELL YOUR MOM I SAID HI, DI'RENI.
MM-HMM. SHE'S ALWAYS ASKING ABOUT YOU.
VZEEW!
AAARGH!
PANT PANT
WHACK
OOPH!

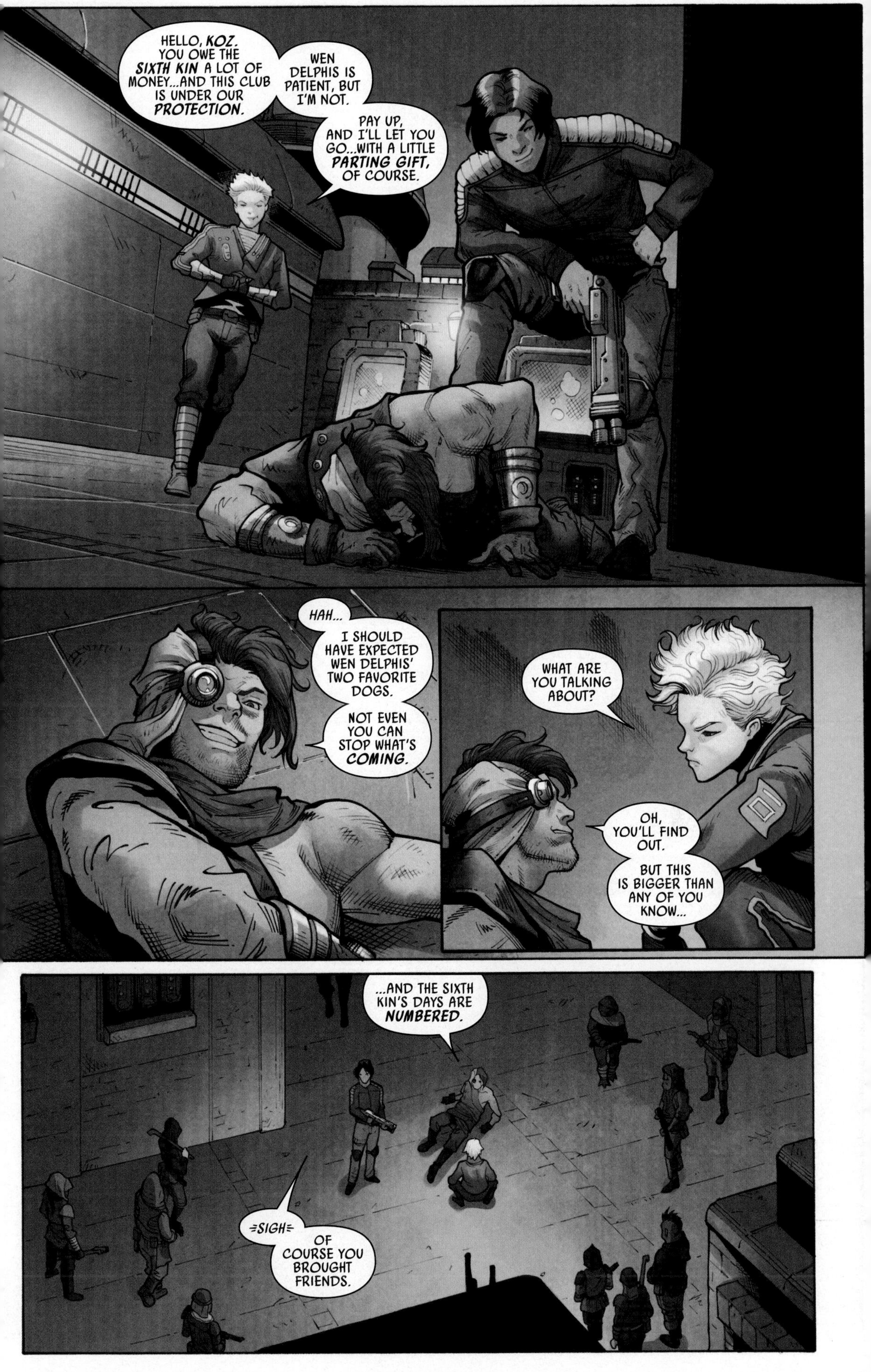
HELLO, KOZ. YOU OWE THE SIXTH KIN A LOT OF MONEY...AND THIS CLUB IS UNDER OUR PROTECTION.
WEN DELPHIS IS PATIENT, BUT I'M NOT.
PAY UP, AND I'LL LET YOU GO...WITH A LITTLE PARTING GIFT, OF COURSE.
HAH...
I SHOULD HAVE EXPECTED WEN DELPHIS' TWO FAVORITE DOGS.
NOT EVEN YOU CAN STOP WHAT'S COMING.
WHAT ARE YOU TALKING ABOUT?
OH, YOU'LL FIND OUT.
BUT THIS IS BIGGER THAN ANY OF YOU KNOW...
...AND THE SIXTH KIN'S DAYS ARE NUMBERED.
=SIGH=
OF COURSE YOU BROUGHT FRIENDS.

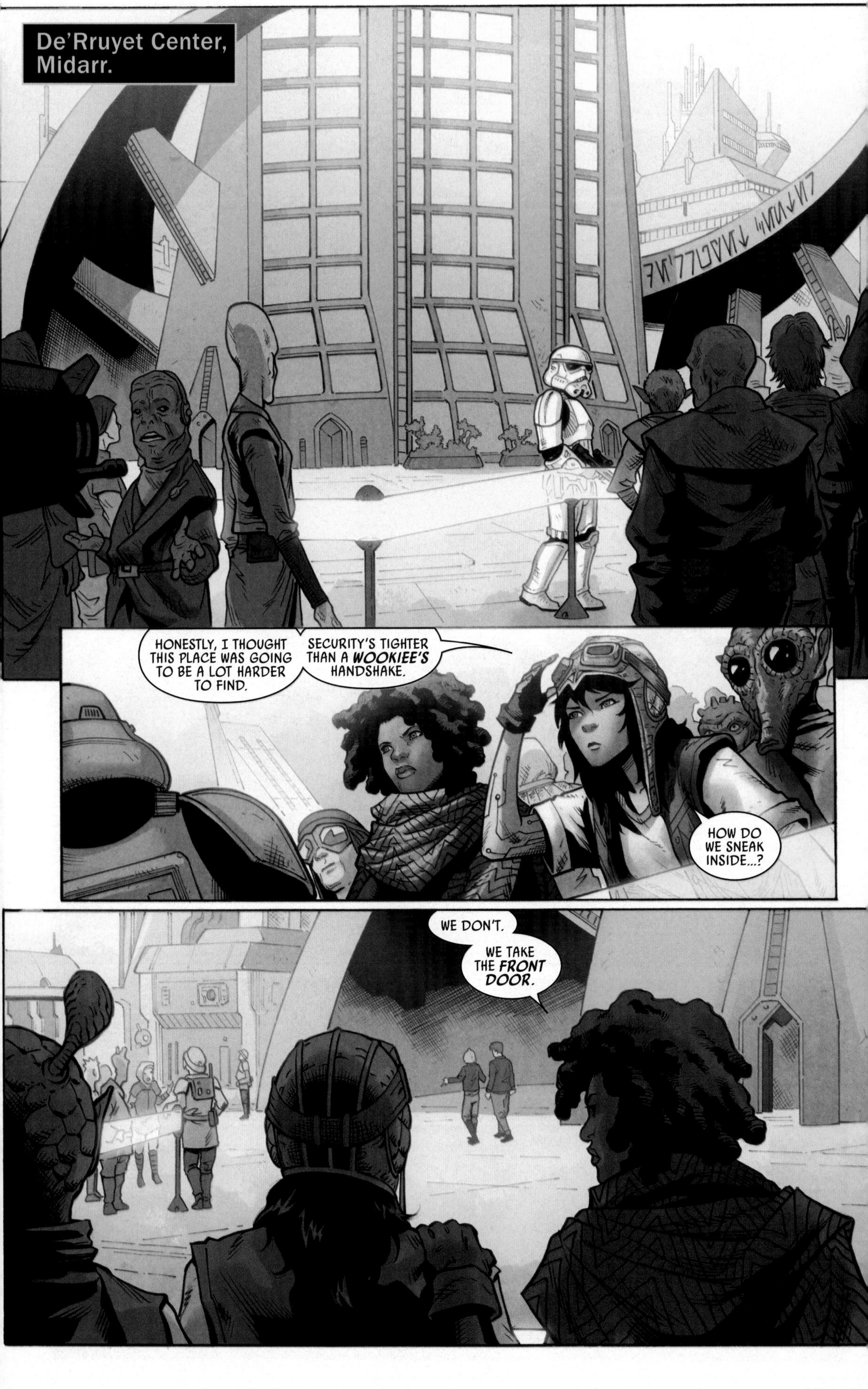
De'Rruyet Center, Midarr.
HONESTLY, I THOUGHT THIS PLACE WAS GOING TO BE A LOT HARDER TO FIND.
SECURITY'S TIGHTER THAN A WOOKIEE'S HANDSHAKE.
HOW DO WE SNEAK INSIDE...?
WE DON'T.
WE TAKE THE FRONT DOOR.

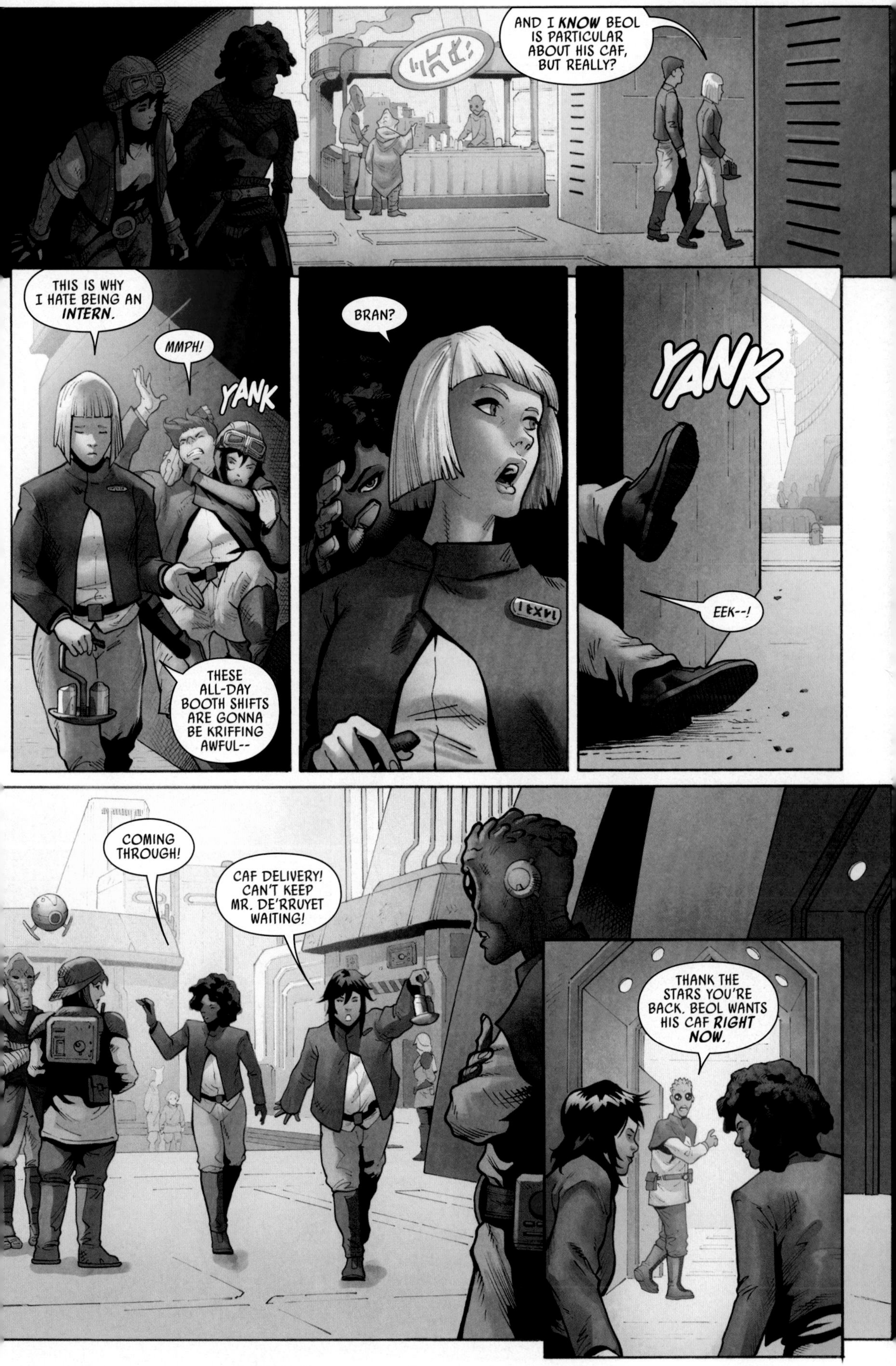
AND I KNOW BEOL IS PARTICULAR ABOUT HIS CAF, BUT REALLY?
THIS IS WHY I HATE BEING AN INTERN.
MMPH!
YANK
THESE ALL-DAY BOOTH SHIFTS ARE GONNA BE KRIFFING AWFUL--
BRAN?
YANK
EEK--!
COMING THROUGH!
CAF DELIVERY! CAN'T KEEP MR. DE'RRUYET WAITING!
THANK THE STARS YOU'RE BACK. BEOL WANTS HIS CAF RIGHT NOW.

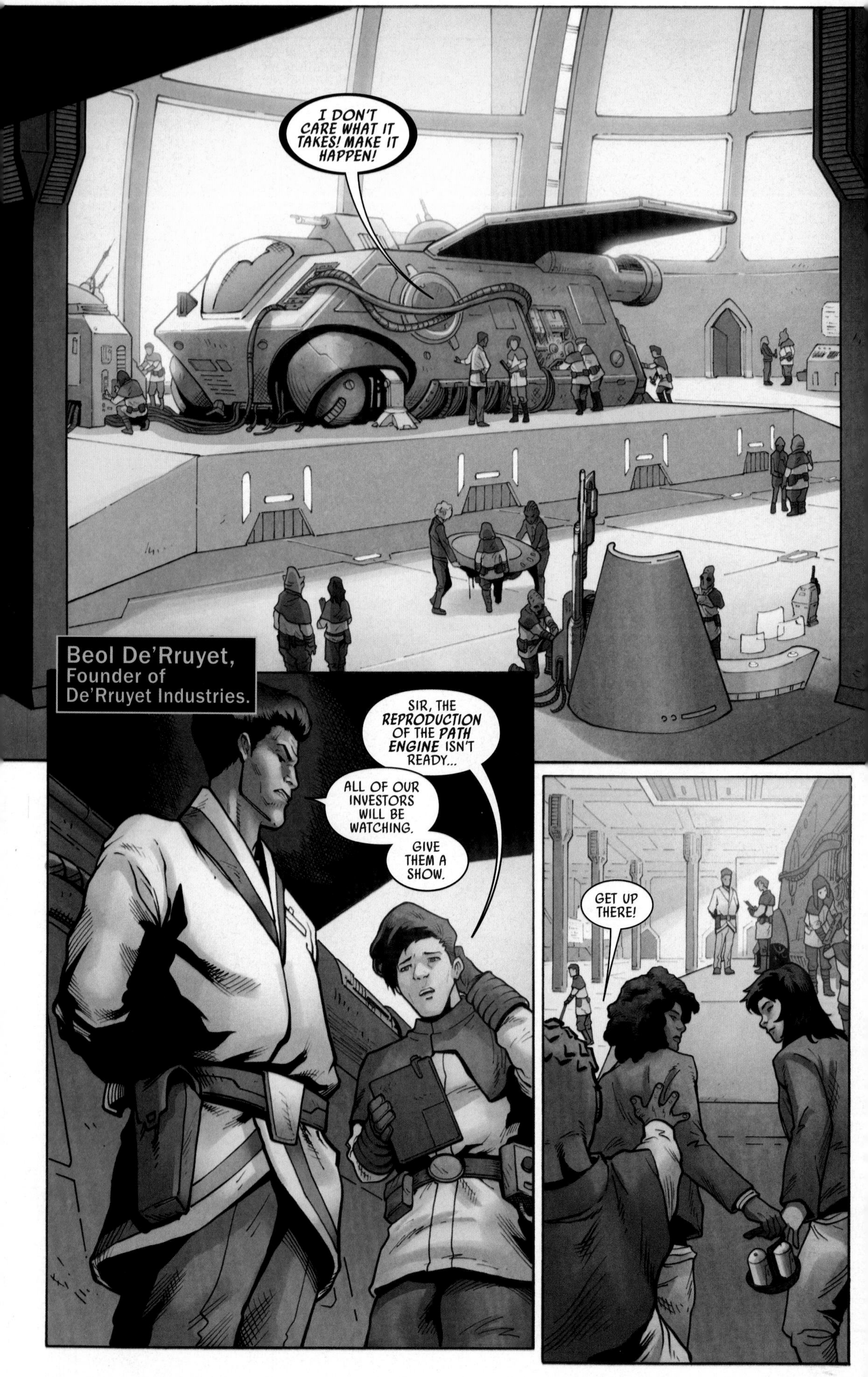
I DON'T CARE WHAT IT TAKES! MAKE IT HAPPEN!
Beol De'Rruyet, Founder of De'Rruyet Industries.
SIR, THE REPRODUCTION OF THE PATH ENGINE ISN'T READY...
ALL OF OUR INVESTORS WILL BE WATCHING.
GIVE THEM A SHOW.
GET UP THERE!

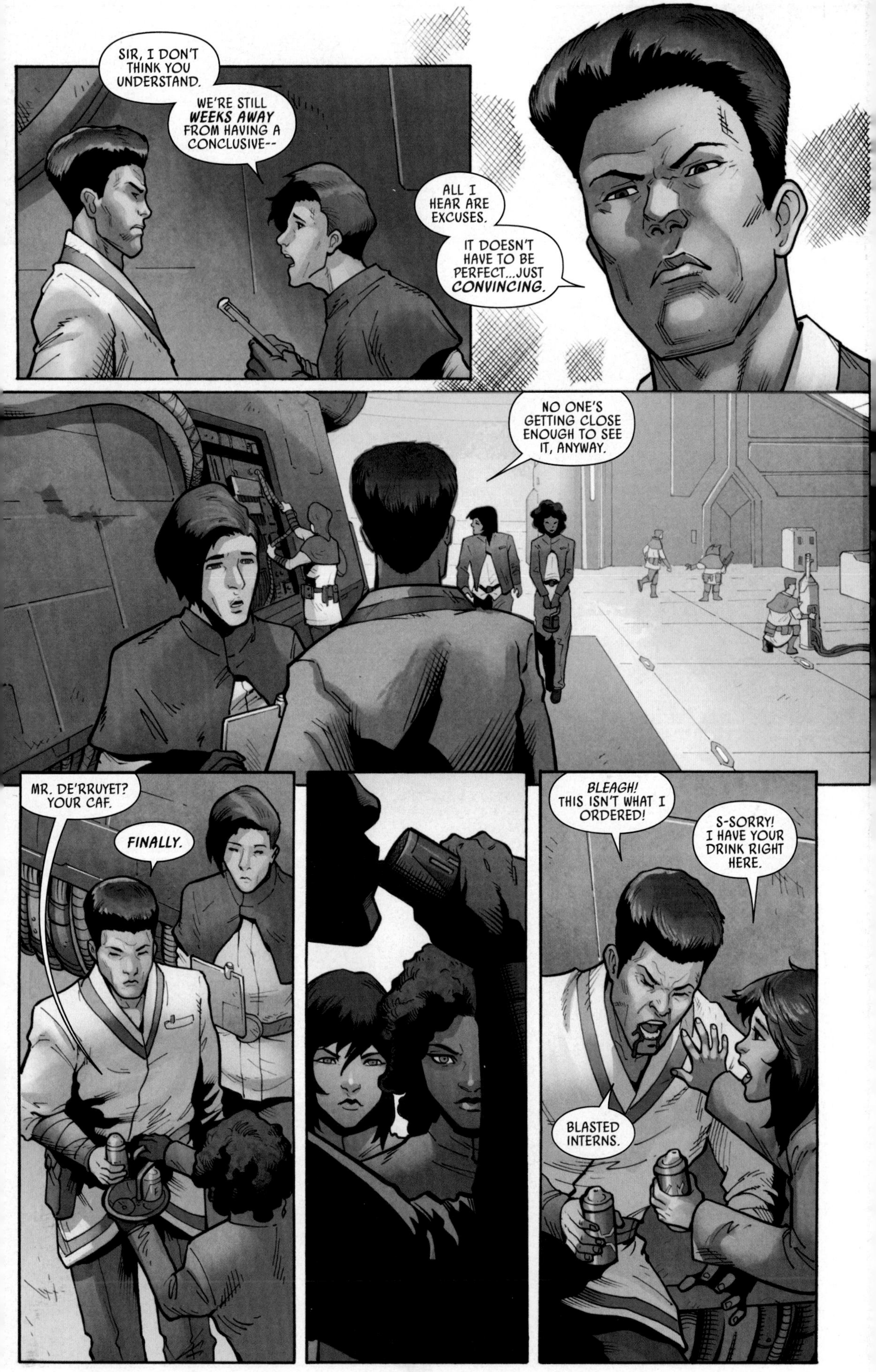
SIR, I DON'T THINK YOU UNDERSTAND.
WE'RE STILL WEEKS AWAY FROM HAVING A CONCLUSIVE--
ALL I HEAR ARE EXCUSES.
IT DOESN'T HAVE TO BE PERFECT...JUST CONVINCING.
NO ONE'S GETTING CLOSE ENOUGH TO SEE IT, ANYWAY.
MR. DE'RRUYET? YOUR CAF.
FINALLY.
BLEAGH! THIS ISN'T WHAT I ORDERED!
S-SORRY! I HAVE YOUR DRINK RIGHT HERE.
BLASTED INTERNS.

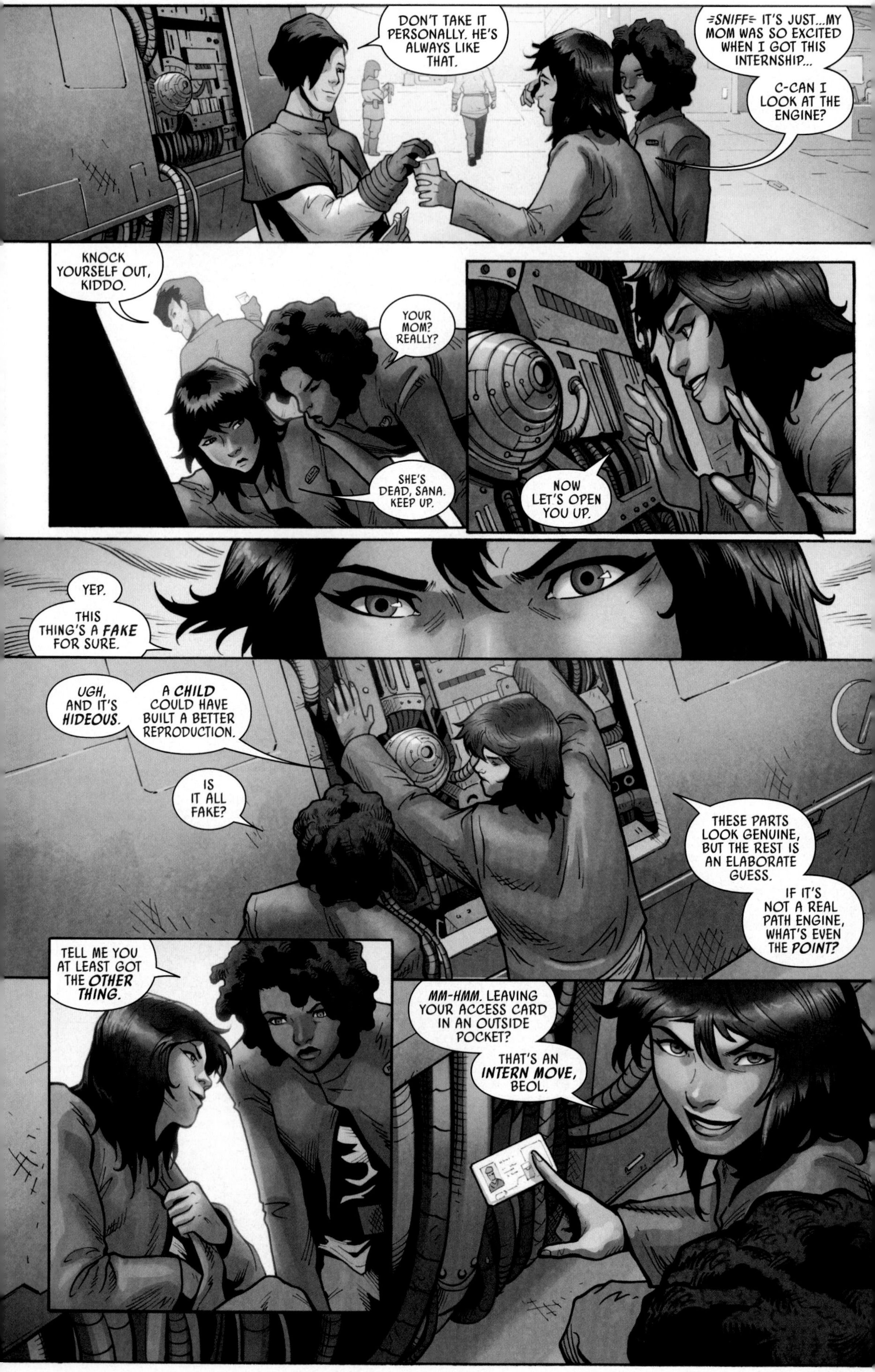
DON'T TAKE IT PERSONALLY. HE'S ALWAYS LIKE THAT.
=SNIFF= IT'S JUST...MY MOM WAS SO EXCITED WHEN I GOT THIS INTERNSHIP...
C-CAN I LOOK AT THE ENGINE?
KNOCK YOURSELF OUT, KIDDO.
YOUR MOM? REALLY?
SHE'S DEAD, SANA. KEEP UP.
NOW LET'S OPEN YOU UP.
YEP.
THIS THING'S A FAKE FOR SURE.
UGH, AND IT'S HIDEOUS.
A CHILD COULD HAVE BUILT A BETTER REPRODUCTION.
IS IT ALL FAKE?
THESE PARTS LOOK GENUINE, BUT THE REST IS AN ELABORATE GUESS.
IF IT'S NOT A REAL PATH ENGINE, WHAT'S EVEN THE POINT?
TELL ME YOU AT LEAST GOT THE OTHER THING.
MM-HMM. LEAVING YOUR ACCESS CARD IN AN OUTSIDE POCKET?
THAT'S AN INTERN MOVE, BEOL.

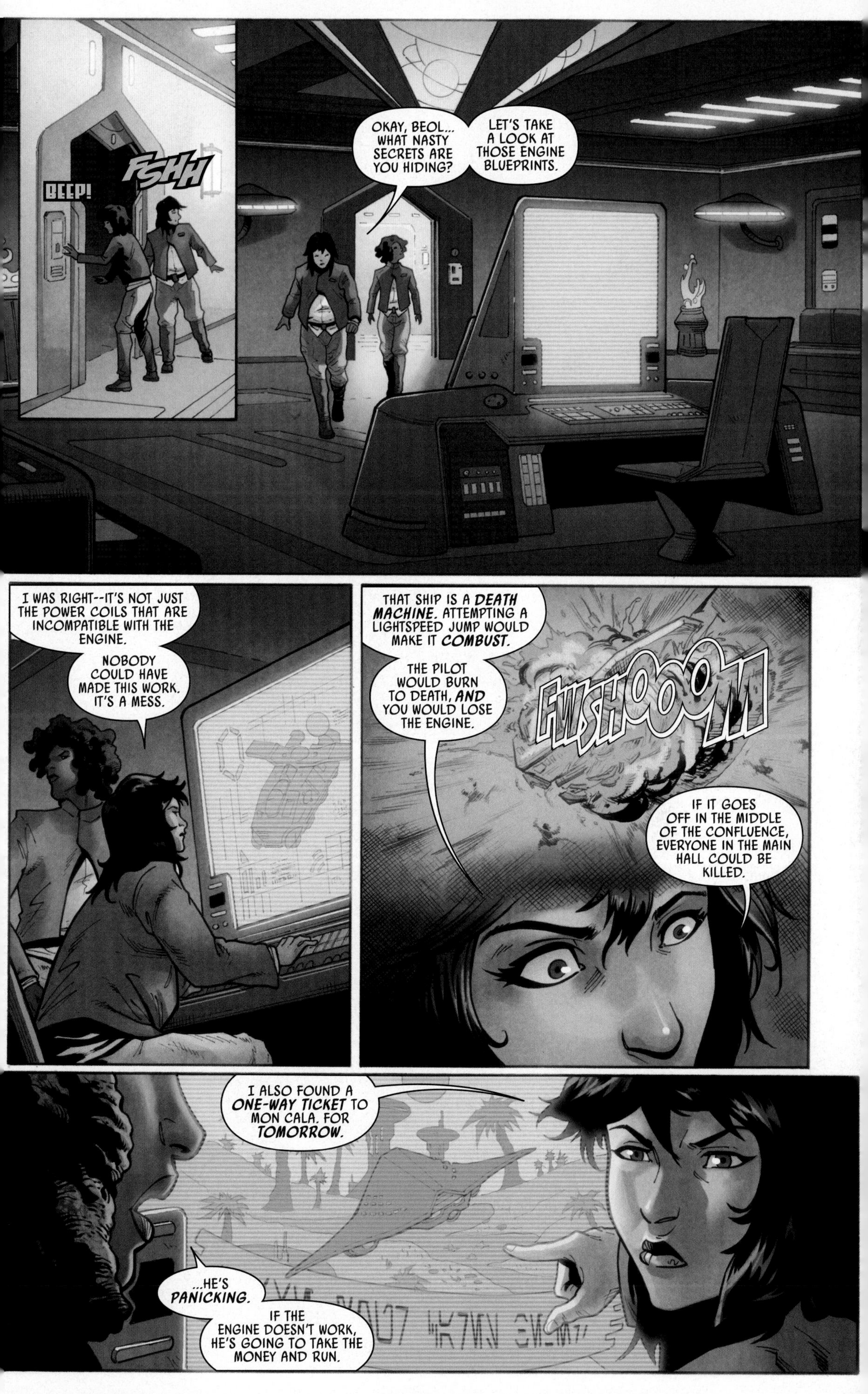
BEEP!
FSHH
OKAY, BEOL... WHAT NASTY SECRETS ARE YOU HIDING?
LET'S TAKE A LOOK AT THOSE ENGINE BLUEPRINTS.
I WAS RIGHT--IT'S NOT JUST THE POWER COILS THAT ARE INCOMPATIBLE WITH THE ENGINE.
NOBODY COULD HAVE MADE THIS WORK. IT'S A MESS.
THAT SHIP IS A DEATH MACHINE. ATTEMPTING A LIGHTSPEED JUMP WOULD MAKE IT COMBUST.
THE PILOT WOULD BURN TO DEATH, AND YOU WOULD LOSE THE ENGINE.
FWSHOOOOM
IF IT GOES OFF IN THE MIDDLE OF THE CONFLUENCE, EVERYONE IN THE MAIN HALL COULD BE KILLED.
I ALSO FOUND A ONE-WAY TICKET TO MON CALA. FOR TOMORROW.
...HE'S PANICKING.
IF THE ENGINE DOESN'T WORK, HE'S GOING TO TAKE THE MONEY AND RUN.

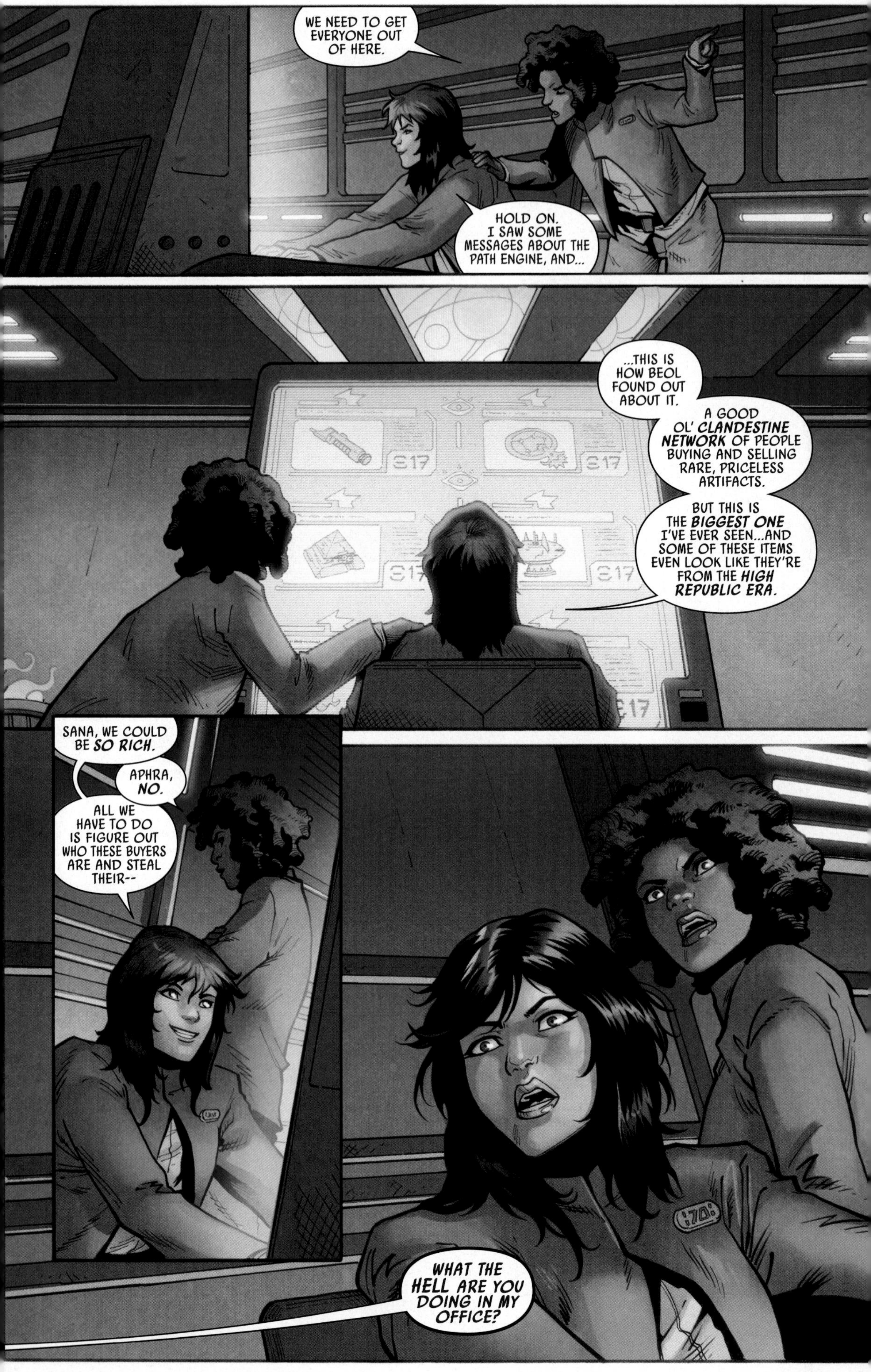
WE NEED TO GET EVERYONE OUT OF HERE.
HOLD ON. I SAW SOME MESSAGES ABOUT THE PATH ENGINE, AND...
...THIS IS HOW BEOL FOUND OUT ABOUT IT.
A GOOD OL' CLANDESTINE NETWORK OF PEOPLE BUYING AND SELLING RARE, PRICELESS ARTIFACTS.
BUT THIS IS THE BIGGEST ONE I'VE EVER SEEN...AND SOME OF THESE ITEMS EVEN LOOK LIKE THEY'RE FROM THE HIGH REPUBLIC ERA.
SANA, WE COULD BE SO RICH.
APHRA, NO.
ALL WE HAVE TO DO IS FIGURE OUT WHO THESE BUYERS ARE AND STEAL THEIR--
WHAT THE HELL ARE YOU DOING IN MY OFFICE?

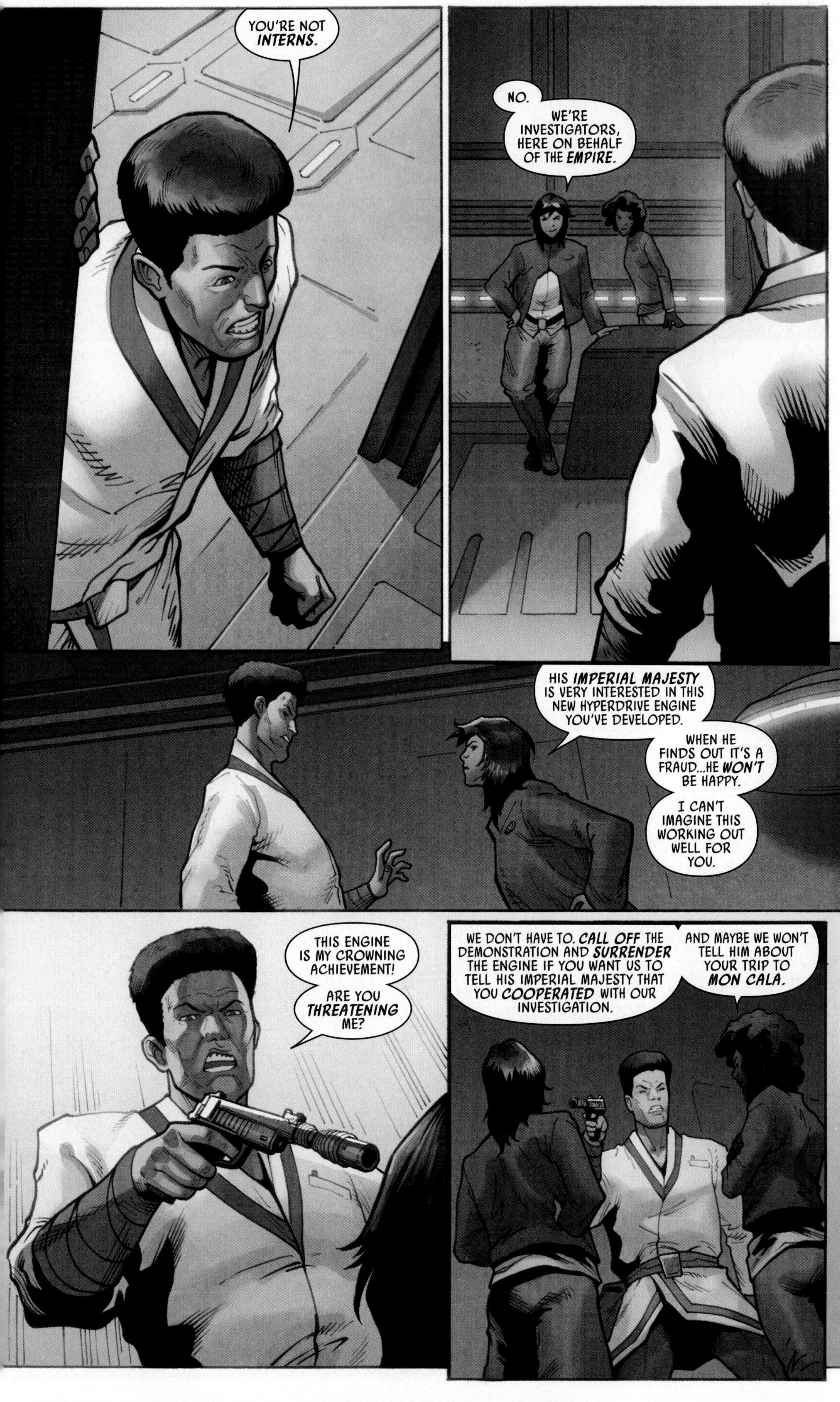
YOU'RE NOT INTERNS.
NO.
WE'RE INVESTIGATORS, HERE ON BEHALF OF THE EMPIRE.
HIS IMPERIAL MAJESTY IS VERY INTERESTED IN THIS NEW HYPERDRIVE ENGINE YOU'VE DEVELOPED.
WHEN HE FINDS OUT IT'S A FRAUD...HE WON'T BE HAPPY.
I CAN'T IMAGINE THIS WORKING OUT WELL FOR YOU.
THIS ENGINE IS MY CROWNING ACHIEVEMENT!
ARE YOU THREATENING ME?
WE DON'T HAVE TO. CALL OFF THE DEMONSTRATION AND SURRENDER THE ENGINE IF YOU WANT US TO TELL HIS IMPERIAL MAJESTY THAT YOU COOPERATED WITH OUR INVESTIGATION.
AND MAYBE WE WON'T TELL HIM ABOUT YOUR TRIP TO MON CALA.

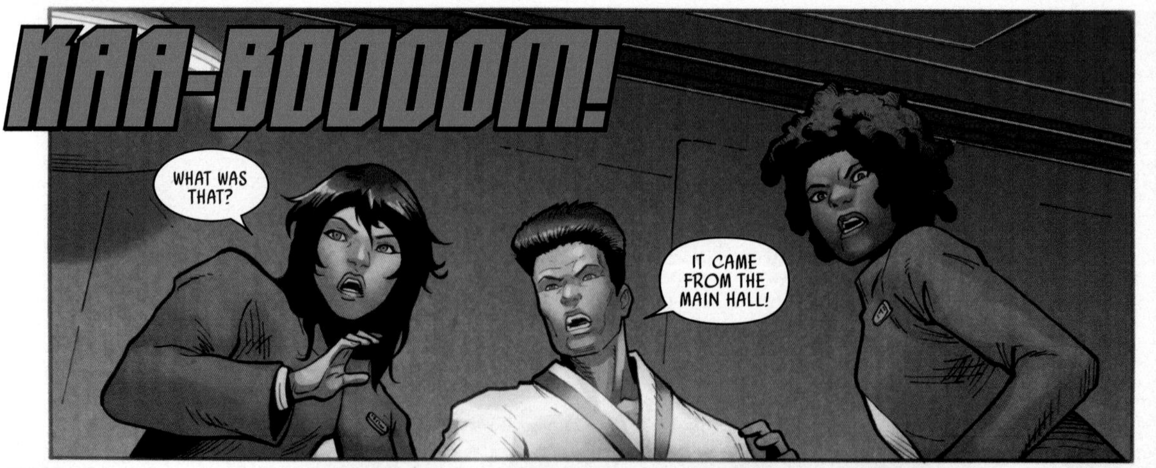
KAA-BOOOOM!
WHAT WAS THAT?
IT CAME FROM THE MAIN HALL!

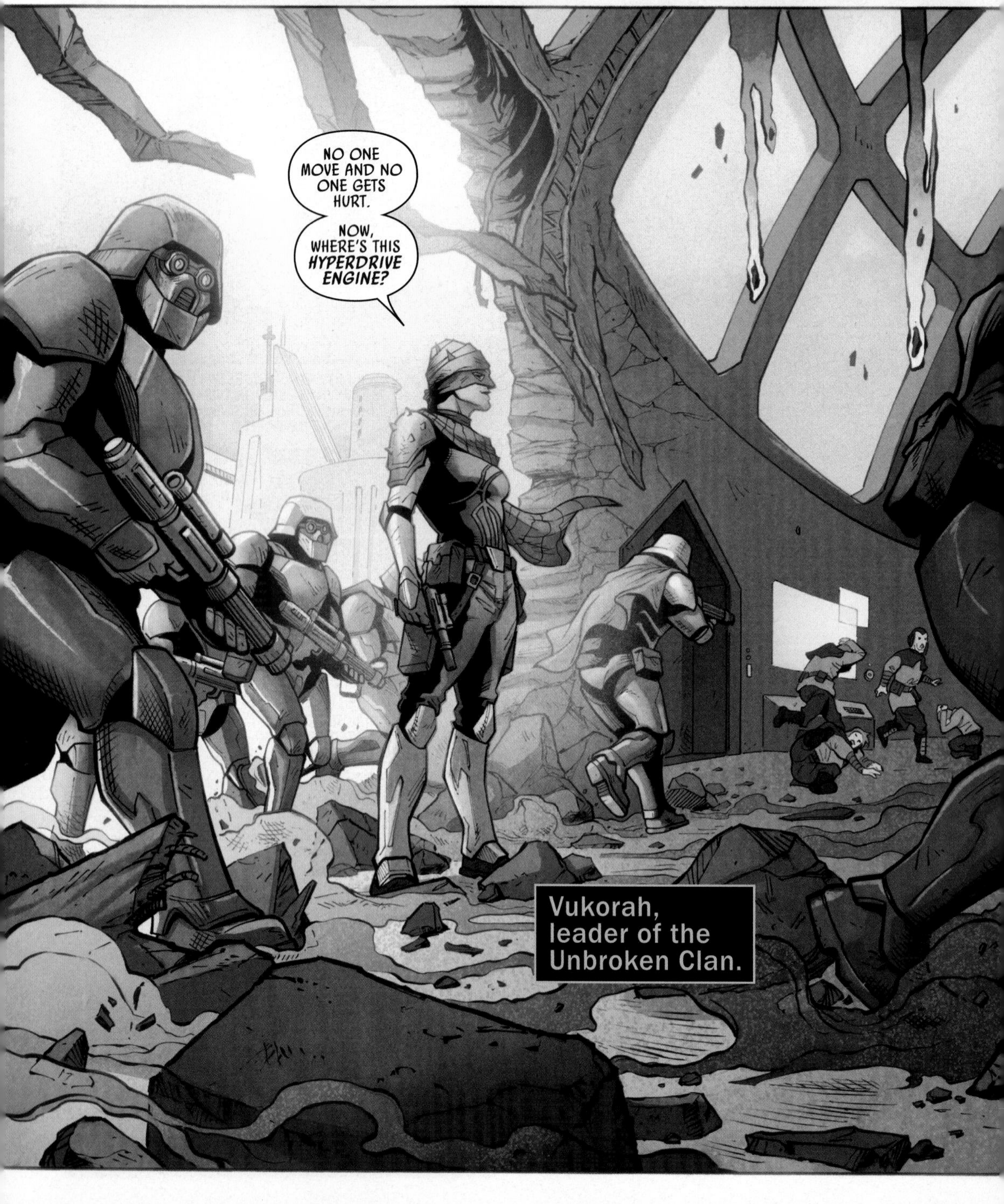
NO ONE MOVE AND NO ONE GETS HURT.
NOW, WHERE'S THIS *HYPERDRIVE ENGINE?*
Vukorah, leader of the Unbroken Clan.

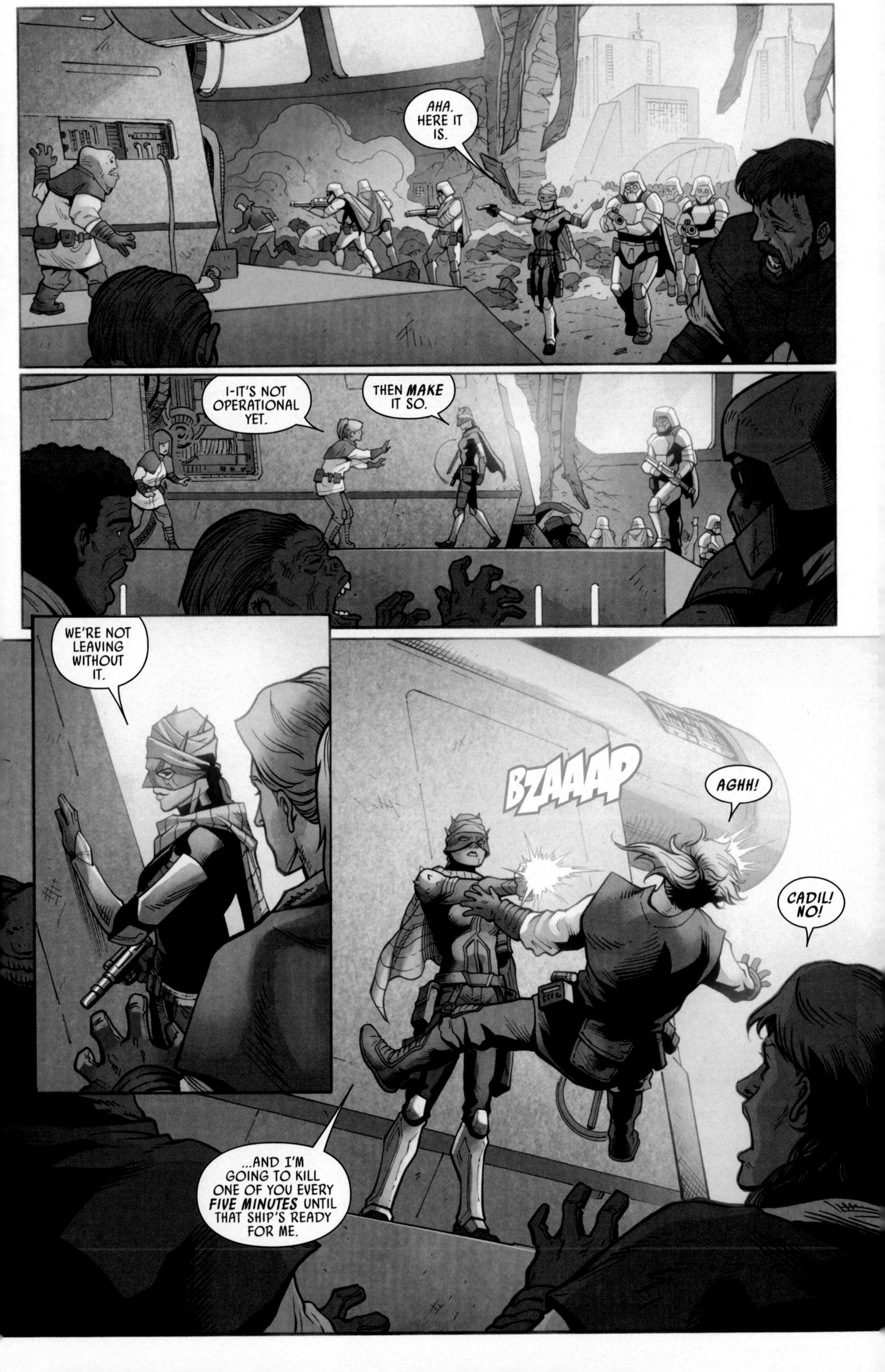
AHA. HERE IT IS.
I-IT'S NOT OPERATIONAL YET.
THEN MAKE IT SO.
WE'RE NOT LEAVING WITHOUT IT.
BZAAAP
AGHH!
CADIL! NO!
...AND I'M GOING TO KILL ONE OF YOU EVERY FIVE MINUTES UNTIL THAT SHIP'S READY FOR ME.

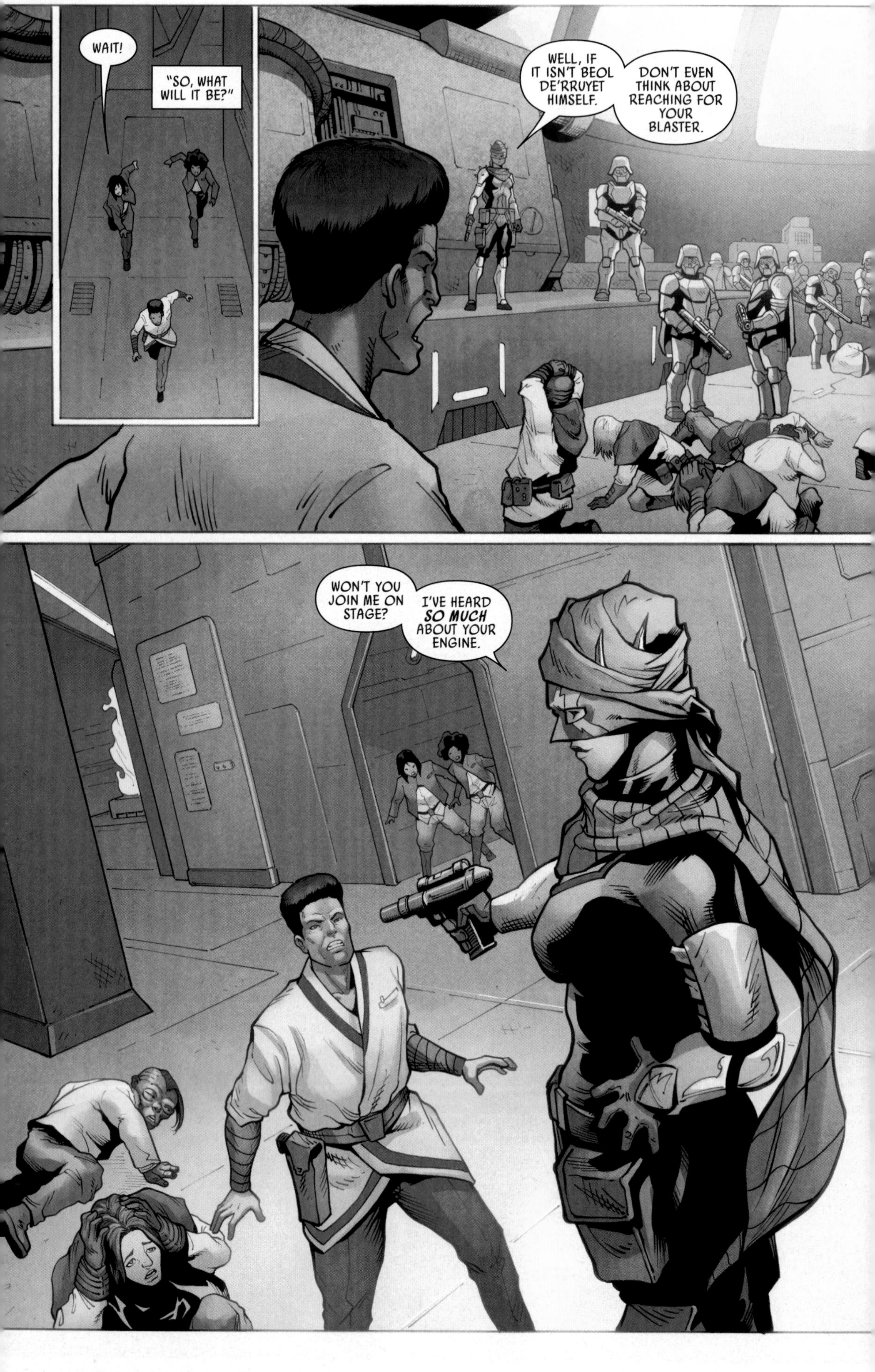
WAIT!
"SO, WHAT WILL IT BE?"
WELL, IF IT ISN'T BEOL DE'RRUYET HIMSELF.
DON'T EVEN THINK ABOUT REACHING FOR YOUR BLASTER.
WON'T YOU JOIN ME ON STAGE?
I'VE HEARD **SO MUCH** ABOUT YOUR ENGINE.

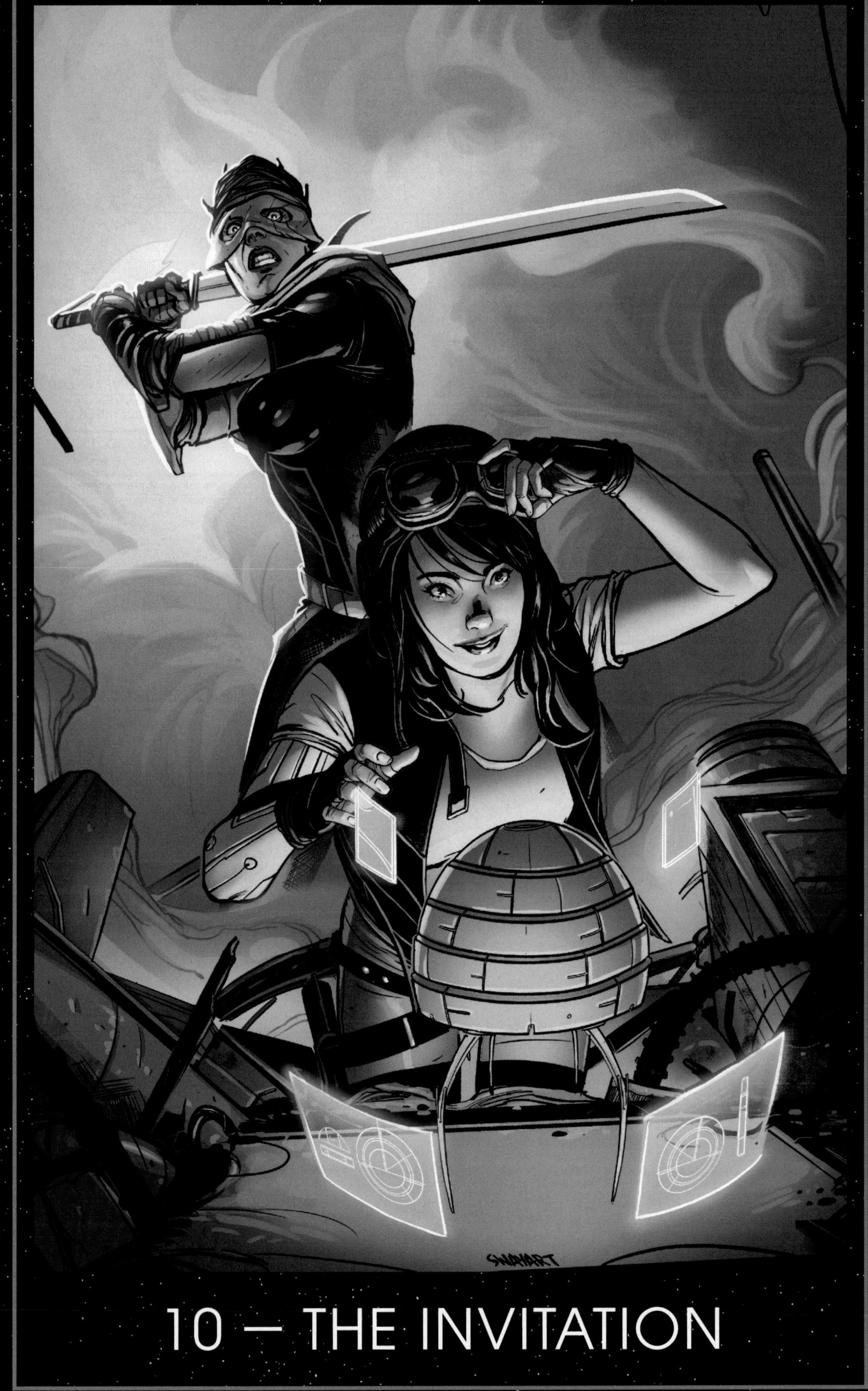

10 — THE INVITATION

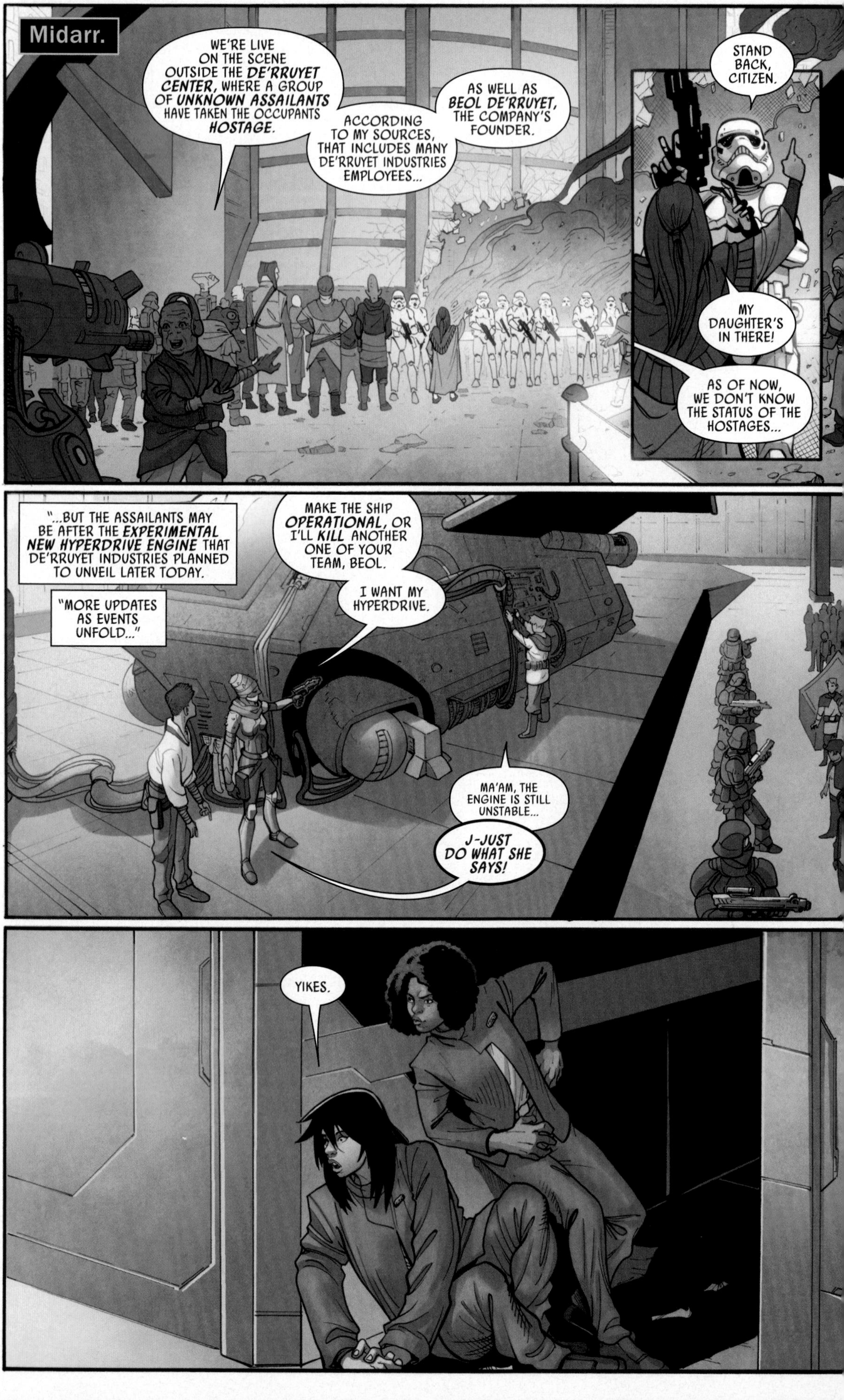
Midarr.
WE'RE LIVE ON THE SCENE OUTSIDE THE DE'RRUYET CENTER, WHERE A GROUP OF UNKNOWN ASSAILANTS HAVE TAKEN THE OCCUPANTS HOSTAGE.
ACCORDING TO MY SOURCES, THAT INCLUDES MANY DE'RRUYET INDUSTRIES EMPLOYEES...
AS WELL AS BEOL DE'RRUYET, THE COMPANY'S FOUNDER.
STAND BACK, CITIZEN.
MY DAUGHTER'S IN THERE!
AS OF NOW, WE DON'T KNOW THE STATUS OF THE HOSTAGES...
"...BUT THE ASSAILANTS MAY BE AFTER THE EXPERIMENTAL NEW HYPERDRIVE ENGINE THAT DE'RRUYET INDUSTRIES PLANNED TO UNVEIL LATER TODAY.
"MORE UPDATES AS EVENTS UNFOLD..."
MAKE THE SHIP OPERATIONAL, OR I'LL KILL ANOTHER ONE OF YOUR TEAM, BEOL.
I WANT MY HYPERDRIVE.
MA'AM, THE ENGINE IS STILL UNSTABLE...
J-JUST DO WHAT SHE SAYS!
YIKES.

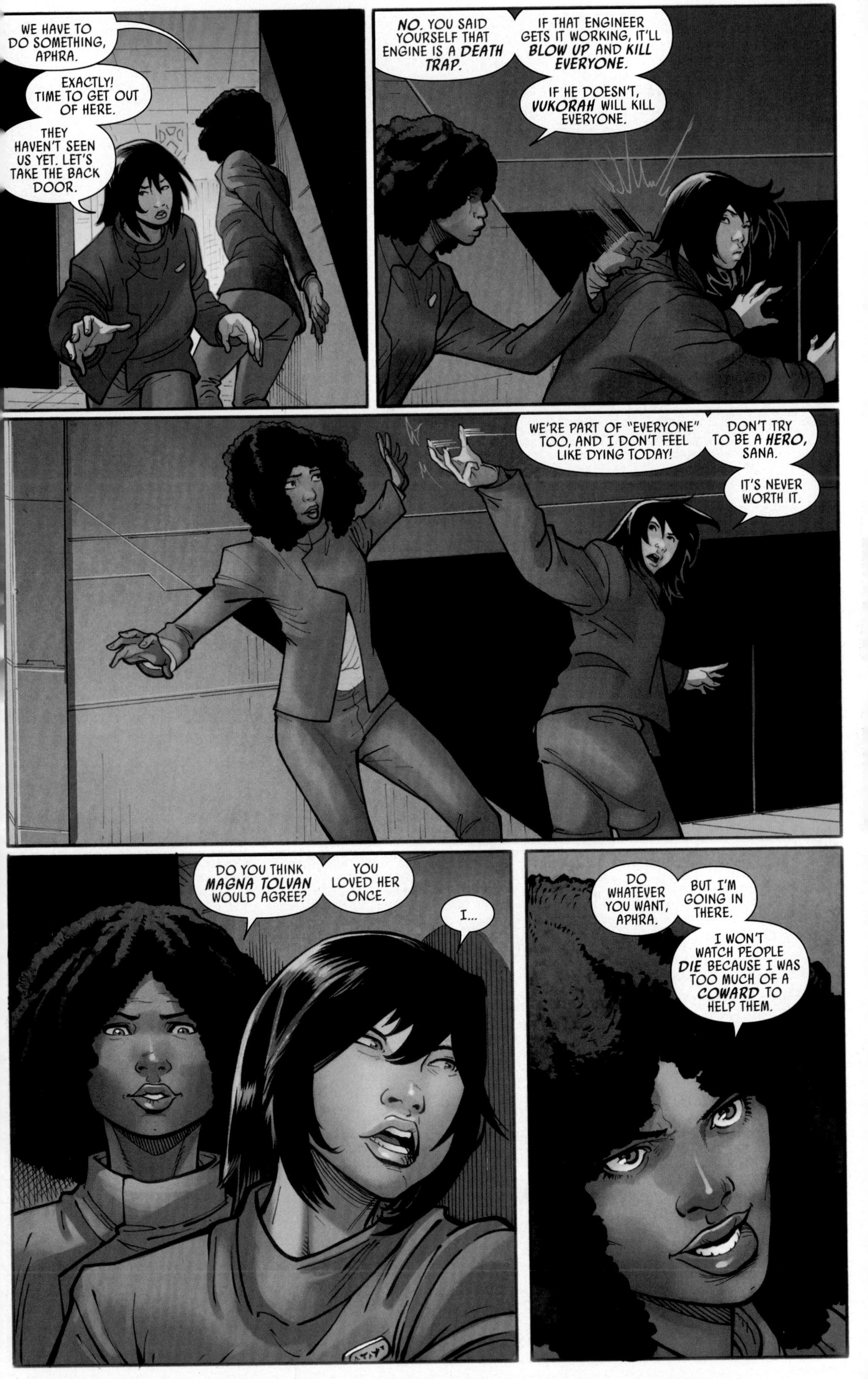
WE HAVE TO DO SOMETHING, APHRA.
EXACTLY! TIME TO GET OUT OF HERE.
THEY HAVEN'T SEEN US YET. LET'S TAKE THE BACK DOOR.
NO. YOU SAID YOURSELF THAT ENGINE IS A DEATH TRAP.
IF THAT ENGINEER GETS IT WORKING, IT'LL BLOW UP AND KILL EVERYONE.
IF HE DOESN'T, VUKORAH WILL KILL EVERYONE.
WE'RE PART OF "EVERYONE" TOO, AND I DON'T FEEL LIKE DYING TODAY!
DON'T TRY TO BE A HERO, SANA.
IT'S NEVER WORTH IT.
DO YOU THINK MAGNA TOLVAN WOULD AGREE?
YOU LOVED HER ONCE.
I...
DO WHATEVER YOU WANT, APHRA.
BUT I'M GOING IN THERE.
I WON'T WATCH PEOPLE DIE BECAUSE I WAS TOO MUCH OF A COWARD TO HELP THEM.

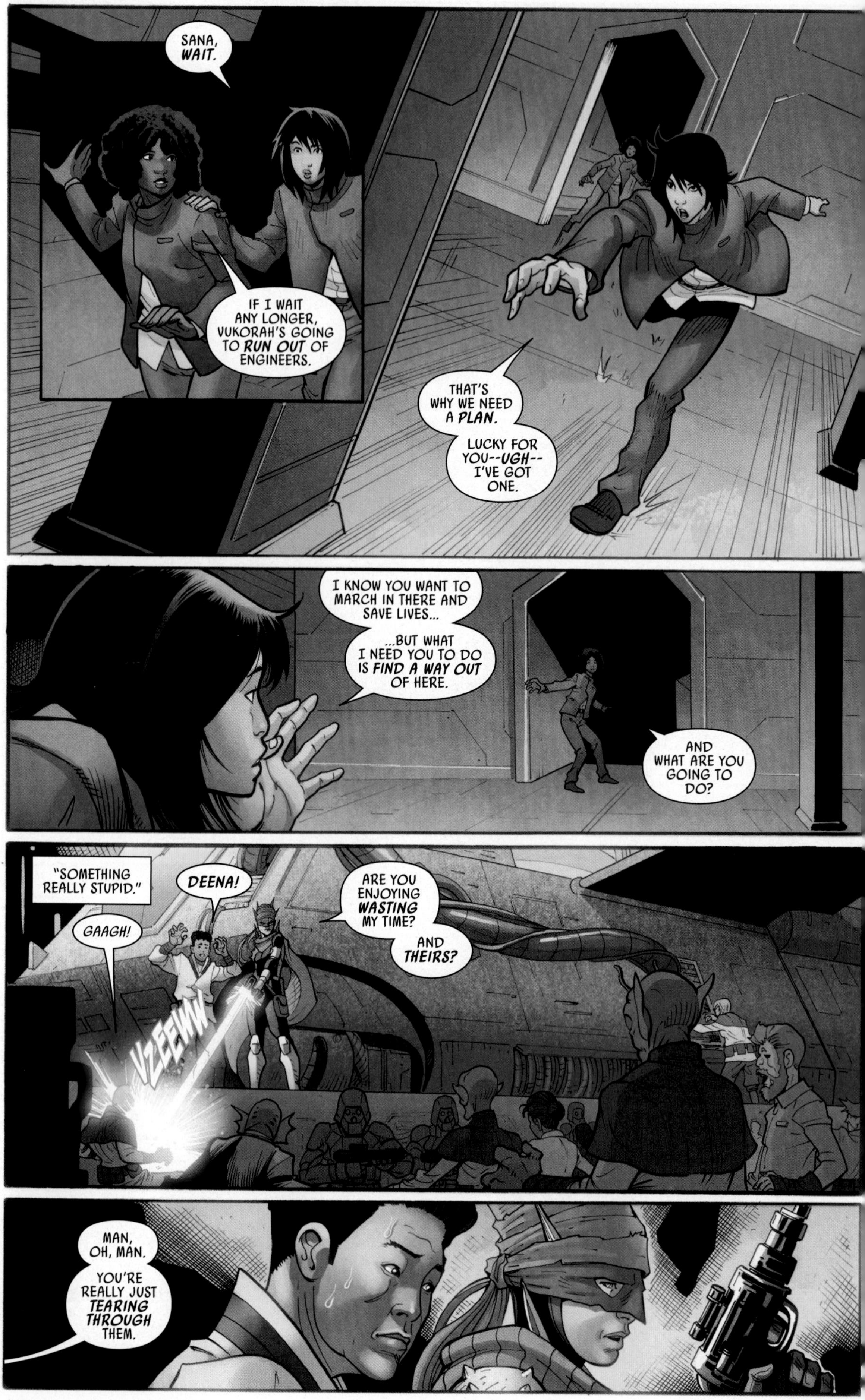
SANA, WAIT.
IF I WAIT ANY LONGER, VUKORAH'S GOING TO RUN OUT OF ENGINEERS.
THAT'S WHY WE NEED A PLAN.
LUCKY FOR YOU--UGH--I'VE GOT ONE.
I KNOW YOU WANT TO MARCH IN THERE AND SAVE LIVES...
...BUT WHAT I NEED YOU TO DO IS FIND A WAY OUT OF HERE.
AND WHAT ARE YOU GOING TO DO?
"SOMETHING REALLY STUPID."
DEENA!
GAAGH!
ARE YOU ENJOYING WASTING MY TIME?
AND THEIRS?
VZEEWW
MAN, OH, MAN.
YOU'RE REALLY JUST TEARING THROUGH THEM.

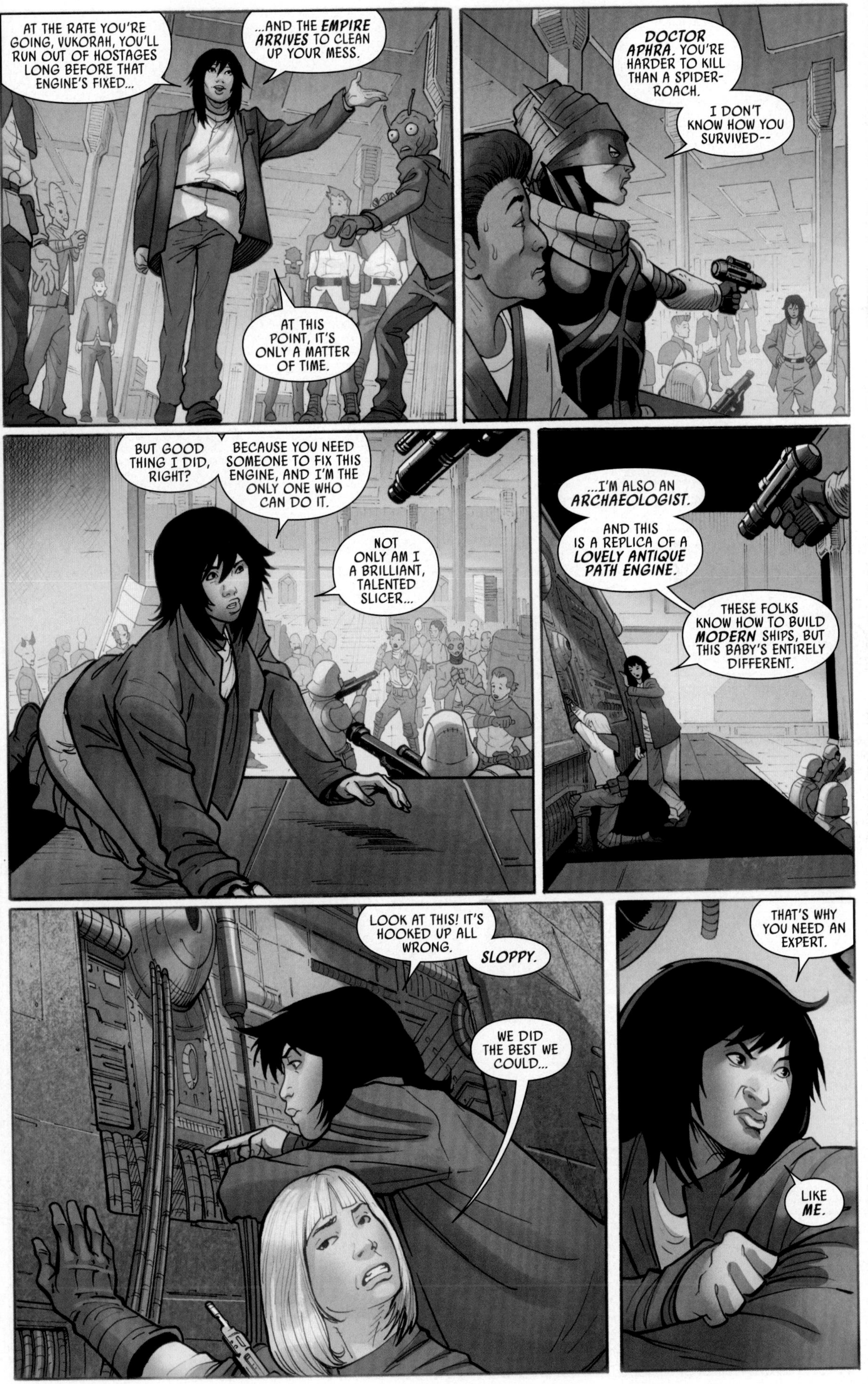
AT THE RATE YOU'RE GOING, VUKORAH, YOU'LL RUN OUT OF HOSTAGES LONG BEFORE THAT ENGINE'S FIXED...
...AND THE EMPIRE ARRIVES TO CLEAN UP YOUR MESS.
AT THIS POINT, IT'S ONLY A MATTER OF TIME.
DOCTOR APHRA. YOU'RE HARDER TO KILL THAN A SPIDER-ROACH.
I DON'T KNOW HOW YOU SURVIVED--
BUT GOOD THING I DID, RIGHT?
BECAUSE YOU NEED SOMEONE TO FIX THIS ENGINE, AND I'M THE ONLY ONE WHO CAN DO IT.
NOT ONLY AM I A BRILLIANT, TALENTED SLICER...
...I'M ALSO AN ARCHAEOLOGIST.
AND THIS IS A REPLICA OF A LOVELY ANTIQUE PATH ENGINE.
THESE FOLKS KNOW HOW TO BUILD MODERN SHIPS, BUT THIS BABY'S ENTIRELY DIFFERENT.
LOOK AT THIS! IT'S HOOKED UP ALL WRONG.
SLOPPY.
WE DID THE BEST WE COULD...
THAT'S WHY YOU NEED AN EXPERT.
LIKE ME.

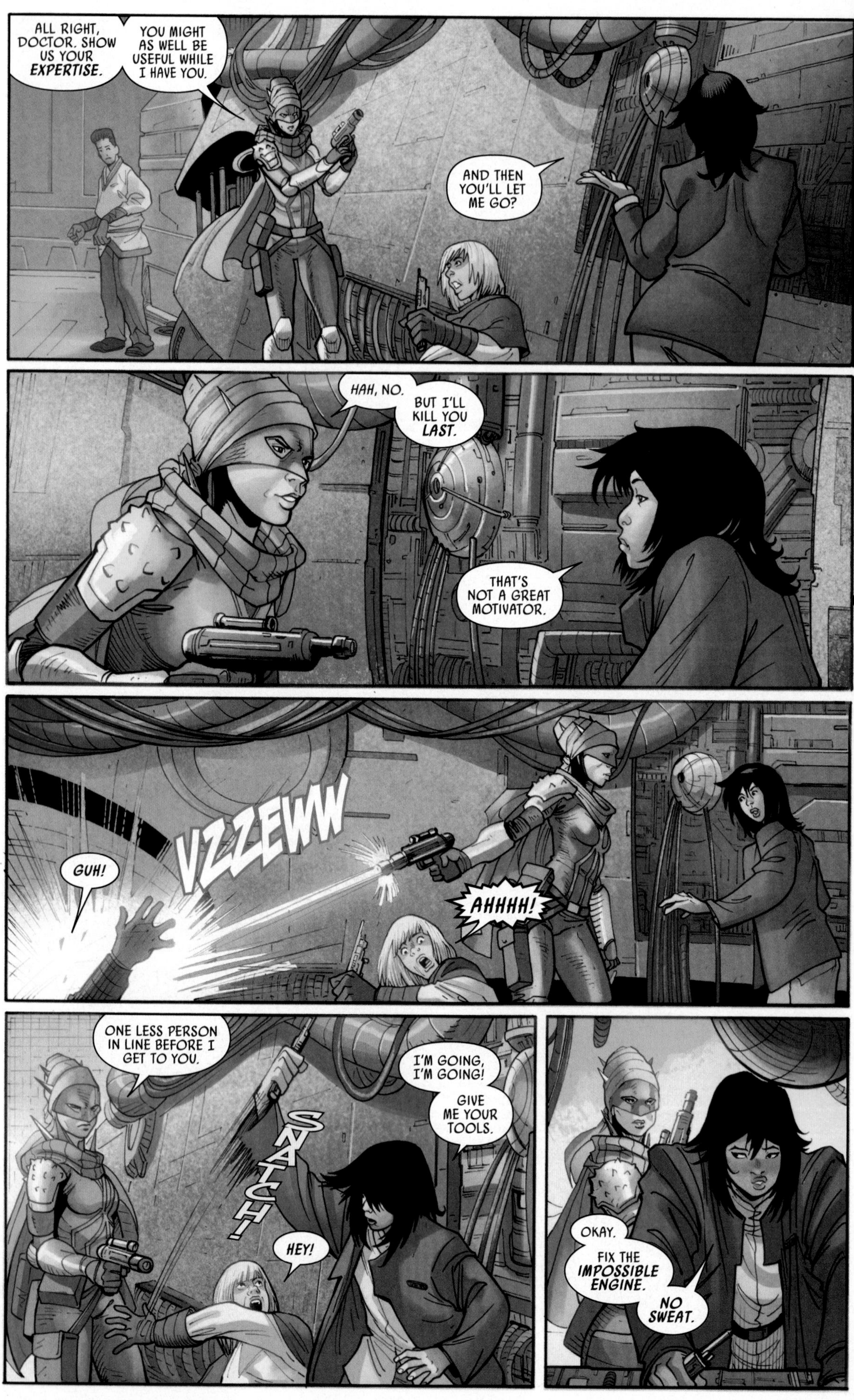
ALL RIGHT, DOCTOR. SHOW US YOUR EXPERTISE.
YOU MIGHT AS WELL BE USEFUL WHILE I HAVE YOU.
AND THEN YOU'LL LET ME GO?
HAH, NO.
BUT I'LL KILL YOU LAST.
THAT'S NOT A GREAT MOTIVATOR.
VZZEWW
GUH!
AHHHH!
ONE LESS PERSON IN LINE BEFORE I GET TO YOU.
I'M GOING, I'M GOING!
GIVE ME YOUR TOOLS.
SNATCH!
HEY!
OKAY.
FIX THE IMPOSSIBLE ENGINE.
NO SWEAT.

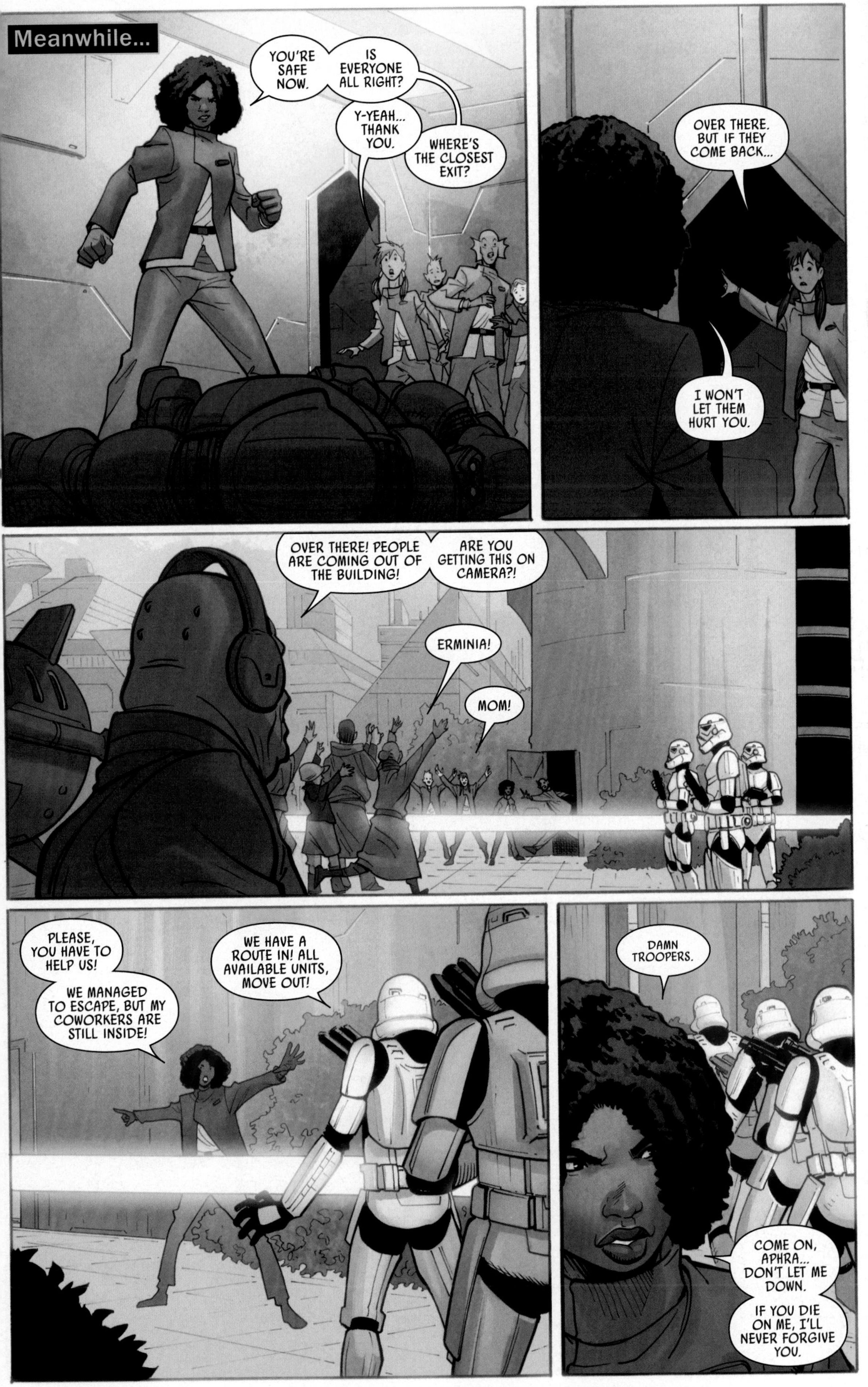
Meanwhile...
YOU'RE SAFE NOW.
IS EVERYONE ALL RIGHT?
Y-YEAH... THANK YOU.
WHERE'S THE CLOSEST EXIT?
OVER THERE. BUT IF THEY COME BACK...
I WON'T LET THEM HURT YOU.
OVER THERE! PEOPLE ARE COMING OUT OF THE BUILDING!
ARE YOU GETTING THIS ON CAMERA?!
ERMINIA!
MOM!
PLEASE, YOU HAVE TO HELP US!
WE MANAGED TO ESCAPE, BUT MY COWORKERS ARE STILL INSIDE!
WE HAVE A ROUTE IN! ALL AVAILABLE UNITS, MOVE OUT!
DAMN TROOPERS.
COME ON, APHRA... DON'T LET ME DOWN.
IF YOU DIE ON ME, I'LL NEVER FORGIVE YOU.

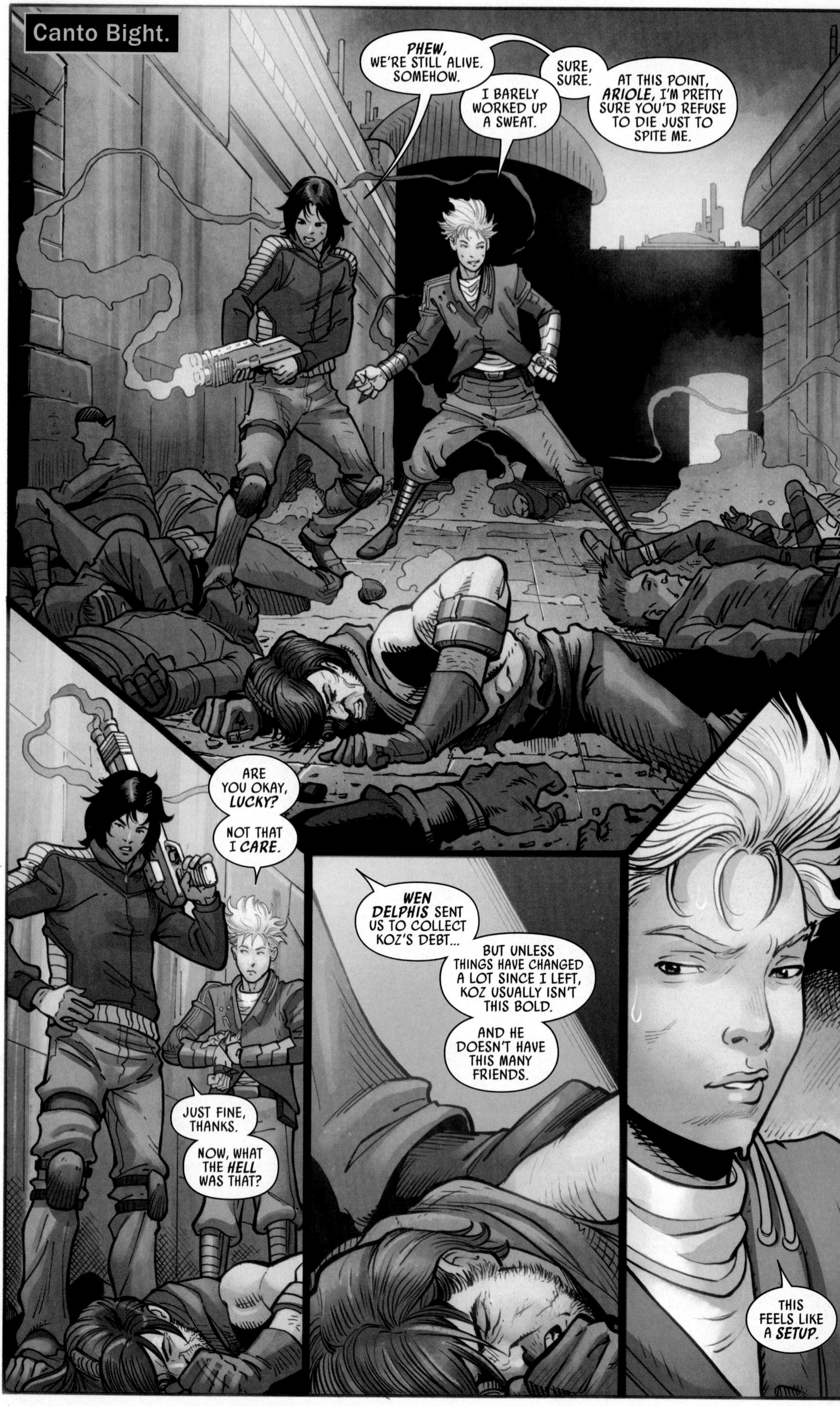
Canto Bight.
PHEW, WE'RE STILL ALIVE. SOMEHOW.
I BARELY WORKED UP A SWEAT.
SURE, SURE.
AT THIS POINT, ARIOLE, I'M PRETTY SURE YOU'D REFUSE TO DIE JUST TO SPITE ME.
ARE YOU OKAY, LUCKY?
NOT THAT I CARE.
JUST FINE, THANKS.
NOW, WHAT THE HELL WAS THAT?
WEN DELPHIS SENT US TO COLLECT KOZ'S DEBT...
BUT UNLESS THINGS HAVE CHANGED A LOT SINCE I LEFT, KOZ USUALLY ISN'T THIS BOLD.
AND HE DOESN'T HAVE THIS MANY FRIENDS.
THIS FEELS LIKE A SETUP.

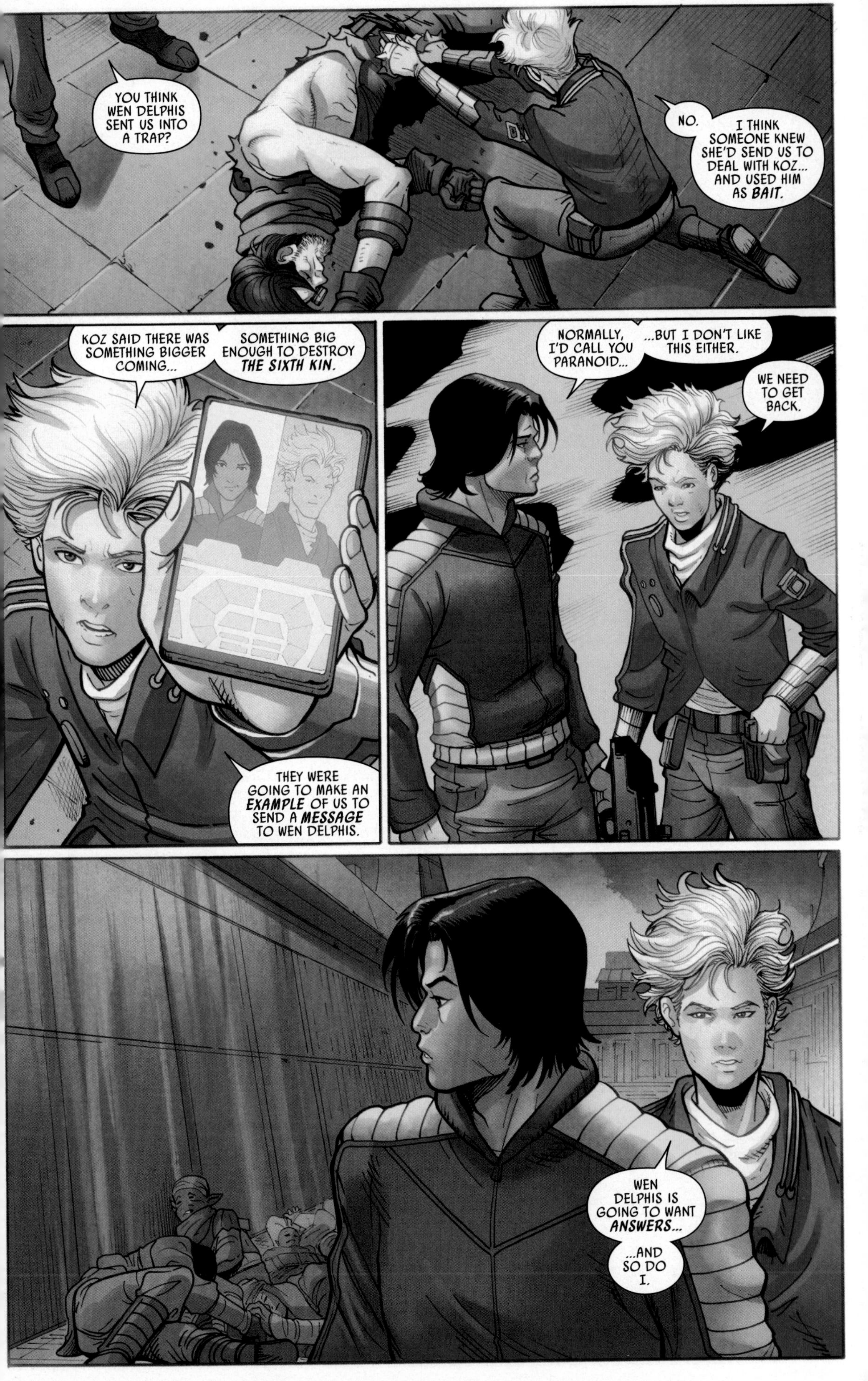
YOU THINK WEN DELPHIS SENT US INTO A TRAP?
NO.
I THINK SOMEONE KNEW SHE'D SEND US TO DEAL WITH KOZ... AND USED HIM AS BAIT.
KOZ SAID THERE WAS SOMETHING BIGGER COMING...
SOMETHING BIG ENOUGH TO DESTROY THE SIXTH KIN.
THEY WERE GOING TO MAKE AN EXAMPLE OF US TO SEND A MESSAGE TO WEN DELPHIS.
NORMALLY, I'D CALL YOU PARANOID...
...BUT I DON'T LIKE THIS EITHER.
WE NEED TO GET BACK.
WEN DELPHIS IS GOING TO WANT ANSWERS...
...AND SO DO I.

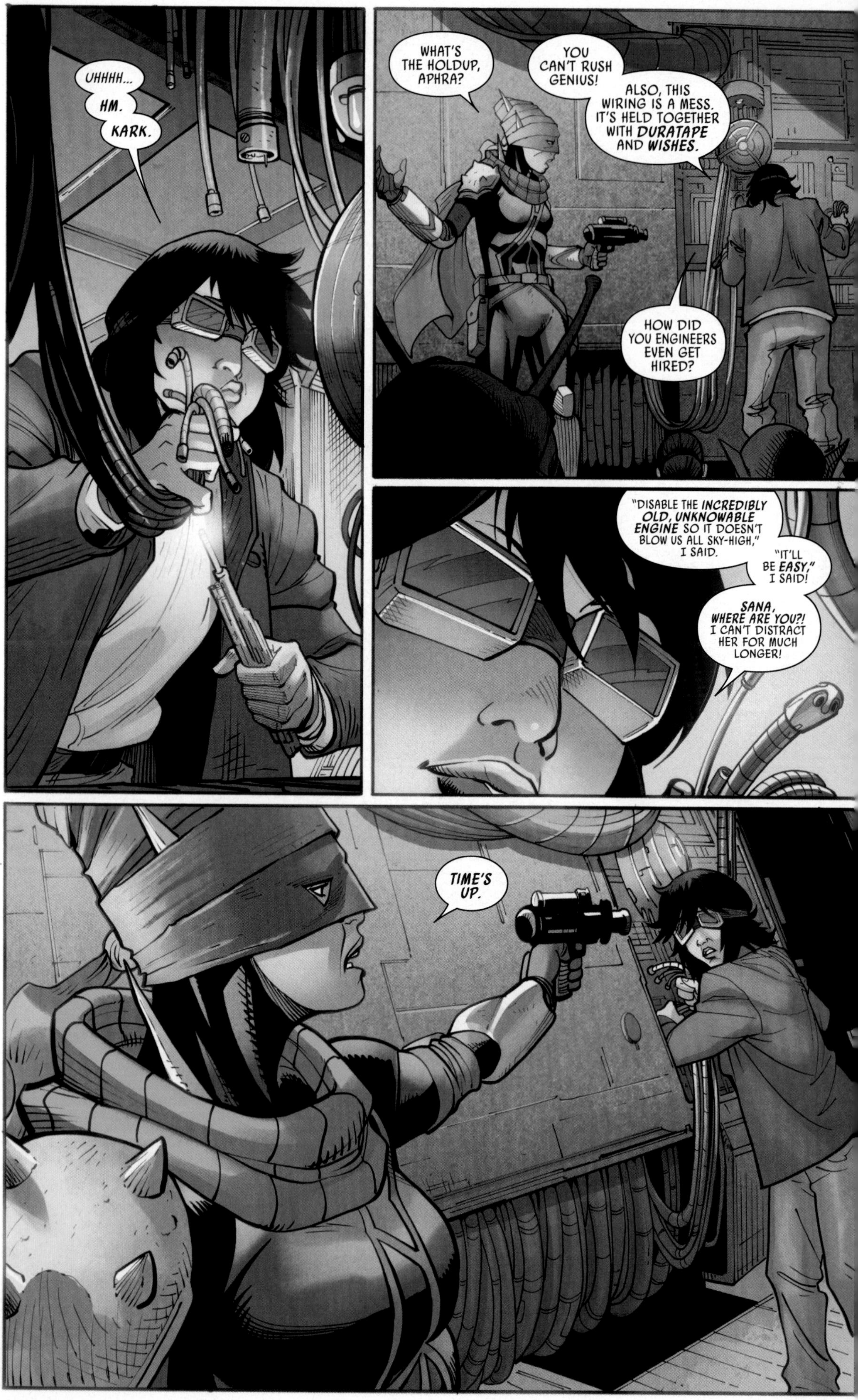
UHHHH...
HM.
KARK.
WHAT'S THE HOLDUP, APHRA?
YOU CAN'T RUSH GENIUS!
ALSO, THIS WIRING IS A MESS. IT'S HELD TOGETHER WITH DURATAPE AND WISHES.
HOW DID YOU ENGINEERS EVEN GET HIRED?
"DISABLE THE INCREDIBLY OLD, UNKNOWABLE ENGINE SO IT DOESN'T BLOW US ALL SKY-HIGH," I SAID.
"IT'LL BE EASY," I SAID!
SANA, WHERE ARE YOU?! I CAN'T DISTRACT HER FOR MUCH LONGER!
TIME'S UP.

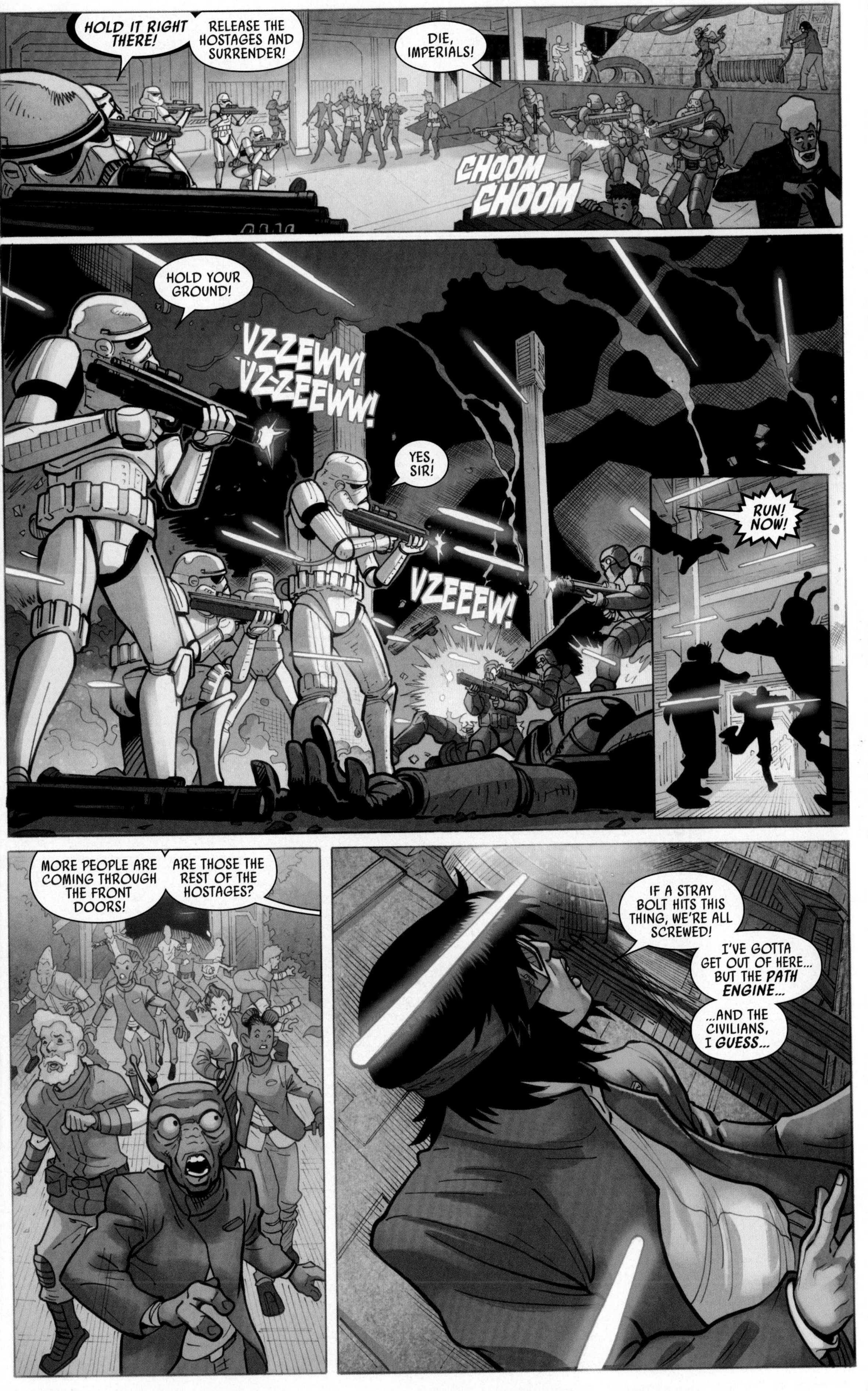
HOLD IT RIGHT THERE!
RELEASE THE HOSTAGES AND SURRENDER!
DIE, IMPERIALS!
CHOOM CHOOM
HOLD YOUR GROUND!
VZZEWW! VZ-ZEEWW!
YES, SIR!
VZEEEW!
RUN! NOW!
MORE PEOPLE ARE COMING THROUGH THE FRONT DOORS!
ARE THOSE THE REST OF THE HOSTAGES?
IF A STRAY BOLT HITS THIS THING, WE'RE ALL SCREWED!
I'VE GOTTA GET OUT OF HERE... BUT THE PATH ENGINE...
...AND THE CIVILIANS, I GUESS...

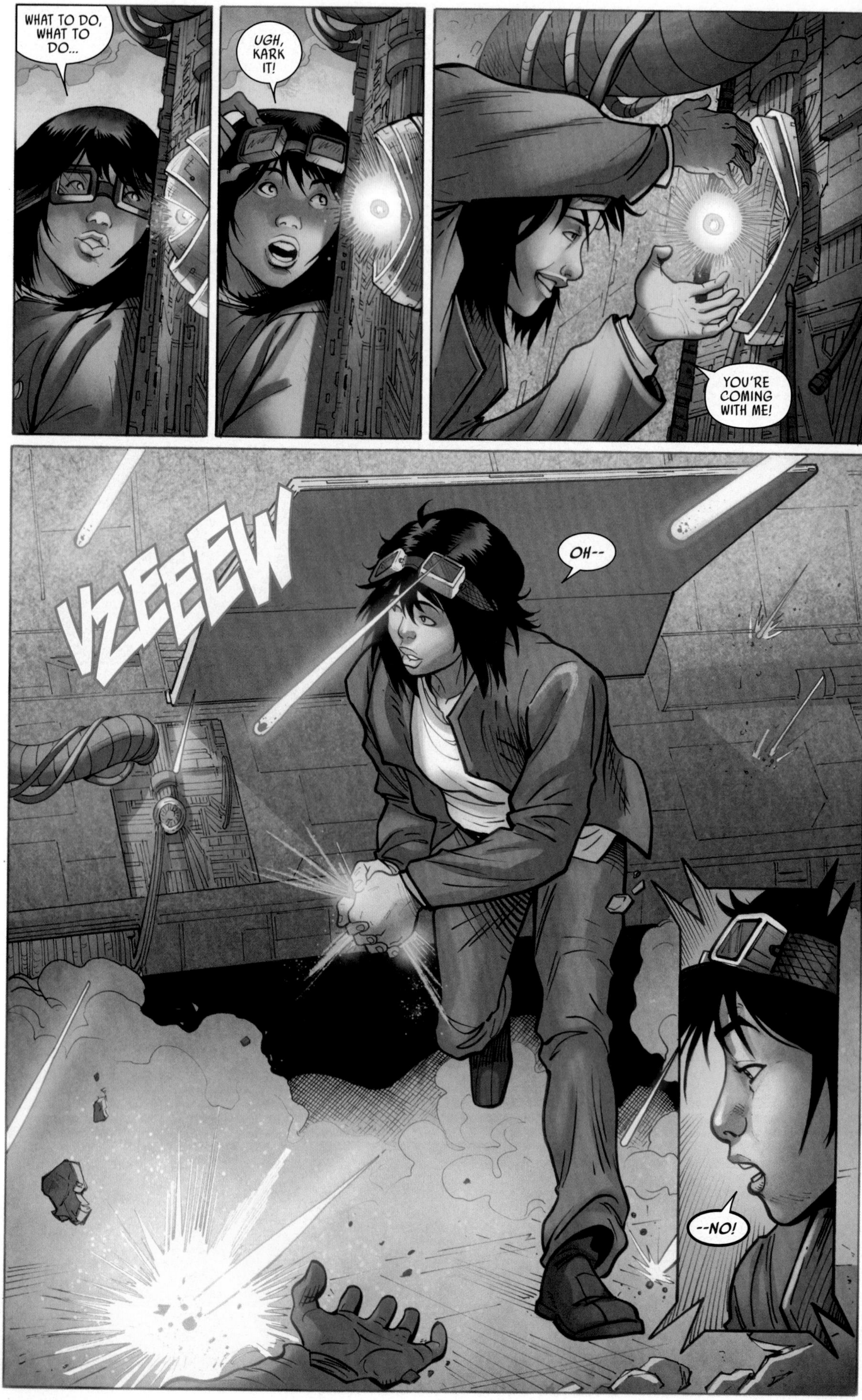
WHAT TO DO, WHAT TO DO...
UGH, KARK IT!
YOU'RE COMING WITH ME!
VZEEEW
OH--
--NO!

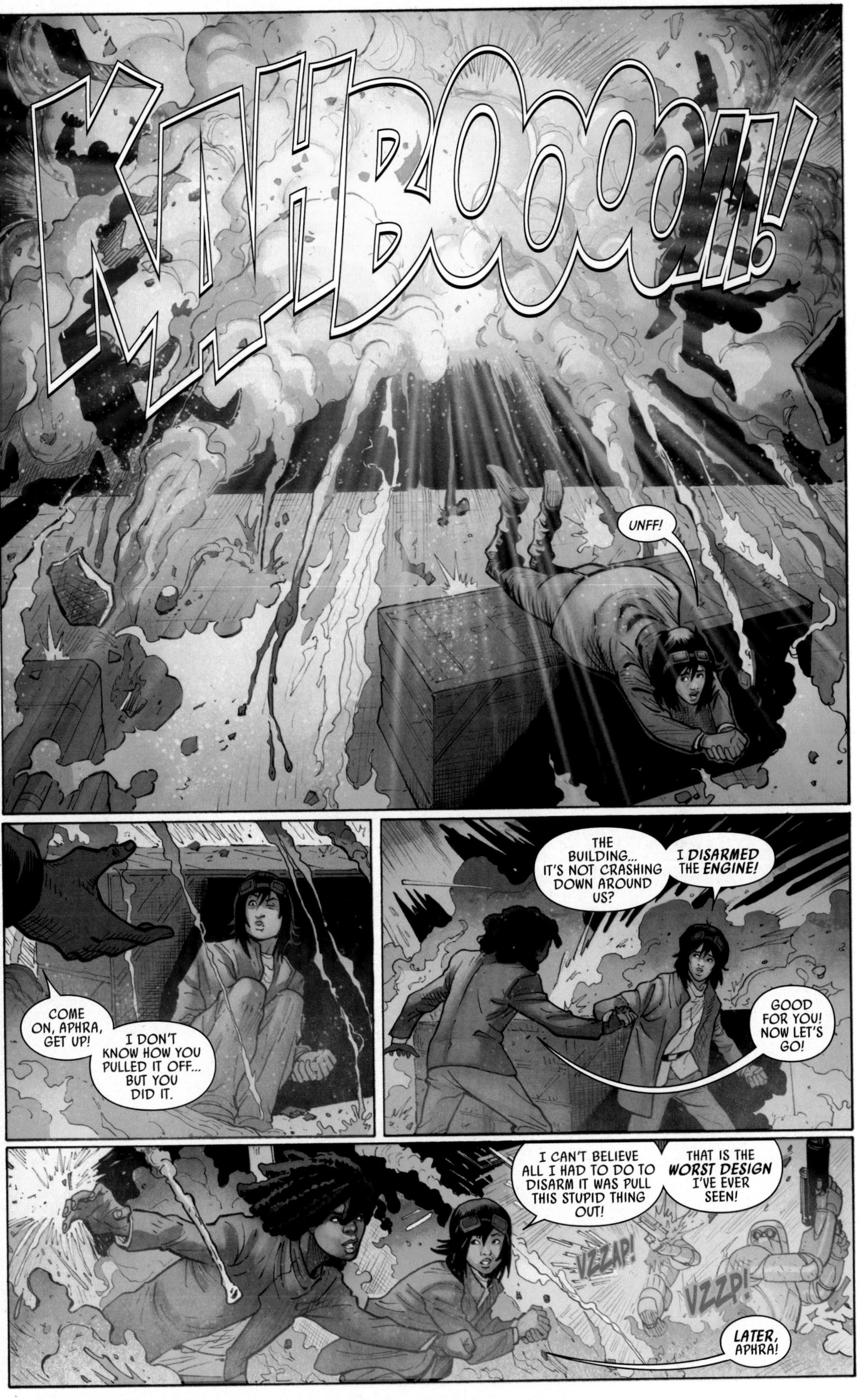
KATHBOOOOM!!
UNFF!
COME ON, APHRA, GET UP!
I DON'T KNOW HOW YOU PULLED IT OFF... BUT YOU DID IT.
THE BUILDING... IT'S NOT CRASHING DOWN AROUND US?
I DISARMED THE ENGINE!
GOOD FOR YOU! NOW LET'S GO!
I CAN'T BELIEVE ALL I HAD TO DO TO DISARM IT WAS PULL THIS STUPID THING OUT!
THAT IS THE WORST DESIGN I'VE EVER SEEN!
VZZAP!
VZZP!
LATER, APHRA!

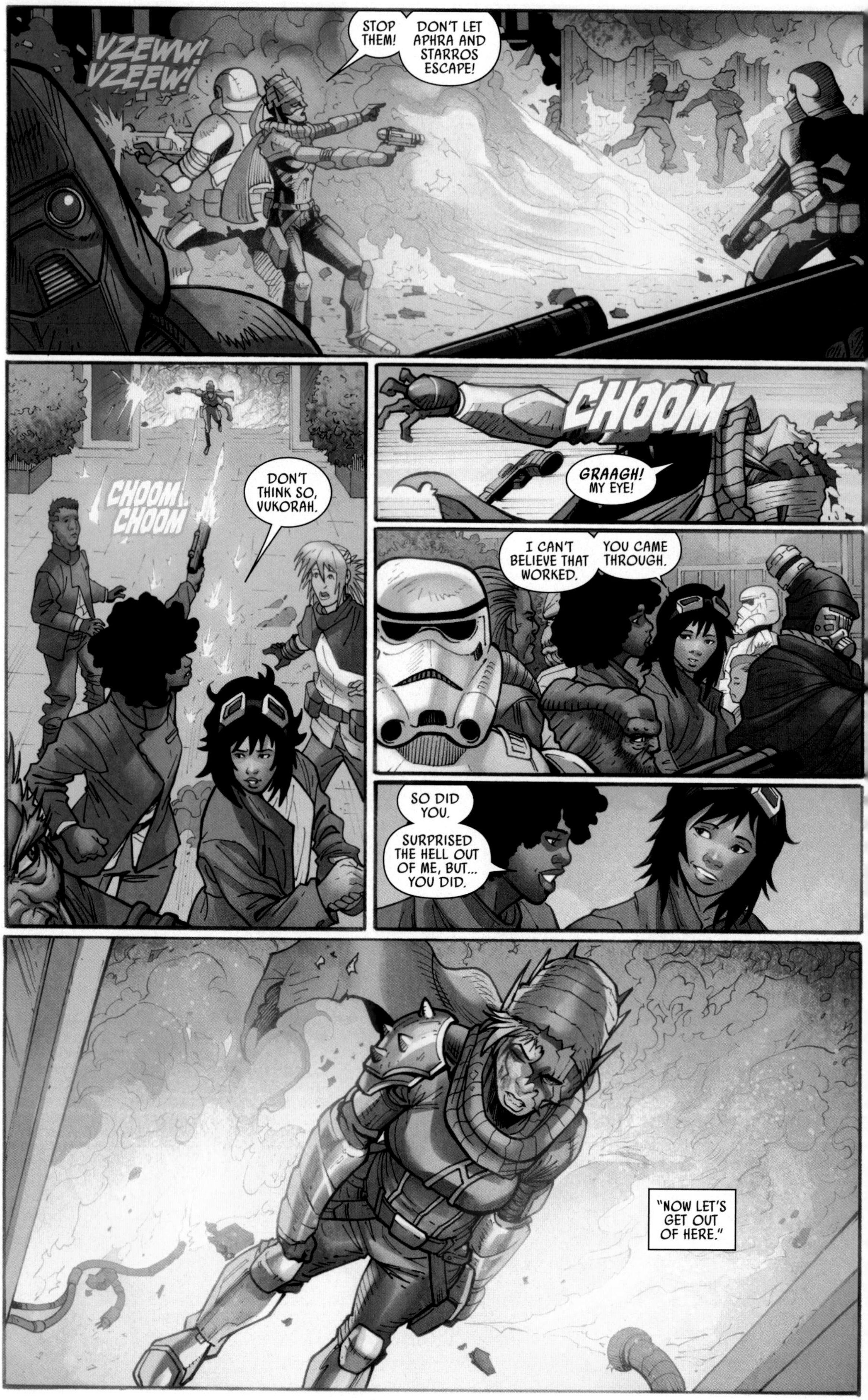
VZEWW! VZEEW!
STOP THEM!
DON'T LET APHRA AND STARROS ESCAPE!
CHOOM CHOOM
DON'T THINK SO, VUKORAH.
CHOOM
GRAAGH! MY EYE!
I CAN'T BELIEVE THAT WORKED.
YOU CAME THROUGH.
SO DID YOU.
SURPRISED THE HELL OUT OF ME, BUT... YOU DID.
"NOW LET'S GET OUT OF HERE."

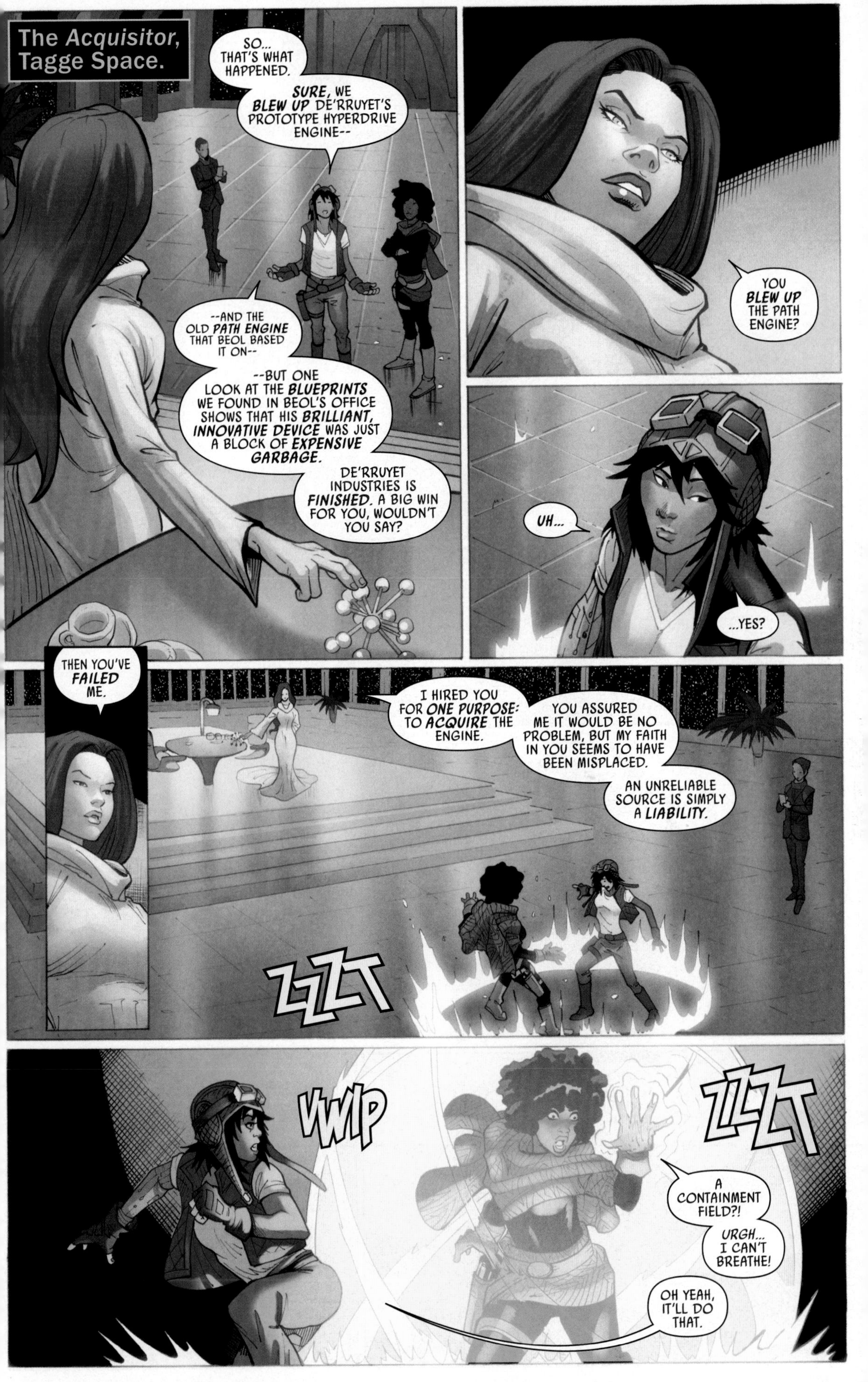
The Acquisitor, Tagge Space.
SO... THAT'S WHAT HAPPENED.
SURE, WE BLEW UP DE'RRUYET'S PROTOTYPE HYPERDRIVE ENGINE--
--AND THE OLD PATH ENGINE THAT BEOL BASED IT ON--
--BUT ONE LOOK AT THE BLUEPRINTS WE FOUND IN BEOL'S OFFICE SHOWS THAT HIS BRILLIANT, INNOVATIVE DEVICE WAS JUST A BLOCK OF EXPENSIVE GARBAGE.
DE'RRUYET INDUSTRIES IS FINISHED. A BIG WIN FOR YOU, WOULDN'T YOU SAY?
YOU BLEW UP THE PATH ENGINE?
UH...
...YES?
THEN YOU'VE FAILED ME.
I HIRED YOU FOR ONE PURPOSE: TO ACQUIRE THE ENGINE.
YOU ASSURED ME IT WOULD BE NO PROBLEM, BUT MY FAITH IN YOU SEEMS TO HAVE BEEN MISPLACED.
AN UNRELIABLE SOURCE IS SIMPLY A LIABILITY.
ZZZT
VWIP
ZZZT
A CONTAINMENT FIELD?!
URGH... I CAN'T BREATHE!
OH YEAH, IT'LL DO THAT.

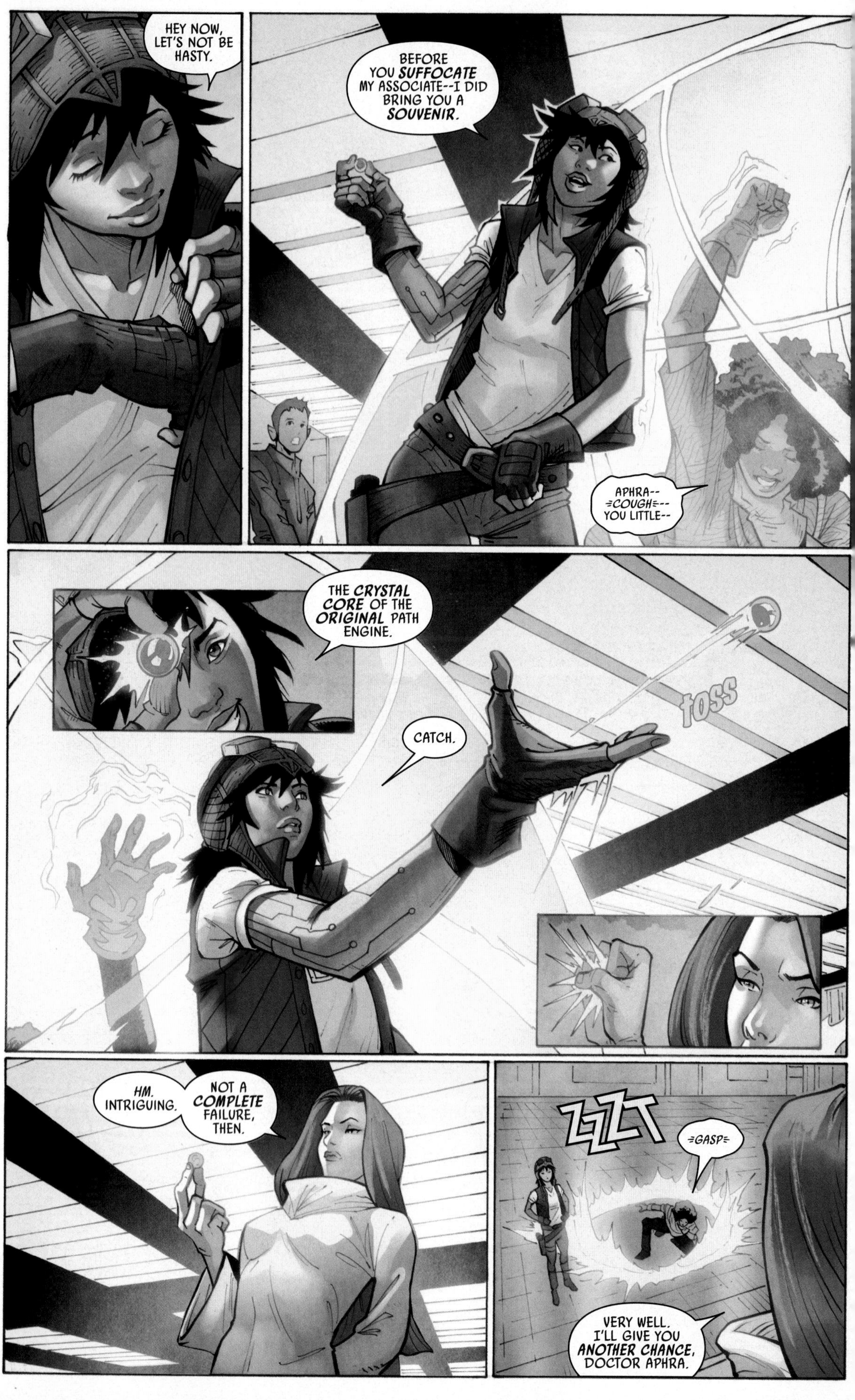
HEY NOW, LET'S NOT BE HASTY.
BEFORE YOU SUFFOCATE MY ASSOCIATE--I DID BRING YOU A SOUVENIR.
APHRA-- =COUGH=-- YOU LITTLE--
THE CRYSTAL CORE OF THE ORIGINAL PATH ENGINE.
toss
CATCH.
HM. INTRIGUING.
NOT A COMPLETE FAILURE, THEN.
ZZZT
=GASP=
VERY WELL. I'LL GIVE YOU ANOTHER CHANCE, DOCTOR APHRA.

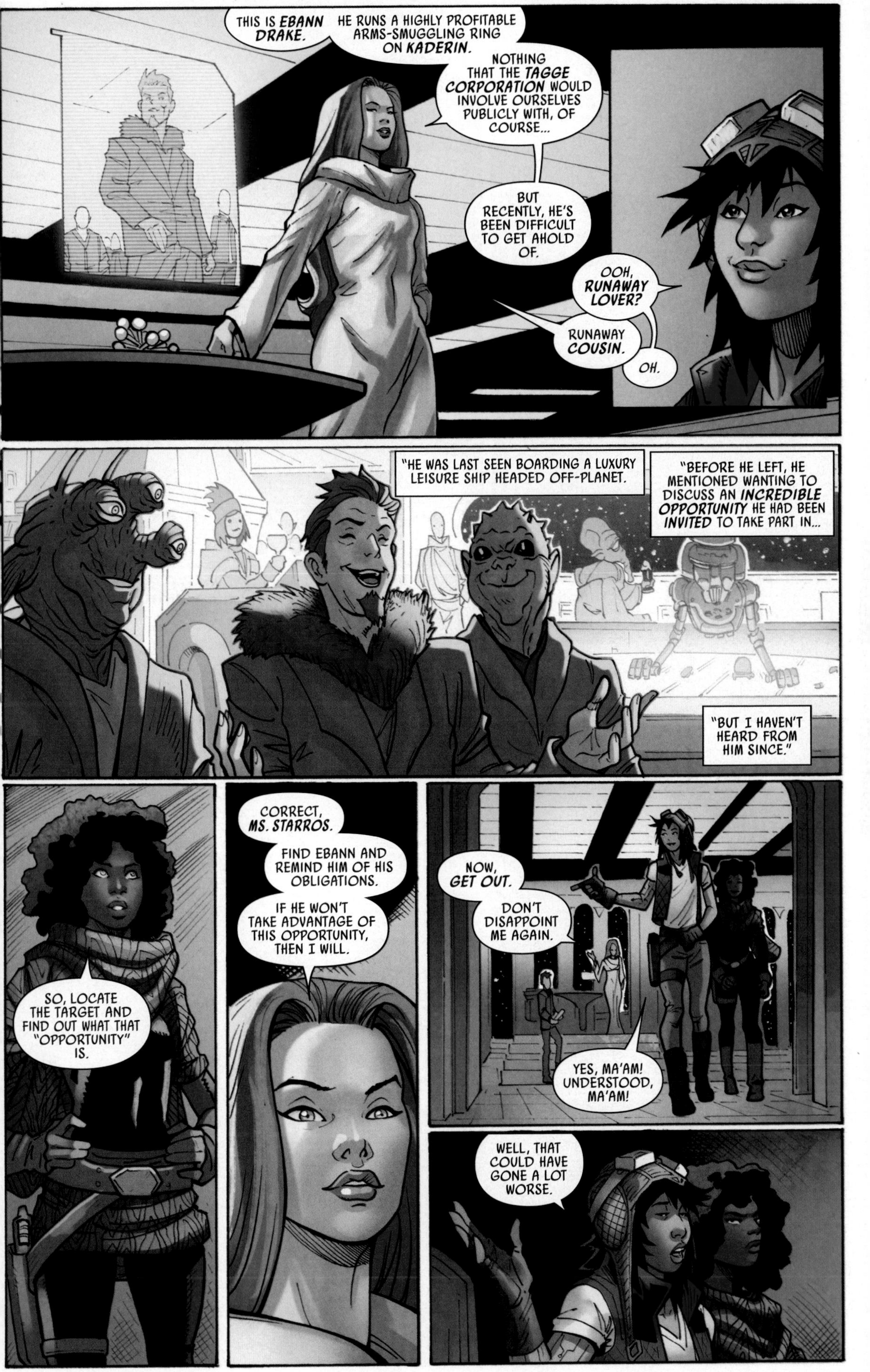

THIS IS EBANN DRAKE.
HE RUNS A HIGHLY PROFITABLE ARMS-SMUGGLING RING ON KADERIN.
NOTHING THAT THE TAGGE CORPORATION WOULD INVOLVE OURSELVES PUBLICLY WITH, OF COURSE...
BUT RECENTLY, HE'S BEEN DIFFICULT TO GET AHOLD OF.
OOH, RUNAWAY LOVER?
RUNAWAY COUSIN.
OH.
"HE WAS LAST SEEN BOARDING A LUXURY LEISURE SHIP HEADED OFF-PLANET.
"BEFORE HE LEFT, HE MENTIONED WANTING TO DISCUSS AN INCREDIBLE OPPORTUNITY HE HAD BEEN INVITED TO TAKE PART IN...
"BUT I HAVEN'T HEARD FROM HIM SINCE."
SO, LOCATE THE TARGET AND FIND OUT WHAT THAT "OPPORTUNITY" IS.
CORRECT, MS. STARROS.
FIND EBANN AND REMIND HIM OF HIS OBLIGATIONS.
IF HE WON'T TAKE ADVANTAGE OF THIS OPPORTUNITY, THEN I WILL.
NOW, GET OUT.
DON'T DISAPPOINT ME AGAIN.
YES, MA'AM! UNDERSTOOD, MA'AM!
WELL, THAT COULD HAVE GONE A LOT WORSE.

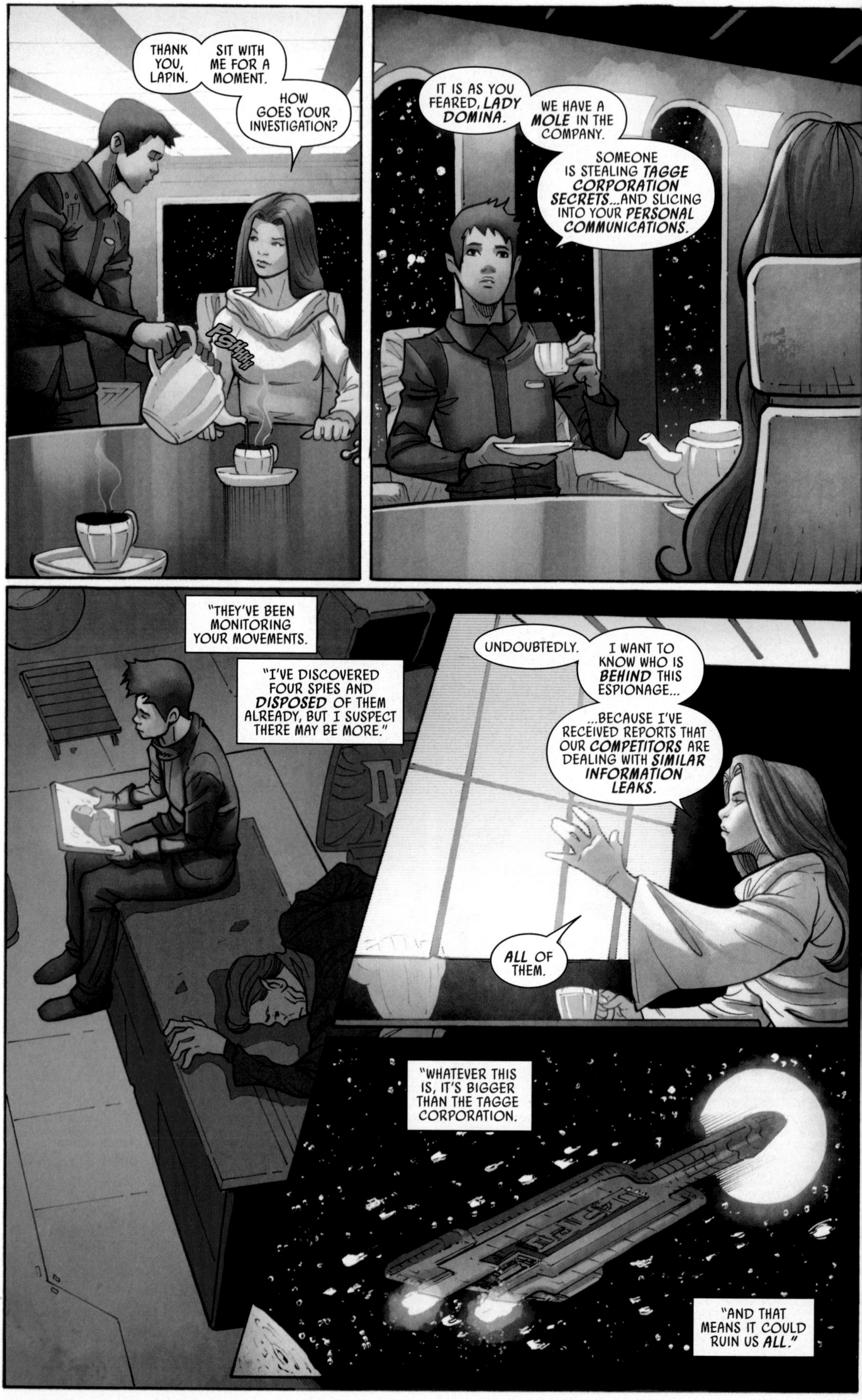
THANK YOU, LAPIN.
SIT WITH ME FOR A MOMENT.
HOW GOES YOUR INVESTIGATION?
FSHHH
IT IS AS YOU FEARED, LADY DOMINA.
WE HAVE A MOLE IN THE COMPANY.
SOMEONE IS STEALING TAGGE CORPORATION SECRETS...AND SLICING INTO YOUR PERSONAL COMMUNICATIONS.
"THEY'VE BEEN MONITORING YOUR MOVEMENTS.
"I'VE DISCOVERED FOUR SPIES AND DISPOSED OF THEM ALREADY, BUT I SUSPECT THERE MAY BE MORE."
UNDOUBTEDLY.
I WANT TO KNOW WHO IS BEHIND THIS ESPIONAGE...
...BECAUSE I'VE RECEIVED REPORTS THAT OUR COMPETITORS ARE DEALING WITH SIMILAR INFORMATION LEAKS.
ALL OF THEM.
"WHATEVER THIS IS, IT'S BIGGER THAN THE TAGGE CORPORATION.
"AND THAT MEANS IT COULD RUIN US ALL."

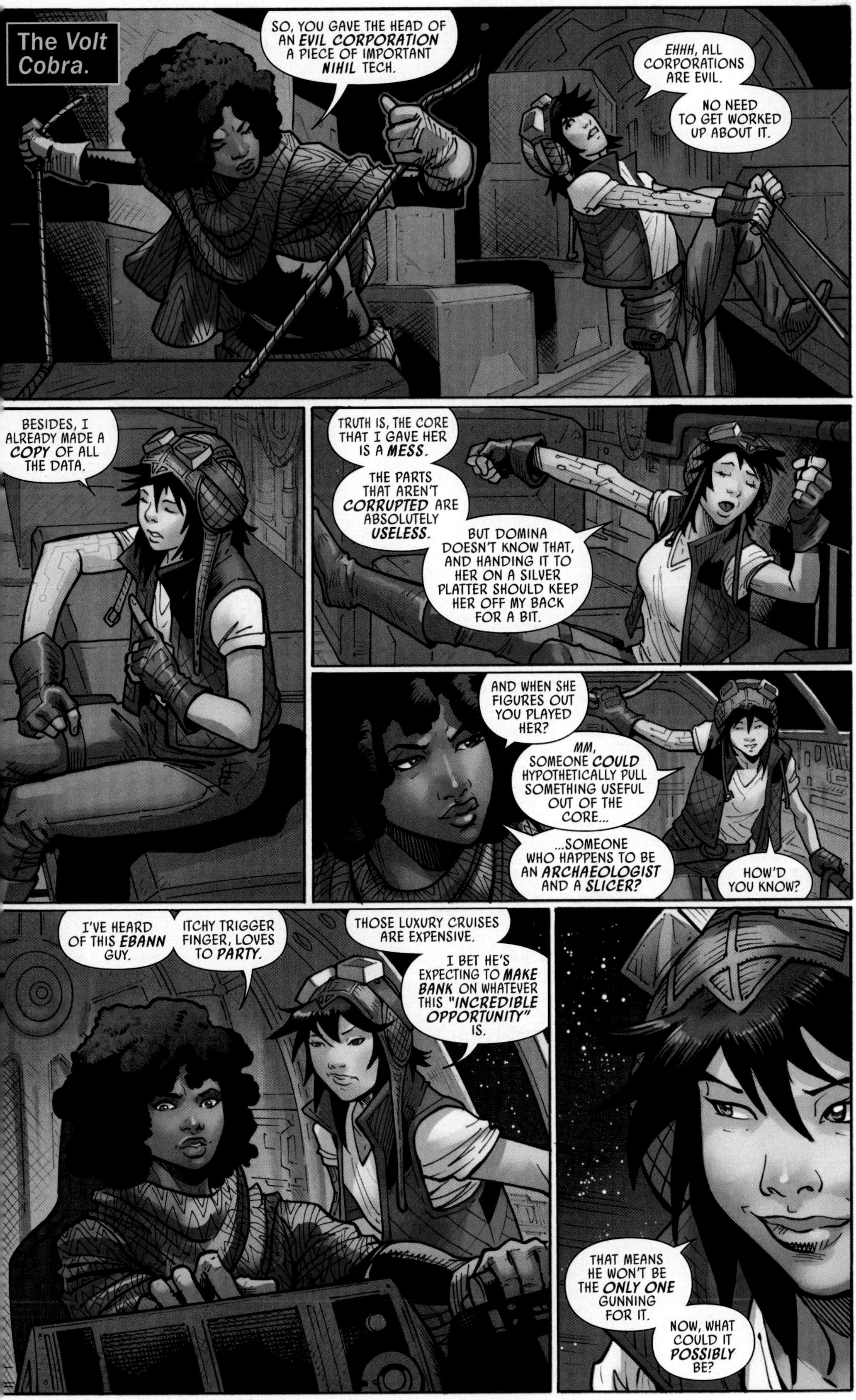
The Volt Cobra.
SO, YOU GAVE THE HEAD OF AN EVIL CORPORATION A PIECE OF IMPORTANT NIHIL TECH.
EHHH, ALL CORPORATIONS ARE EVIL.
NO NEED TO GET WORKED UP ABOUT IT.
BESIDES, I ALREADY MADE A COPY OF ALL THE DATA.
TRUTH IS, THE CORE THAT I GAVE HER IS A MESS.
THE PARTS THAT AREN'T CORRUPTED ARE ABSOLUTELY USELESS.
BUT DOMINA DOESN'T KNOW THAT, AND HANDING IT TO HER ON A SILVER PLATTER SHOULD KEEP HER OFF MY BACK FOR A BIT.
AND WHEN SHE FIGURES OUT YOU PLAYED HER?
MM, SOMEONE COULD HYPOTHETICALLY PULL SOMETHING USEFUL OUT OF THE CORE...
...SOMEONE WHO HAPPENS TO BE AN ARCHAEOLOGIST AND A SLICER?
HOW'D YOU KNOW?
I'VE HEARD OF THIS EBANN GUY.
ITCHY TRIGGER FINGER, LOVES TO PARTY.
THOSE LUXURY CRUISES ARE EXPENSIVE.
I BET HE'S EXPECTING TO MAKE BANK ON WHATEVER THIS "INCREDIBLE OPPORTUNITY" IS.
THAT MEANS HE WON'T BE THE ONLY ONE GUNNING FOR IT.
NOW, WHAT COULD IT POSSIBLY BE?

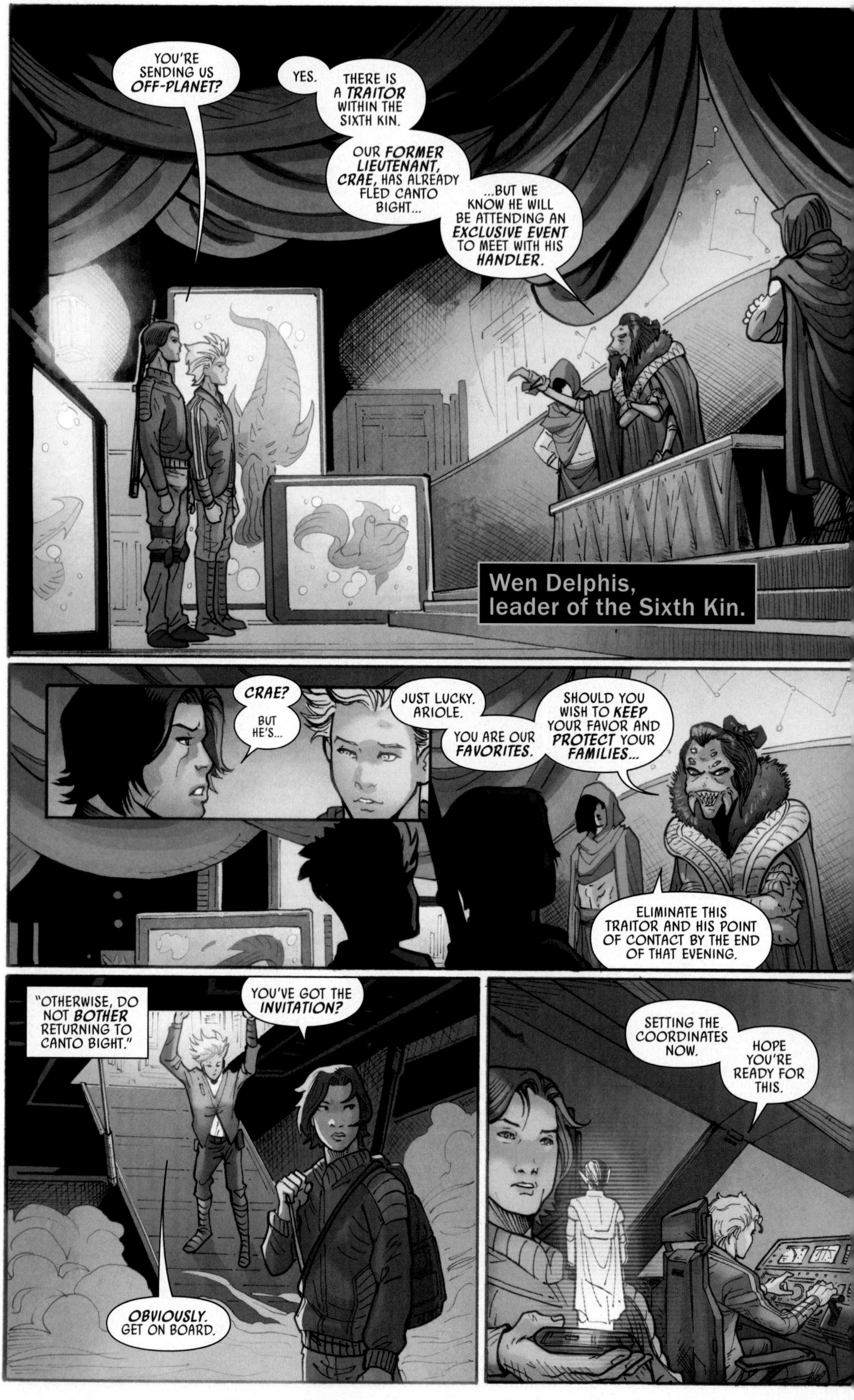
YOU'RE SENDING US OFF-PLANET?
YES.
THERE IS A TRAITOR WITHIN THE SIXTH KIN.
OUR FORMER LIEUTENANT, CRAE, HAS ALREADY FLED CANTO BIGHT...
...BUT WE KNOW HE WILL BE ATTENDING AN EXCLUSIVE EVENT TO MEET WITH HIS HANDLER.
Wen Delphis, leader of the Sixth Kin.
CRAE?
BUT HE'S...
JUST LUCKY. ARIOLE.
YOU ARE OUR FAVORITES.
SHOULD YOU WISH TO KEEP YOUR FAVOR AND PROTECT YOUR FAMILIES...
ELIMINATE THIS TRAITOR AND HIS POINT OF CONTACT BY THE END OF THAT EVENING.
"OTHERWISE, DO NOT BOTHER RETURNING TO CANTO BIGHT."
YOU'VE GOT THE INVITATION?
OBVIOUSLY. GET ON BOARD.
SETTING THE COORDINATES NOW.
HOPE YOU'RE READY FOR THIS.

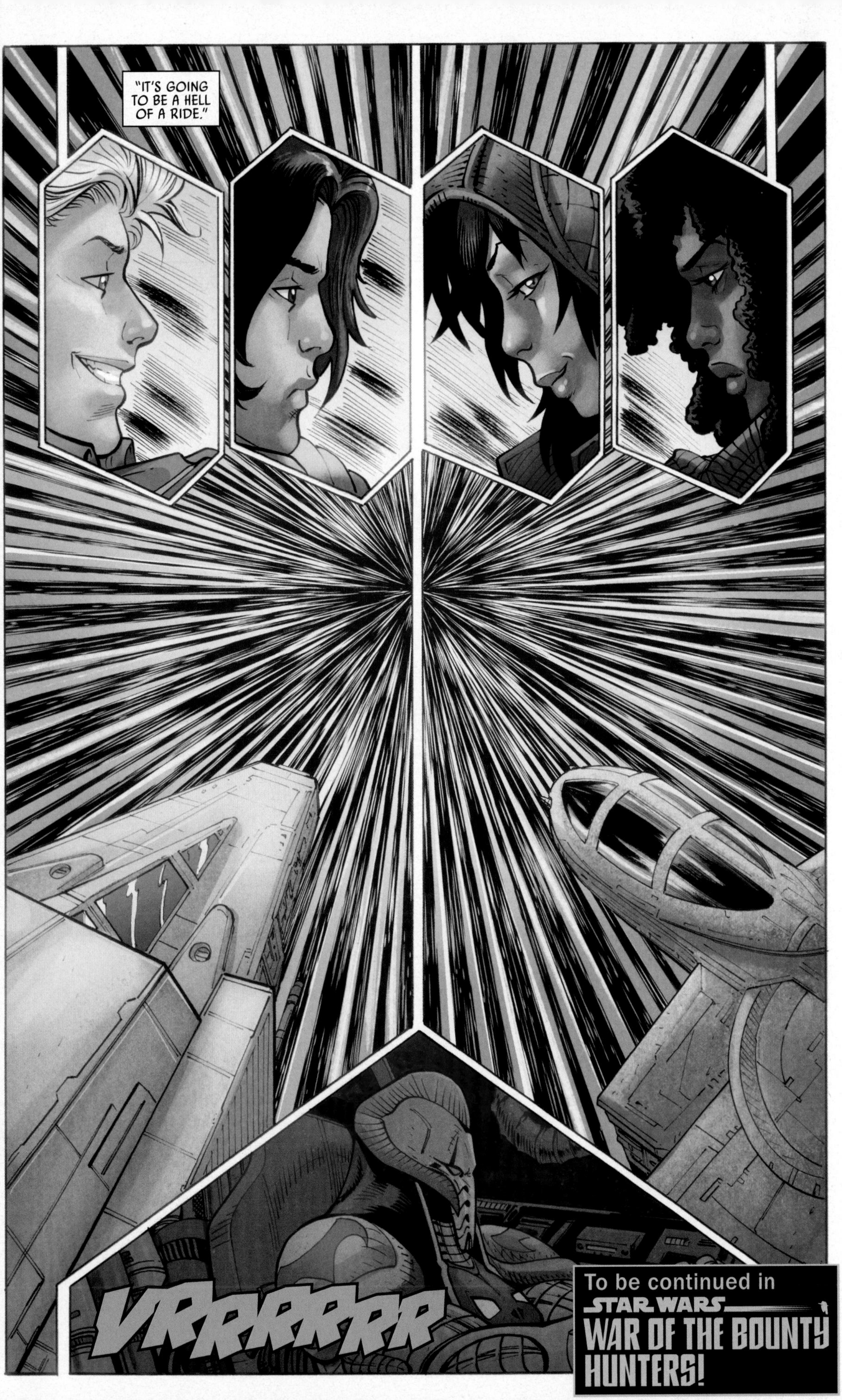
"IT'S GOING TO BE A HELL OF A RIDE."
VRRRRRR
To be continued in
STAR WARS
WAR OF THE BOUNTY HUNTERS!

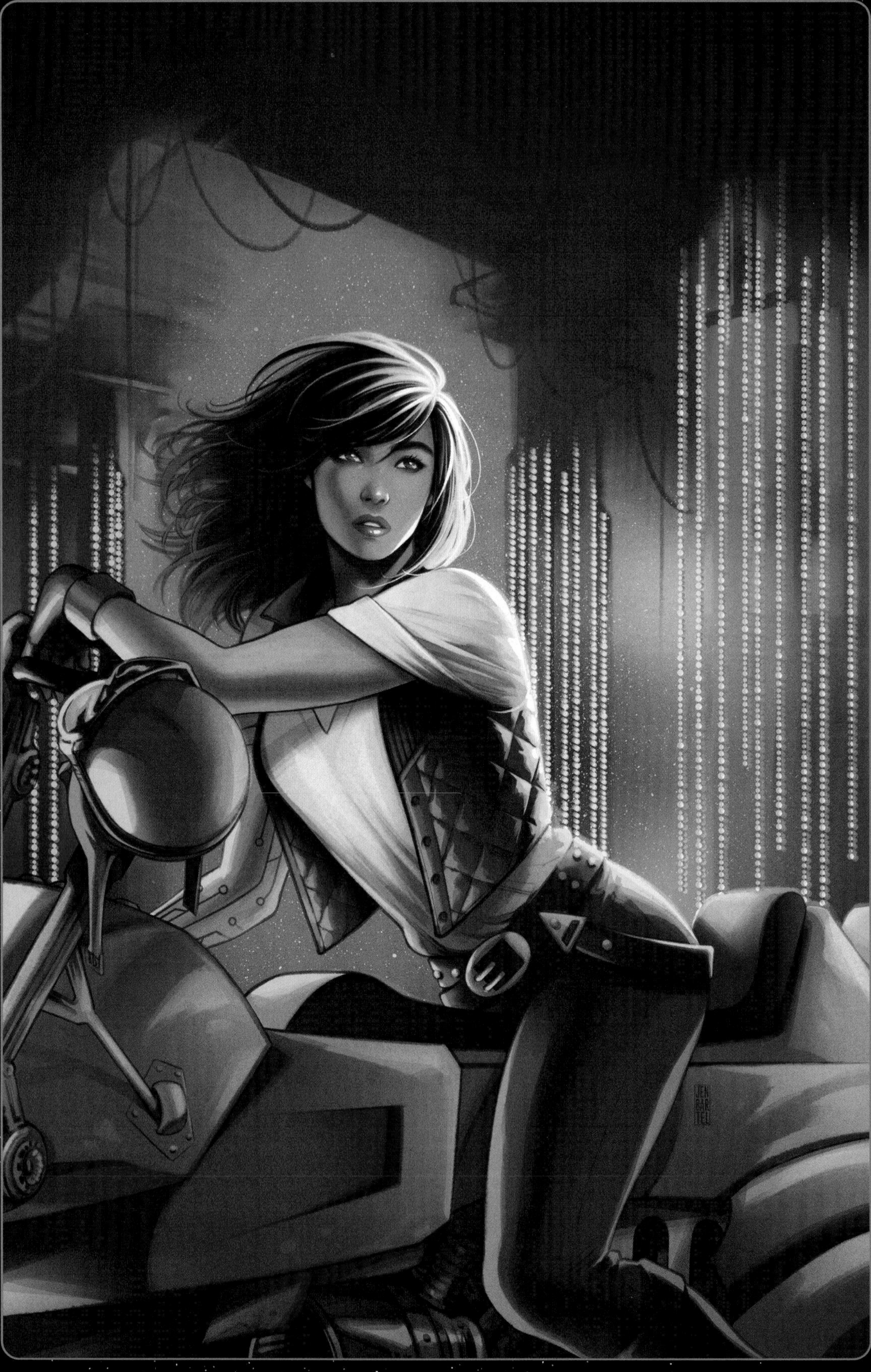

#6 Variant by
JEN BARTEL

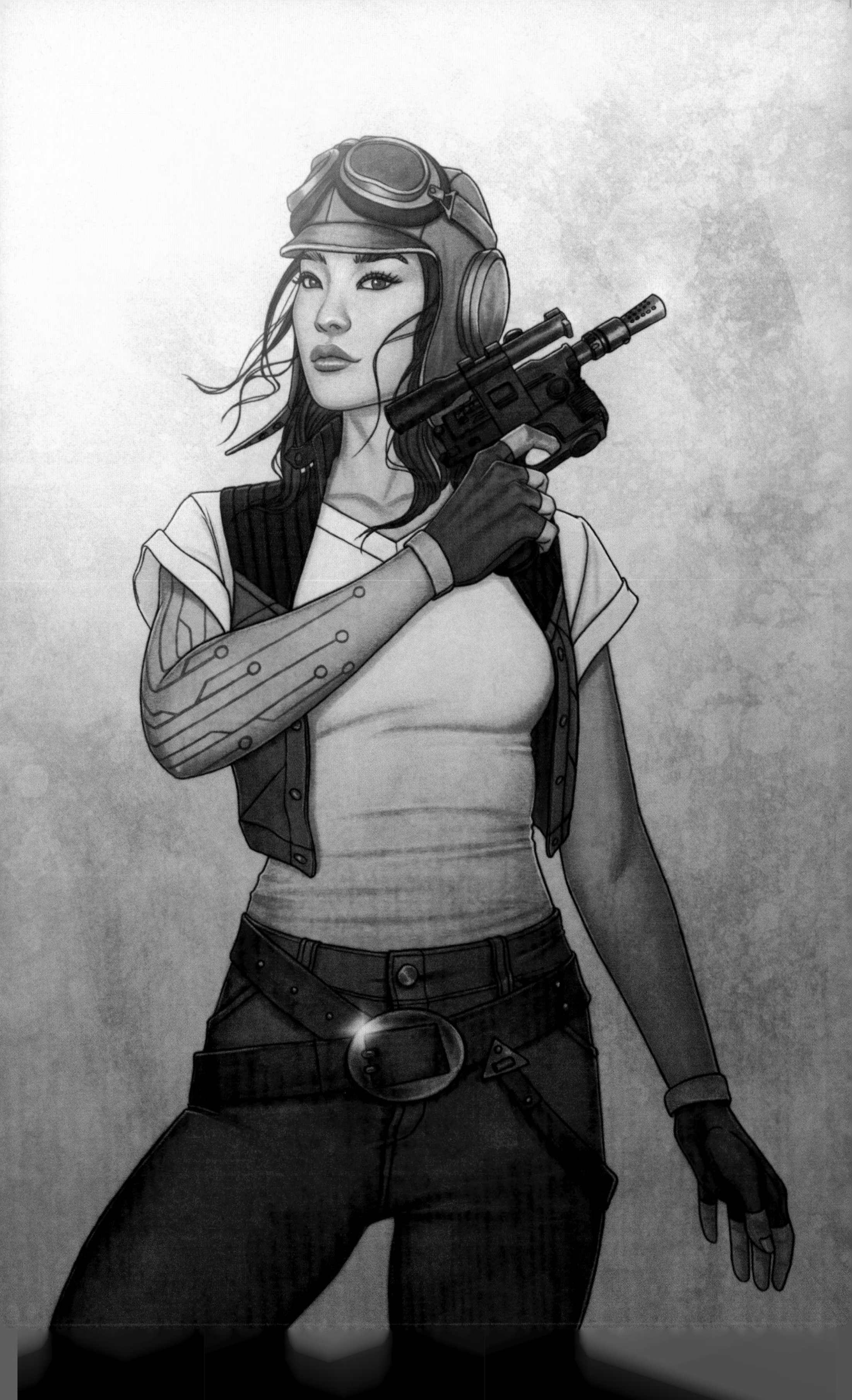

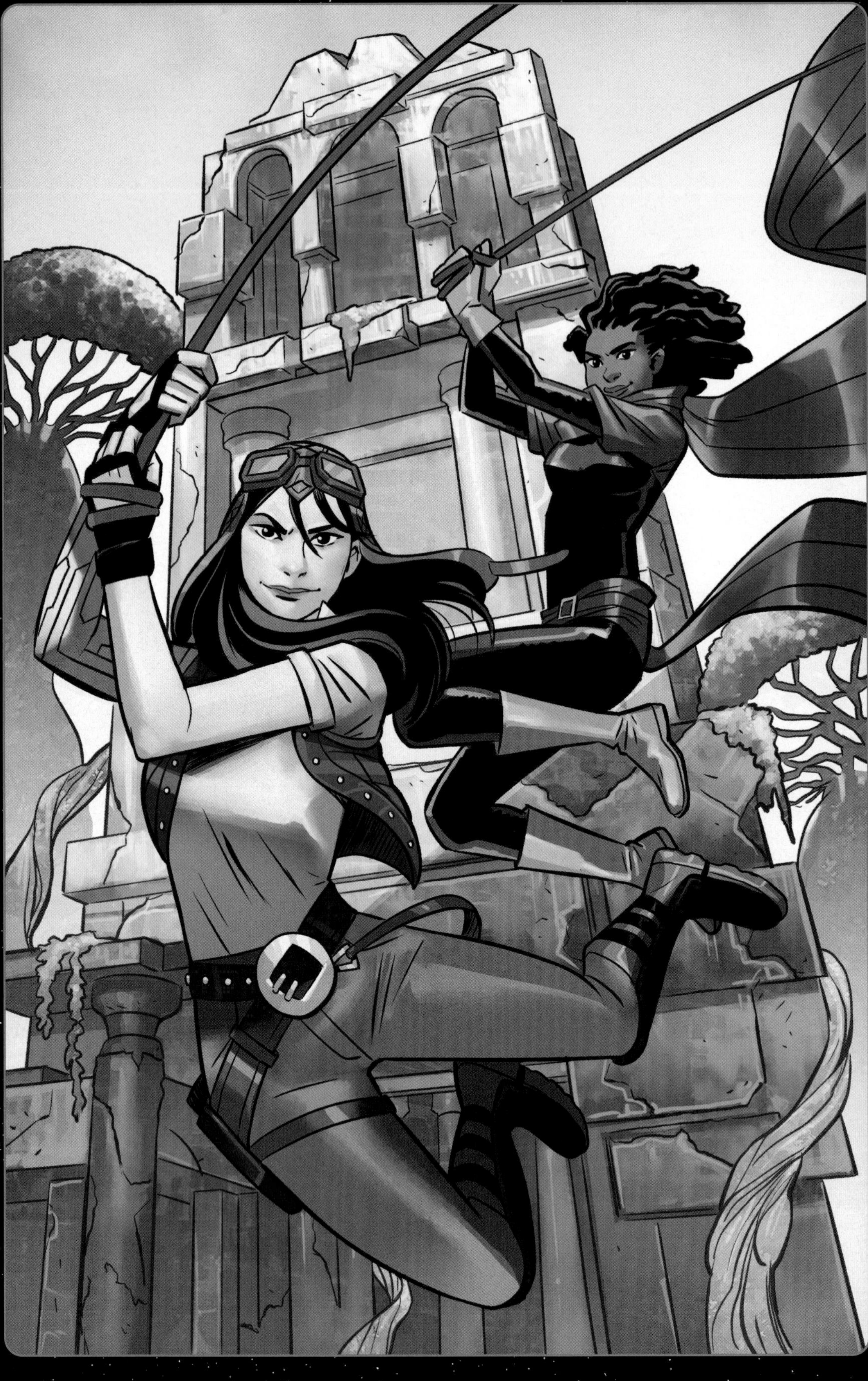

#8 Variant by
NATACHA BUSTOS & ROMULO FAJARDO JR.

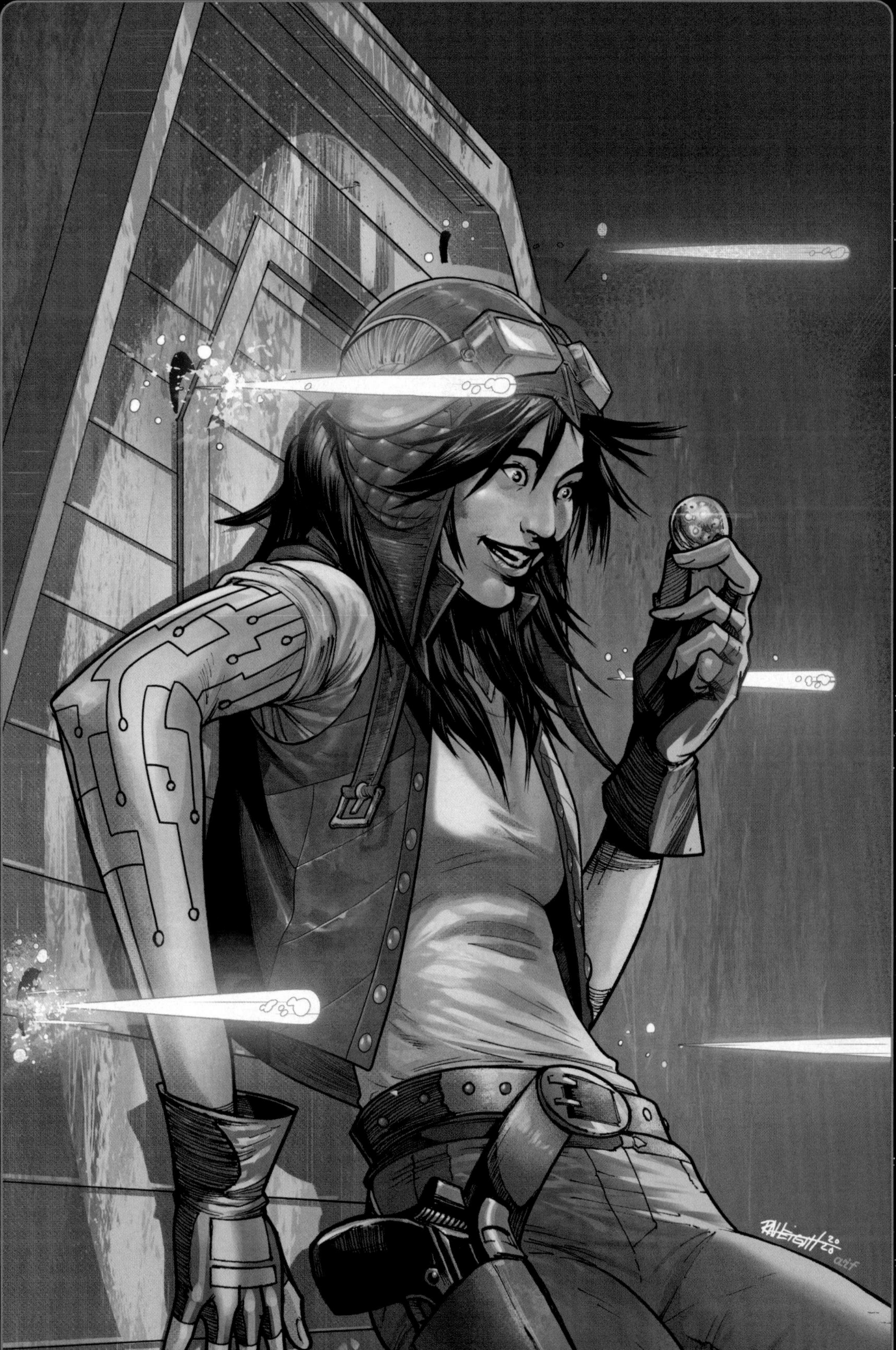

#9 Variant by
RAY-ANTHONY HEIGHT & **ARIF PRIANTO**

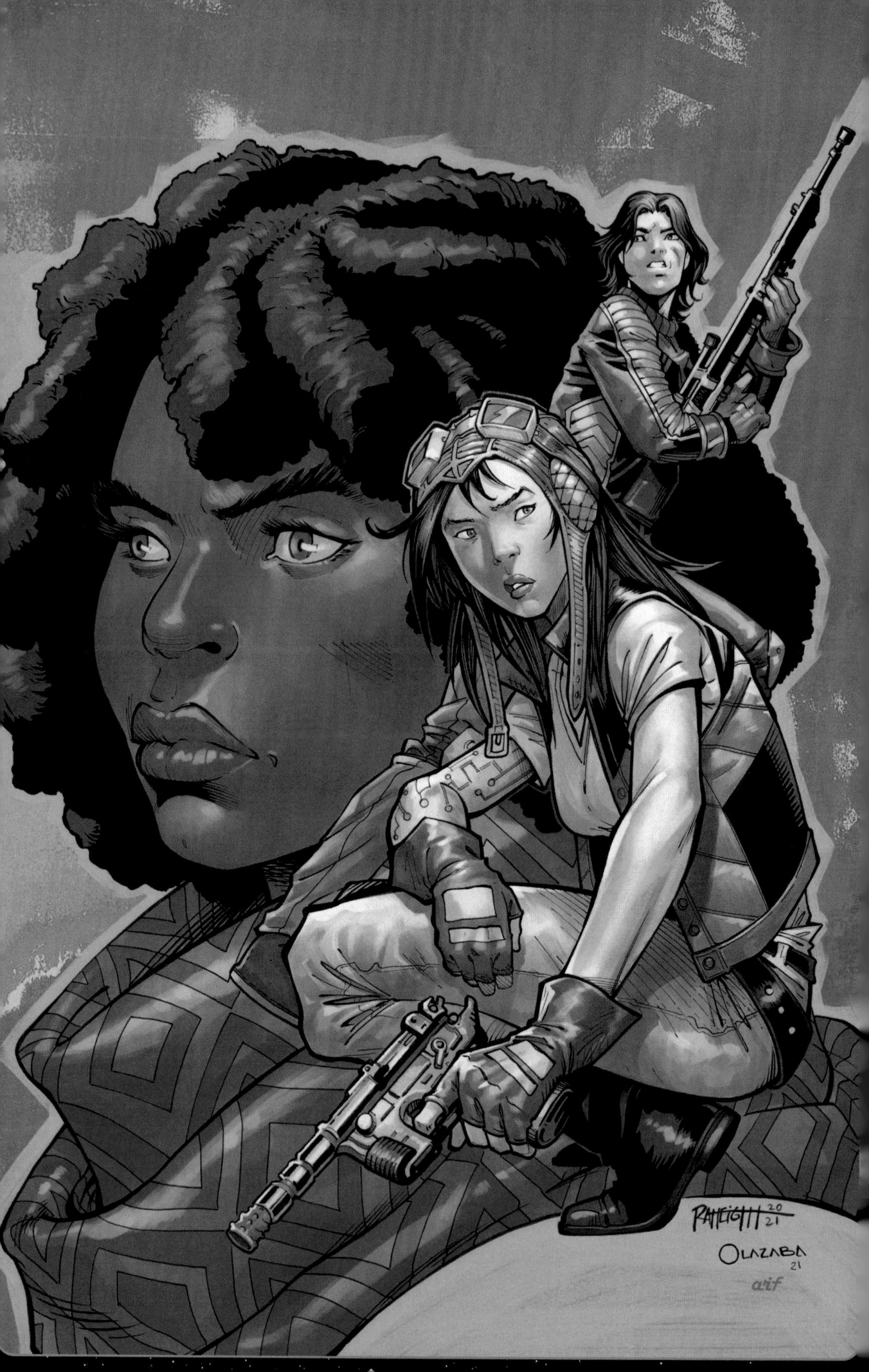
OLAZABA
21
arif

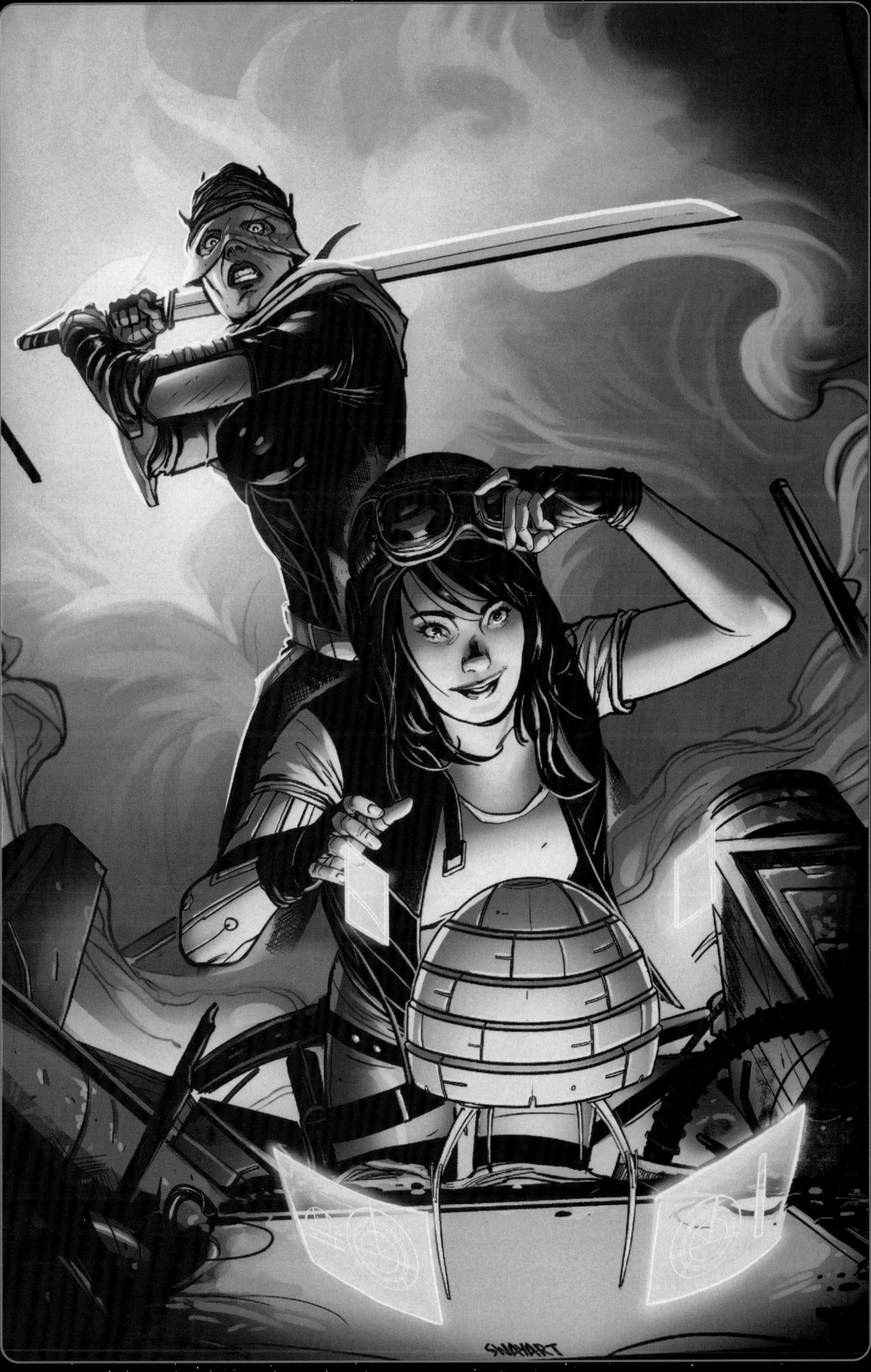

#10 Crimson Variant by
JOSHUA "SWAY" SWABY & **GURU-eFX**

ROGUE ARCHAEOLOGIST DOCTOR APHRA THIEVES HER WAY ACROSS THE GALAXY!

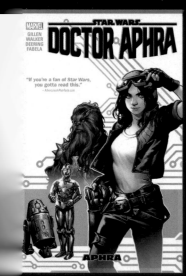

MARVEL
GILLEN
WALKER
DEERING
FABELA
STAR WARS
DOCTOR APHRA
"If you're a fan of Star Wars, you gotta read this."
APHRA

STAR WARS: DOCTOR APHRA VOL. 1 – APHRA TPB

ISBN: 978-1302913212

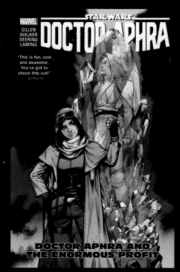

MARVEL
GILLEN
WALKER
DEERING
LAMING
STAR WARS
DOCTOR APHRA
"This is fun, cool and awesome. You've got to check this out!"
DOCTOR APHRA AND THE ENORMOUS PROFIT

STAR WARS: DOCTOR APHRA VOL. 2 – DOCTOR APHRA AND THE ENORMOUS PROFIT TPB

ISBN: 978-1302907631

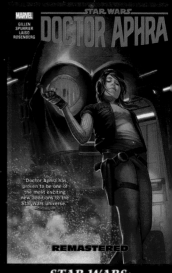

MARVEL
GILLEN
SPURRIER
LAISO
ROSENBERG
STAR WARS
DOCTOR APHRA
"Doctor Aphra has proven to be one of the most exciting new additions to the Star Wars universe."
REMASTERED

STAR WARS: DOCTOR APHRA VOL. 3 REMASTERED TPB

ISBN: 978-1302911522

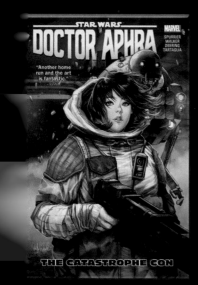

STAR WARS
DOCTOR APHRA
MARVEL
SPURRIER
WALKER
DEERING
TARTAGLIA
"Another home run and the art is fantastic."
THE CATASTROPHE CON

STAR WARS: DOCTOR APHRA VOL. 4 – THE CATASTROPHE CON TPB

ISBN: 978-1302911539

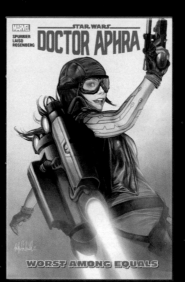

MARVEL
SPURRIER
LAISO
ROSENBERG
STAR WARS
DOCTOR APHRA
WORST AMONG EQUALS

STAR WARS: DOCTOR APHRA VOL. 5 – WORST AMONG EQUALS TPB

ISBN: 978-1302914875

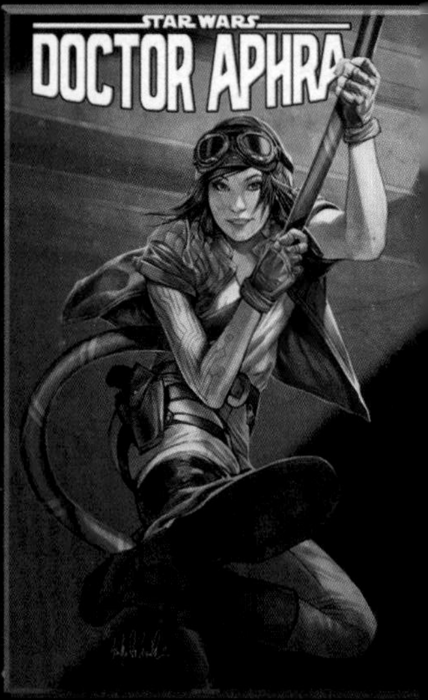

STAR WARS

STAR WARS: DOCTOR APHRA VOL. 6 UNSPEAKABLE REBEL SUPERWEAPON TPB

ISBN: 978-1302914882

ON SALE NOW

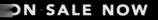

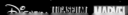

WANT TO KNOW THE BEST WAY TO EXPLORE THE MARVEL STAR WARS UNIVERSE?

THIS GUIDE WILL SHOW YOU WHERE TO BEGIN!

FOLLOW THE ADVENTURES OF LUKE, HAN AND LEIA IN THESE

STAR WARS™

COLLECTED EDITIONS!

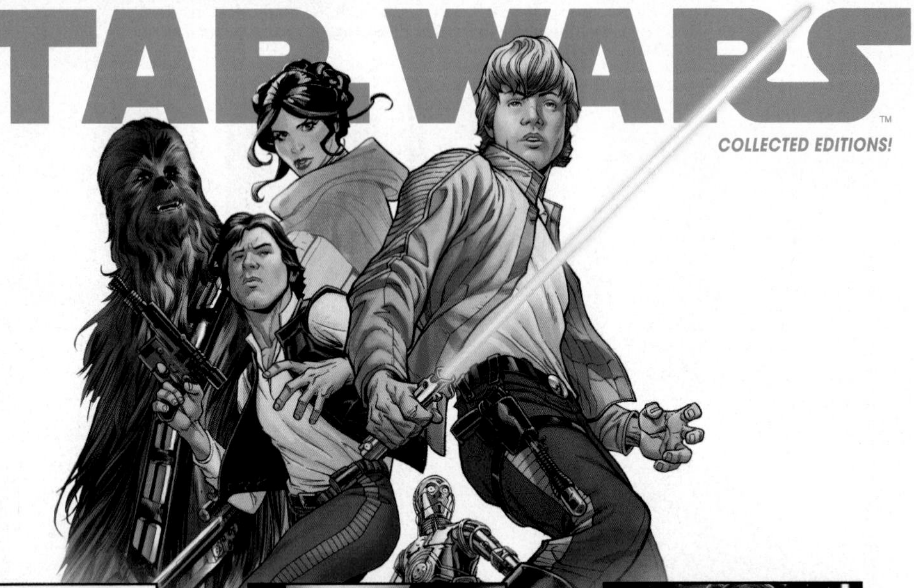

START HERE

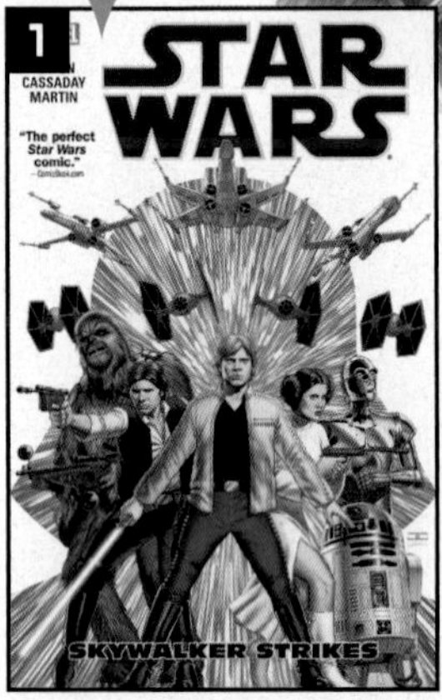
1
CASSADAY
MARTIN
STAR WARS
"The perfect Star Wars comic."
SKYWALKER STRIKES

Star Wars Vol. 1:
Skywalker Strikes

ISBN 978-0-7851-9213-8

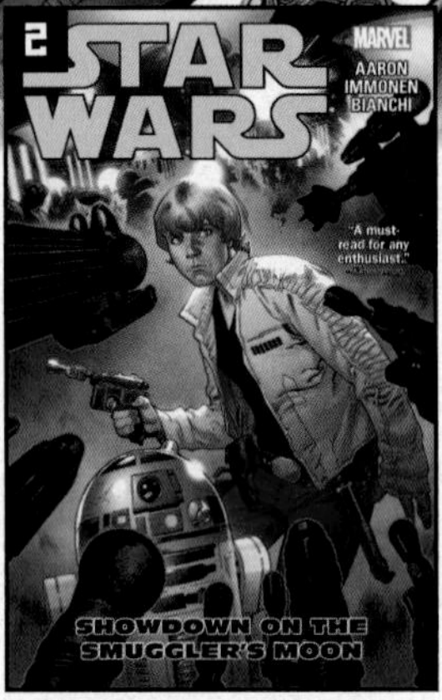
2
STAR WARS
MARVEL
AARON
IMMONEN
BIANCHI
"A must-read for any enthusiast."
SHOWDOWN ON THE SMUGGLER'S MOON

Star Wars Vol. 2:
Showdown on the Smuggler's Moon

ISBN 978-0-7851-9214-5

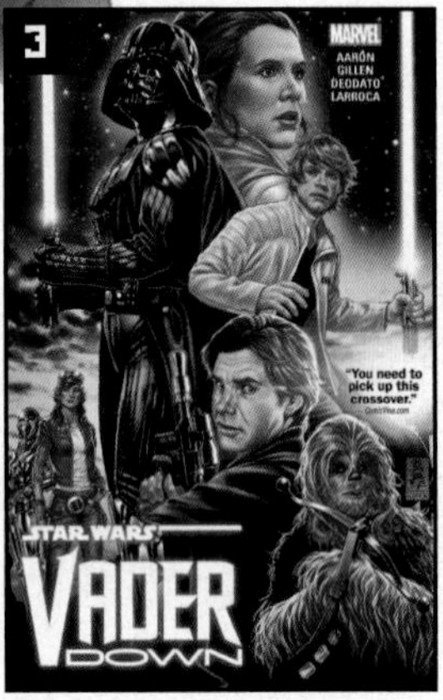
3
MARVEL
AARON
GILLEN
DEODATO
LARROCA
"You need to pick up this crossover."
STAR WARS
VADER
DOWN

Star Wars:
Vader Down

ISBN 978-0-7851-9789-8

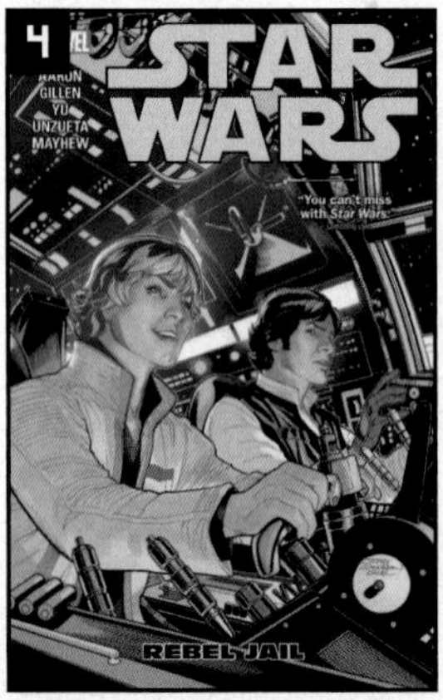
4
GILLEN
YU
UNZUETA
MAYHEW
STAR WARS
"You can't miss with Star Wars."
REBEL JAIL

Star Wars Vol. 3:
Rebel Jail

ISBN 978-0-7851-9983-0

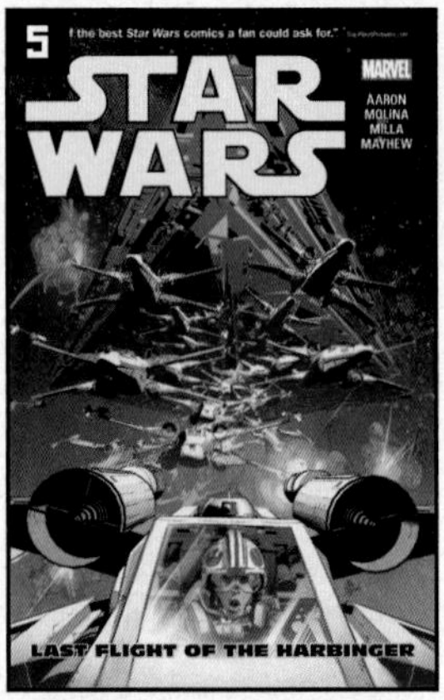
5
STAR WARS
MARVEL
AARON
MOLINA
MILLA
MAYHEW
LAST FLIGHT OF THE HARBINGER

Star Wars Vol. 4:
Last Flight of the Harbinger

ISBN 978-0-7851-9984-7

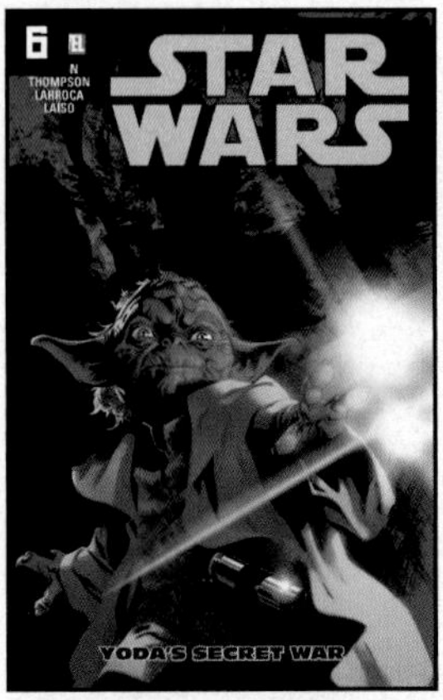
6
THOMPSON
LARROCA
LAISO
STAR WARS
YODA'S SECRET WAR

Star Wars Vol. 5:
Yoda's Secret War

ISBN 978-1-302-90265-0

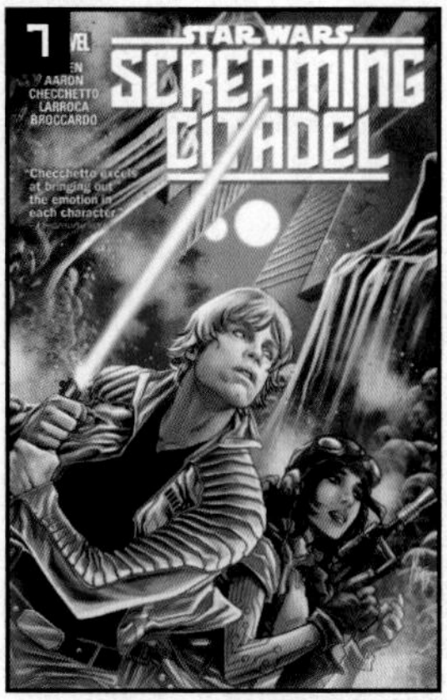
7
STAR WARS
SCREAMING CITADEL

Star Wars:
The Screaming Citadel
ISBN 978-1-302-90678-8

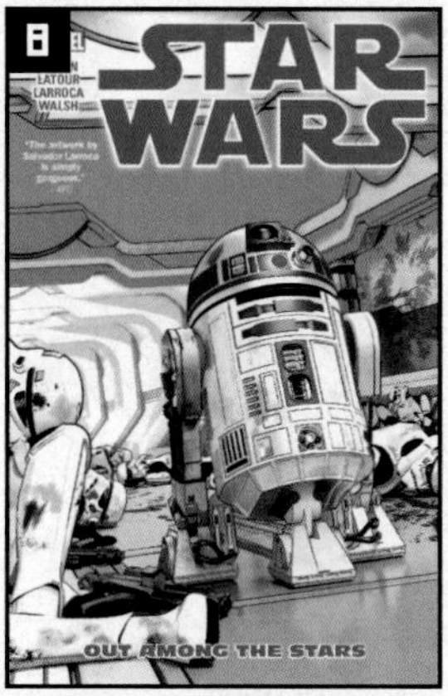
8
STAR WARS
OUT AMONG THE STARS

Star Wars Vol. 6:
Out Among the Stars
ISBN 978-1-302-90553-8

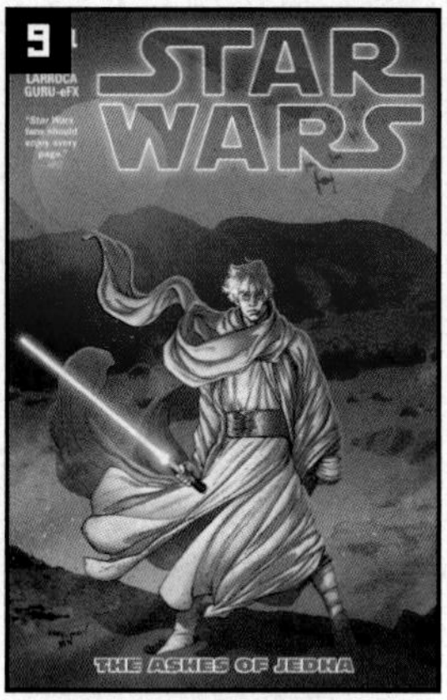
9
STAR WARS
THE ASHES OF JEDHA

Star Wars Vol. 7:
The Ashes of Jedha
ISBN 978-1-302-91052-5

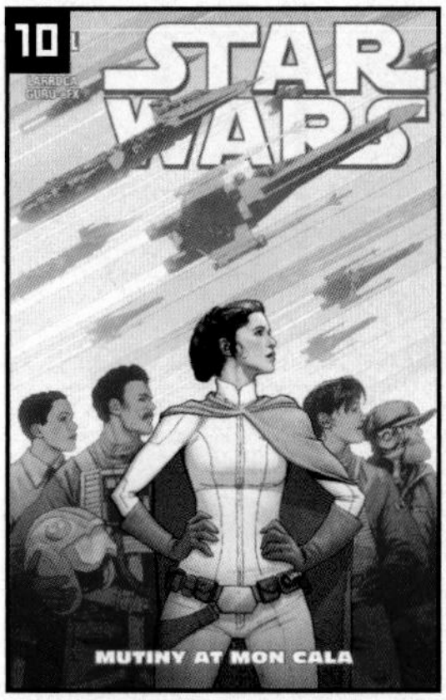
10
STAR WARS
MUTINY AT MON CALA

Star Wars Vol. 8:
Mutiny at Mon Cala
ISBN 978-1-302-91053-2

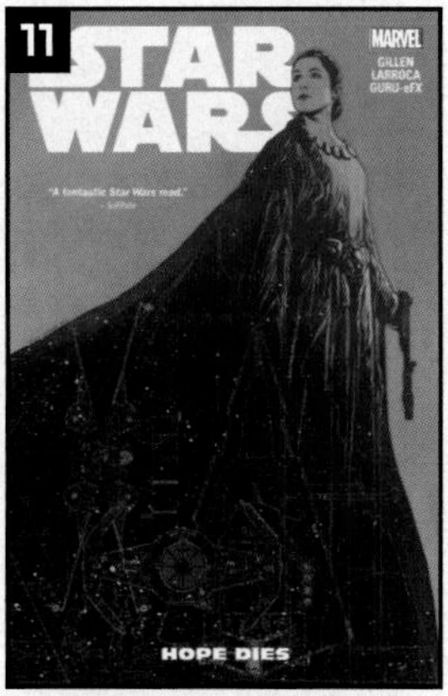
11
STAR WARS
MARVEL
GILLEN
LARROCA
GURU-eFX
HOPE DIES

Star Wars Vol. 9:
Hope Dies
ISBN 978-1-302-91054-9

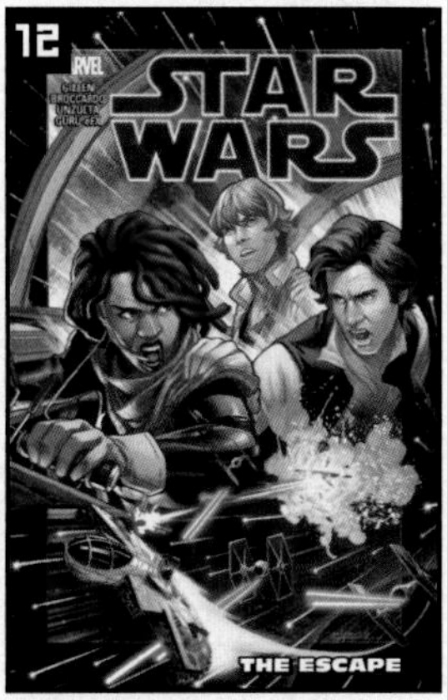
12
STAR WARS
THE ESCAPE

Star Wars Vol. 10:
The Escape
ISBN 978-1-302-91449-3

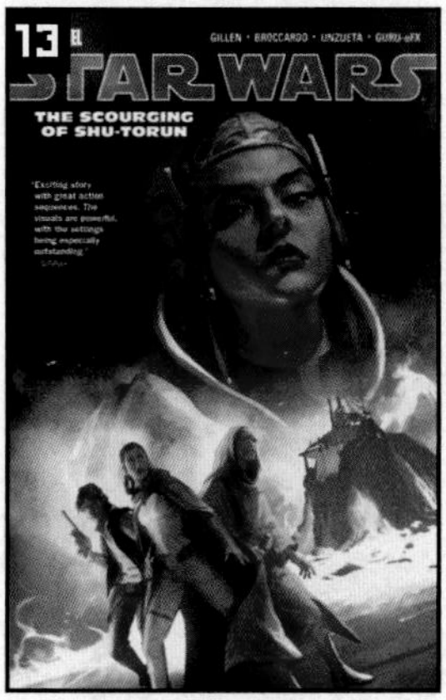
13
GILLEN · BROCCARDO · UNZUETA · GURU-eFX
STAR WARS
THE SCOURGING OF SHU-TORUN

Star Wars Vol. 11:
The Scourging of Shu-Torun
ISBN 978-1-302-91450-9

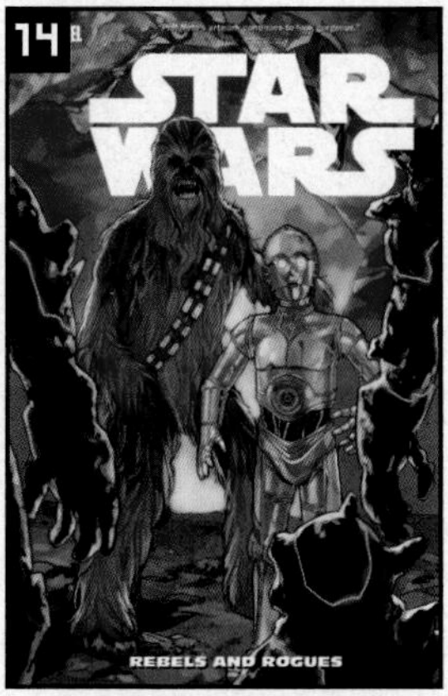
14
STAR WARS
REBELS AND ROGUES

Star Wars Vol. 12:
Rebels and Rogues
ISBN 978-1-302-91451-6

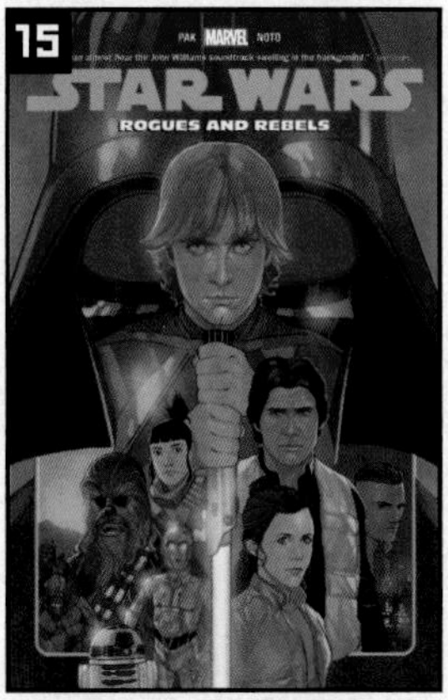
15
PAK MARVEL NOTO
STAR WARS
ROGUES AND REBELS

Star Wars Vol. 13:
Rogues and Rebels
ISBN 978-1-302-91450-9

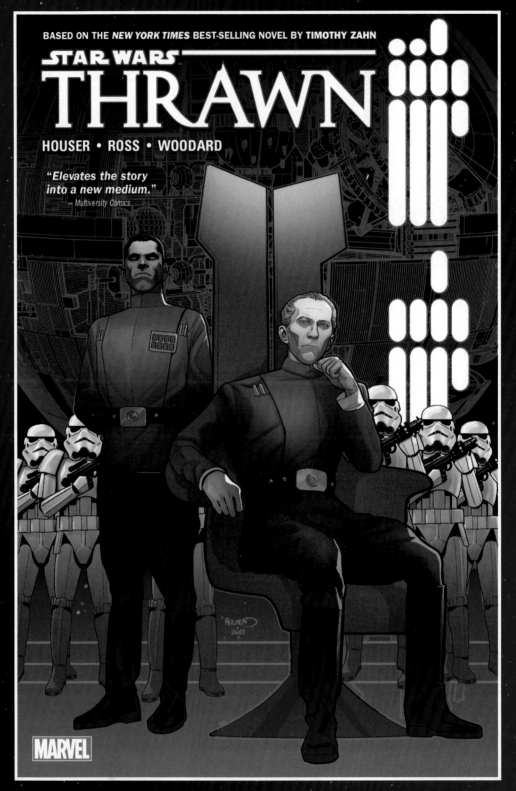